Lecture Notes in Business Information Processing 58

Series Editors

Matthew L. Nelson   Michael J. Shaw
Troy J. Strader (Eds.)

Sustainable e-Business Management

16th Americas Conference on Information Systems,
AMCIS 2010, SIGeBIZ track
Lima, Peru, August 12-15, 2010
Selected Papers

Springer

Volume Editors

Matthew L. Nelson
Illinois State University
College of Business
Normal, IL 61790, USA
E-mail: mlnelso@ilstu.edu

Michael J. Shaw
University of Illinois
College of Business
Champaign, IL, 61820, USA
E-mail: mjshaw@illinois.edu

Troy J. Strader
Drake University
College of Business and Public Administration
Des Moines, IA 50311, USA
E-mail: troy.strader@drake.edu

Library of Congress Control Number: 2010932031

ACM Computing Classification (1998): J.1, K.4.4, H.3.5

ISSN 1865-1348
ISBN-10 3-642-15140-X Springer Berlin Heidelberg New York
ISBN-13 978-3-642-15140-8 Springer Berlin Heidelberg New York

springer.com

Printed in Germany

Typesetting: Camera-ready by author, data conversion by Scientific Publishing Services, Chennai, India
Printed on acid-free paper 06/3180 5 4 3 2 1 0

Preface

With high hopes that the worst of the financial crisis is now behind us, our efforts looking forward must be more vigilant. Change is constant in the electronic business management landscape and we must continue to look for organizational efficiencies, competitive strength, strategic differentiation and value creation in both intra-organizational and collaborative settings. Seeking new and innovative application areas of information technology, in general, and e-business management solutions, in particular, while simultaneously critically evaluating and constantly challenging our own research contributions, methods and practices. It is for these reasons (and many more) that we are particularly excited about and grateful for the collection of papers included in this volume, LNBIP 58, on Sustainable e-Business Management.

The papers selected in this volume address these emerging e-business issues and have been organized into three research lines: *e-Business Models and IS in Financial Markets, e-Commerce Use and Design,* and *e-Business Research Issues and Methods.* We are delighted to kick off the first group of papers *e-Business Models and IS in Financial Markets* with a study by Masao Kakihara of Yahoo Research in Japan, proposing a dynamic revenue model framework and design. This section also includes a fresh look into two pressing e-business areas with Doerr, Benlian, Vetter and Hess's examination of content provider pricing of music as a service and Dutta and Menon's interesting study of the determinants of customer acquisition and e-tailer revenue. This section closes with two papers examining the use of *IS in Financial Markets* with Lewandowska's study of adoption factors of a centralized infrastructure for post-trade processing (appropriately set in an after-the-credit-crisis setting) and Shaper and Chlistalla's assessment of the evolving landscape of information technology's impact on European post-trading.

The second section *e-Commerce Design and Use* includes papers examining five richly diverse, yet critically important, areas of e-commerce. The first provides a fascinating look into the usability analysis of an anonymity network by Fabian, Goertz, Kunz, Müller and Nitzsche. The second paper is by Ayalew, Lessa and Yigzaw and provides a comprehensive and unprecedented readiness assessment of the emerging Ethiopian e-commerce market. Brecht, Cudreasova and Zhou's paper is next with their incredibly insightful and fresh examination of the usage and characteristics of modern-day corporate blogging. This section closes with two papers that investigate e-commerce design considerations in vastly diverse settings. Roßnagel, Zibuschka and Junker propose an intriguing agent-based simulation for the evaluation and design of mobile emergency management systems. Brecht and Schafer provide an extremely enlightening look into the use of ontologies in end-user interfaces in e-commerce design.

The third section *e-Business Research Issues and Methods* provides three areas of self-examination (if you will) of research issues and methods in e-business research disciplines. The first is Pfugler and Turowski's intriguing literature survey and analysis of recent research in B2B electronic marketplaces in supply chain management. The second is Bell and Nguyen's profound and important connections established between business intelligence and the semantic web. Finally, this section closes with Kaewkitipong's candid and very timely look at the gaps between theory versus practice of disintermediation in the tourism industry.

The papers in this LNBIP volume were selected exclusively from the e-Commerce and e-Business (eBIZ SIG) tracks at the 16th Americas Conference on Information Systems (AMCIS), which was held in Lima, Peru on August 12–15, 2010. Overall, 48 papers were submitted to eBIZ SIG related tracks at AMCIS 2010, 28 were accepted for the conference and 13 were selected for this volume.

We would like to thank the contributing authors, the eBIZ SIG track chairs and the reviewers who contributed to this effort. We would also like to thank Ralf Gerstner and Christine Reiβ from Springer for their support in the production of this LNBIP volume.

June 2010

Matthew L. Nelson
Michael J. Shaw
Troy J. Strader

Table of Contents

e-Business Models and IS in Financial Markets

e-Commerce Use and Design

e-Business Research Issues and Methods

Dynamic Revenue Model Design in the Online Services Business: Two Cases in Japan

Masao Kakihara

Yahoo! JAPAN Research
mkakihar@yahoo-corp.jp

Abstract. This paper addresses the dynamic nature of business model design in the online services business. It particularly focuses on *revenue models* as a critical driver for mobilizing the dynamics of business models in high-velocity market environments. It argues that a dynamic revenue model design should be a fundamental strategic practice especially for online services that face significant market and technological uncertainties. To discuss implications of dynamic revenue model design in real business contexts, we examine two Japanese online service businesses: Yahoo! JAPAN and GREE. We found that the framework of dynamic revenue model design offers both researchers and practitioners ean adaptable business perspective on turbulent online service businesses.

Keywords: Revenue model, Dynamic design, Online services, Japan.

1 Introduction

In the last decade or so, research on business models has proliferated and a variety of definitions, conceptions, and frameworks have been developed. This trend clearly shows that along with traditional strategic factors such as competence, resources, core assets, etc., the design and implementation of business models have become critical considerations for a firm's growth and success in the contemporary business environment. Without exception, today's firms are faced with rapid changes in their competitive environment. Competitive advantages resulting from long and continuous effort can be wiped out in a very short period of time by unpredictable changes in customer demand. Changes are often driven by the advent of dramatically innovative new technologies from relatively small firms. In particular, all business players, be they hardware-based, software-based, or service-oriented, in every industrial field face the risk of 'disruptive innovations' (Bower & Christensen, 1995; Christensen & Overdorf, 2000) that bring about sudden changes in their environment.

ICT-related businesses are perhaps the most turbulent; the pace of technological advances in this industry is faster than in other technology-oriented industries. For example, cloud computing and mobile technologies have recently begun to overshadow client-PC-based systems. In such a competitive environment, the potential source of sustainable competitiveness is not the tangible, hardware-based assets, but rather 'architectures' of doing business and making money, namely, *business models*. Therefore, it is natural that much of the research on business models has been conducted in technology-oriented fields such as information systems and e-commerce.

M.L. Nelson et al. (Eds.): Sustainable e-Business Management, LNBIP 58, pp. 1–12, 2010.

However, as only a few scholars have pointed out, the research on business models has failed to take into account an important factor that characterizes ICT-related businesses as distinct from others: the *dynamics of business models*. Even though ICT-related businesses are in a turbulent and competitive environment, business model researchers have implicitly taken a static and linear perspective on their business model design. In reality, though, firms must continuously redesign their business models to survive in a highly competitive market. This is particularly true in the online services business, where many companies, from small startups to mega corporations like Google, Yahoo!, and Facebook, are in severe competition with each other.

This paper emphasizes the dynamic nature of business models in the online services business. In so doing, we particularly look at *revenue models* as a critical driver for mobilizing the dynamics of business models. We argue that a dynamic revenue model design should be a fundamental strategic practice for online service businesses that face considerable market and technological uncertainty. We examine two Japanese online service businesses, Yahoo! JAPAN and GREE, and discuss the implications of dynamic revenue model design in these real business contexts.

2 A Call for a Simple and Dynamic Perspective for Business Models

Although the idea was already in the air, few people would deny that Timmers (1998) initiated scholarly discussions on business models. Following Timmers' article, researchers have discussed the roles and significance of business models in contemporary business contexts, and they have tried to define and classify business models. Throughout the last decade, the scholarly debate on business models has searched for a 'definitive' answer for what a business model is. Despite their efforts, there is still a lack of consensus.

Al-Debei et al. (2008) examine a wide range of definitions from various researchers and their underpinning theories and offer the following ten guidelines in the hope of establishing a consensus in subsequent business model discussions:

1) A way in which organizations create value;
2) A way in which an organization generates revenue;
3) An abstraction of the existing business and a future planned business;
4) An architecture for the organization, including its assets, products, services, and information flow;
5) A business logic relating to the ways in which businesses are being conducted;
6) A way in which an organization enables transactions through the coordination and collaboration among parties and multiple companies;
7) An organization's strategy or set of strategies;
8) An interface or a theoretical layer between the business strategy and the business processes;
9) A conceptual tool, a business abstraction, and a blueprint;
10) A way of understanding a single organization or a network of organizations.

As these guidelines imply, the discussions on what a business model is and what role it plays in actual business are so multifaceted that the researchers have been trying to define them in altogether diverse ways. We believe this can only result in further confusion about the definitions and roles of business model concepts. To make good use of a concept and realize its full potential, we need a simplified approach that avoids hype and buzzwords.

Hence, in this paper, we will not propose alternative definitions or classifications of business model concepts since doing so would only complicate things. Rather, we shall critically look at a fundamental assumption underpinning conceptualizations of business models, i.e., their static nature, or lack of dynamics.

With few exceptions (e.g. MacInnes, 2005; Bouwman & MacInnes, 2006; de Reuver et al., 2009), discussions relating to business models have adopted a *static* and *linear* perspective on their design. By static, we mean that a conceptualization sees a business model as unchanging over time, even in a rapidly changing environment. By linear, we mean that it assumes that a business model follows from higher levels of strategic decision-making, i.e., from missions, objectives, and strategies. This assumption is based on conventional frameworks of strategic management research that presuppose, explicitly or implicitly, a 'waterfall' model of strategic decision making.

Various perspectives in strategic management hold to the assumption that the competitive environment around the firm is stable and mostly unchanging. The position-based perspective of competitive strategy based on industrial economics (e.g. Porter, 1980; 1985) assumes that the economic structure of competition is stable and that taking a superior position to competitors is of paramount importance. The resource-based perspective of firms' capability also assumes stable competitive environments (e.g. Barney, 1991; Grant, 1991). By its nature, a firm's resources cannot be enhanced in a short period of time. Although some recent studies have tried to take environmental dynamics into account (e.g. Brandenburger & Nalebuff, 1996; Eisenhardt and Martin, 2000), they still presuppose a linear, 'waterfall' model of strategic decision making that goes from *missions* and *objectives* to *strategies* and *tactics* (the everyday operations of a firm's business) (See Figure 1).

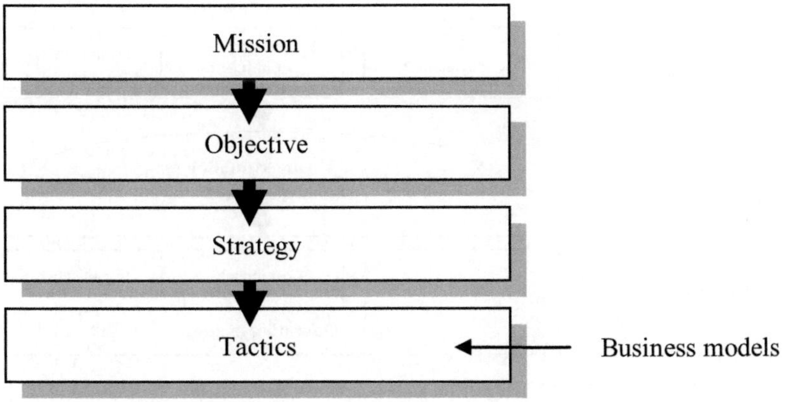

Fig. 1. The conventional 'waterfall' model of strategic decision making

However, given that competitive environments are rapidly changing and technological innovations such as digital and network technologies are accelerating this change, we believe that the setting of concrete missions and objectives or even of strategies is no longer a critical task in strategic management. In a fast-moving environment, missions, objectives, and strategies might have to be continuously revised over time, and the firm would have to focus on tactics rather than strategy. The faster the environmental changes are, the more important the firm's practical ways of value creation and value capture become. That is, for businesses to survive in rapidly changing, highly competitive environments, their business models have to be 'tactically' designed and operationalized.

To cope with rapidly changing competitive environments, particularly in ICT-driven businesses, we need a simpler, more dynamic and non-linear perspective for design and operationalization of business models, not the static and linear ones upon which most of the previous business models have relied.

Here, we shall employ one of the simplest business model concepts. Weill et al. (2005)'s definition consists of two elements: (a) *what the business does*, and (b) *how the business makes money doing these things*. Whereas many researchers have tried to expand this definition to make it more comprehensive and general, we will keep the concept as is, i.e., simple and practical enough for real business settings. Weill et al.'s definition of the business model concept consists of two core elements: *operation* and *value*.

The researchers of Boston Consulting Group offer a sophisticated conception of a business model (Lindgardt et al., 2009). Through their research on business model innovations in various firms, they identified two essential elements that a business model should have: the *value proposition* and the *operating model*, each of which has three sub-elements. The value proposition consists of the *target segment(s)*, *product or service offering*, and *revenue model*. The operating model consists of the *value chain*, *cost model*, and *organization* (See Figure 2). This framework is intended to be a general one that can be applied to many other businesses besides ICT-related ones.

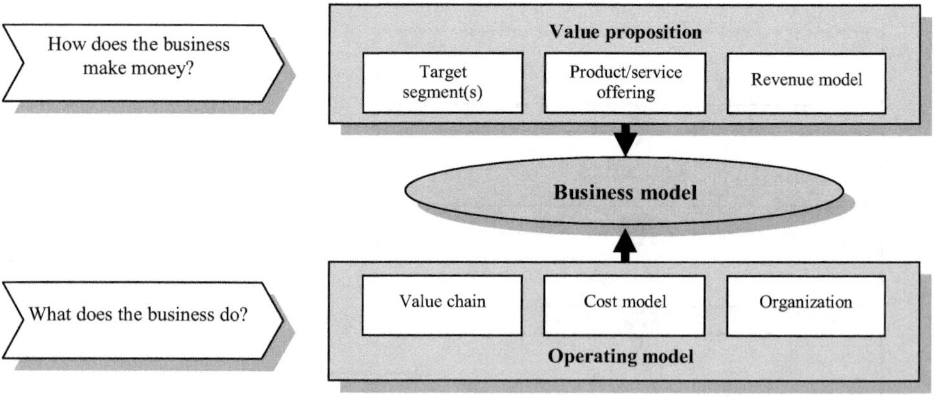

Fig. 2. A simple framework of a business model (After Weill et al., 2006 and Lindgardt et al., 2009)

3 Dynamic Revenue Model Design for Online Service Business

The online services business is one of the most competitive markets today. Its advent more or less coincided with the release of the first beta version of Netscape Navigator in 1994 and Windows 95 in 1995. These systems enabled ordinary people to browse World Wide Web services on their personal computers. It has since taken only fifteen years or so for many online service businesses to emerge, and some have developed into mega corporations, e.g., Yahoo!, eBay, Amazon.com, Google, MySpace, and Facebook. It should be noted too that even more online service businesses disappeared during the same time.

There are a variety of online services, ranging from traditional services such as portals, search engines, and e-commerce sites to emerging online services such as SaaS (Software-as-a-Service), social computing tools and services, and virtual worlds (Lyons et al., 2009). The proliferation of online services has been accelerated by the rise of social stream media such as Twitter and location-based services such as Four-Square.

Besides being associated with the rapid pace of changes in the market, technology, and regulation, the online services business has the characteristic of *dynamic design of revenue models*.

As the stories of Google, Yahoo!, and many other firms clearly show, most online services businesses start operations without a clear revenue model. For example, the two young Stanford graduate students who founded Google in 1998 had no particular revenue model in mind. The company existed on venture capital (VC) until it started selling keyword advertisements two years later (Battelle, 2005). The case of Google is typical. Most of the successful online service firms did not have a clear revenue model when they began operations. Rather, they developed cutting-edge, technology-driven services and offered them free to customers. Then, they rapidly improved their customer's experience to get a good reputation as soon as possible. The latest example of this sort of development is Twitter, a text-based micro-blogging service that has rapidly expanded since beginning in 2007. Although Twitter has millions of monthly unique visitors, it still lacks a concrete revenue model and just announced their potential revenue model, 'promoted tweets,' in April 2010.

There seem to be two reasons for the absence of revenue models at the beginning. Firstly, online services typically do not require a lot of assets and/or funding to start up. By using commercial infrastructural services such as server hosting, online storage, and database services, people can start an online service with a limited amount of initial funding. Secondly, online services need to get a widespread and favorable customer reputation as quickly as possible because network externalities among customers can be a critical driver for service expansion (Chun & Hahn, 2006). Therefore, online services companies tend to put much more effort, tangible or intangible, on how to gather customers quickly rather than how to monetize themselves, particularly in the first phase of their business.

As discussed above, post-launch, dynamic design of revenue models is probably the most distinctive characteristic of the online services business. It should be noticed too that revenue models in the online services business can be designed independently of other business model elements. For instance, the service may remain the same but different revenue models may be implemented within the business model (See Figure 3).

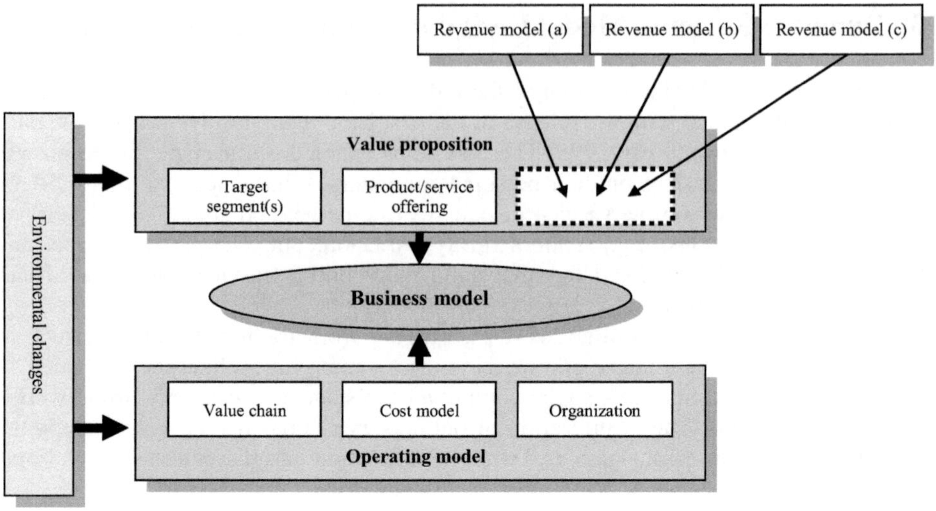

Fig. 3. Dynamic Revenue Model Design in the Online Services Business

4 Main Revenue Models for Online Service Business

Scholars have paid little attention to how revenue models are associated with business models. Although some see revenue models as an important element in business model design (e.g. Rappa, 2000; Alt & Zimmermann, 2001; Magretta, 2002), they do not see them as 'critical' to the design and operationalization of business models in real markets. As indicated above, making money through effective value creation and delivery is of paramount importance for competitiveness in high-velocity market environments. Therefore, we here examine several revenue models especially for the online services business.

The mainstream revenue model in the online services business is the *advertising model*. Almost all online services have at one time been offered to customers for free. In the advertising model, third-party advertisers pay money to service providers to utilize the service's media functions for promoting their products and/or services. The advertising model has been so dominant in the online services business that many people tend to think all the online services should be free, just like TV broadcasting (not cable TV services).

The global financial crisis of 2009 has been a significant problem for any business relying on the advertising model as their primary revenue model. Big advertisers, e.g., large consumer product manufacturers and service providers, have reduced their advertising expenditures on mass media such as TV, newspapers, and magazines. This has directly hit the revenues of advertising-based businesses, and the online services business is no exception. It is time for online service firms to embrace dynamic redesign of their revenue models so that they can adapt to and take advantage of the environmental changes.

Online services have several potential revenue models (See Table 1). As mentioned above, the *advertising model* is the most widely used model for monetization of online services. It creates revenues by providing media functions of the services to advertisers. Display ads (banner ads) are a traditional form of online ads, whereas search ads and content-match ads are new forms. The *brokerage model* is widely utilized for e-commerce and auction services, and it monetizes by matching shoppers and sellers of services. The *platform* model is a way of offering a business platform to third-party service providers and end users. As the success of Facebook and Apple's iTunes Store shows, the accumulation of products/services and potential customers can heighten the value of the platform itself.

The advertising, brokerage, and platform revenue models all presuppose 'multi-sided markets', where two or more distinct user groups interact with each other for their own benefit (Eisenmann et al., 2006; Boudreau & Hagiu, 2009). In contrast, the *service/content sales model* is a direct approach to sell certain values to a single user group. Multi-sided market models are common in the online services business, whereas the direct-to-user sales model is still largely unexplored.

Table 1. Revenue models in the online services business

	Mechanism	*Core sources of value*	*Multi-sided/single-side market*	*Examples*
Advertising model [AD]	- Offers advertisers promotional media functions - Offers users online services for free or low price	- Site traffic (the number of visitors)	- Multi-sided (advertisers, users)	- Display ads - Search ads - Content-match ads
Brokerage model [BR]	- Offers market participants intermediary functions for matching their demands	- Scale and frequency of transactions - Efficiency of matching	- Multi-sided (different market participants)	- E-commerce - Auction
Platform model [PT]	- Offers service providers a platform for doing business - Offers users a wide range of services	- High level of accumulation of content/services and (potential) customers	- Multi-sided (service providers, users)	- Facebook widgets - iTunes Store
Service/content sales model [SA]	- Offers users certain pay services/content	- Direct value to users for usage/possession of the service/content	- Single-side (direct users)	- Subscription fees - Utility fees for SaaS - Content sales

5 Two Cases in the Japanese Online Services Business

Japan's broadband internet access and 3G mobile networks are comparatively better than those of other developed countries. As a result, Japanese online services have been highly competitive and have developed rapidly (OECD, 2008; Kakihara, 2008). A rigid strategy employing a static business model cannot sustain a firm's development in a situation where numerous internet-driven start-ups arise and severely compete with each other. As examples of dynamic revenue model design, therefore, the online services *Yahoo! JAPAN* and *GREE* are particularly worth looking at; they succeeded in dynamically redesigning their business operations and prospering a highly turbulent and competitive market.

For each case, two dimensions will be examined: *core business domains* that accommodate continuous revenue streams for their constant business operations, and *revenue models* that actually create those streams. Publicly available online financial information was used in this analysis. The operating models including cost models will not be discussed in this paper.

5.1 Yahoo! Japan: Diversifying Revenue Models

Yahoo! JAPAN (www.yahoo.co.jp) is Japan's largest online portal service and one of Japan's most successful companies in the last decade in terms of expansion of revenue and market capitalization. Since its debut in 1996, Yahoo! JAPAN has expanded by continuously redesigning its business models. The 2008 fiscal year (ended in March 2009) was Yahoo! JAPAN's 12th consecutive year of record sales and profits, and this achievement was despite the global financial and economic downturn. It is also important for us to note that whereas Google, Amazon, eBay, and other online services are popular or even dominating the markets in most of the Western countries, Yahoo! JAPAN is still the top online service in Japan in search, web-based email, online news, and auctions (Yahoo! JAPAN, 2009).

The most striking difference of Yahoo! JAPAN from other online service companies is that it has well-balanced, multiple revenue models (See Table 2 and Figure 4). The company started operations as a portal, and its initial revenue model was advertising. It launched Japan's first online auction service, Yahoo! Auction in 1999, and it followed that development with an ISP service, Yahoo! BB, and a search advertising business in 2001. These new businesses have posted steady revenues since 2001, and like many other online services, they have adopted new revenue models, i.e., *personal services* and *business services*. Thanks to this revenue model diversification, Yahoo! JAPAN prospered in severe market environment after the bursting of the dot-com bubble. Moreover, Yahoo! JAPAN invested in emerging business domains much more swiftly than its competitors did. It launched new-generation ad services (e.g. behavioral targeting ads) and consumer-generated media services like social Q&A services, which further expanded its ad sales.

Table 2. The evolution of Yahoo! JAPAN's business

	1996-2000	2001 - 2005	2006 -
Core business domains	- Portal	- Portal + - *Auction* - *E-commerce* - *ISP* - *Search*	- Portal - Auction - E-commerce - ISP - Search + - *New-generation ads services (Behavioral targeting etc.)* - *CGM services etc.*
Revenue models	- Display ads [AD]	- Display ads [AD] + - *Search ads [AD]* - *Personal services [SA]* - *Business services [BR, PT]*	- Display ads [AD] - Search ads [AD] - Personal services [SA] - Business services [BR, PT] + - *Behavioral targeting ads [AD]* - *Content-matching ads [AD]*

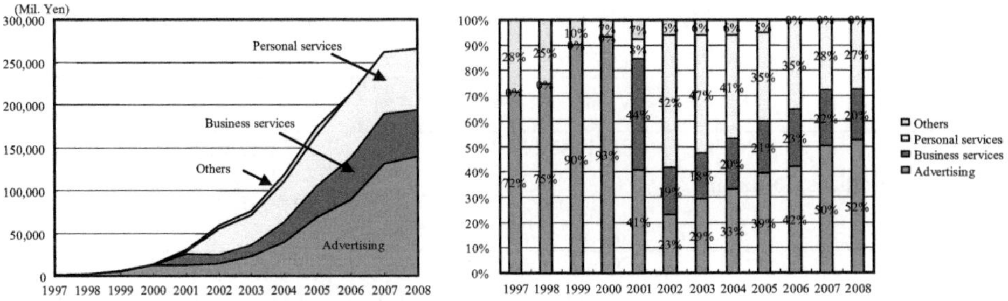

Fig. 4. Trend of Yahoo! JAPAN's revenue models

The case of Yahoo! JAPAN clearly shows that in severe economic situations, diverse revenue models can be a significant driver of growth and stabilization of online companies. Even though strong competitors like Google and eBay have been in the Japanese online services market since the early 2000s, Yahoo! JAPAN, through its dynamic and continuous reconfiguration of its revenue models, has maintained a significant competitive advantage and has had superior financial performance.

5.2 Gree: Switching Revenue Models

As of March 2010, *GREE* (gree.jp) is the second largest SNS in Japan, with 17 million subscribed users. GREE's financial performance in the past year has been nothing less than spectacular. In fiscal 2008 (ended in June 2009), this relatively small company with less than 200 staff generated 14 billion yen in annual revenue, a 375% increase from the previous fiscal year, and even more surprisingly, it had 8 billion in operating income, a 696% increase from the previous year (GREE, 2010).

GREE's dramatic growth since 2007 is due to its strategic shift in business domains (See Table 3 and Figure 5). At its launch in 2004, GREE was a SNS for desktop PCs. Over the next two years, GREE struggled with slow growth of its user base, and it was outpaced by its largest competitor, *mixi*. As mentioned before, online services need to garner a widespread and favorable customer reputation as quickly as possible because network externalities among customers are a critical driver of growth. By 2006, GREE had clearly lost in the initial PC-based phase of the SNS business in Japan.

However, instead of folding operations, its officers decided to concentrate almost all their effort on an emerging business domain: mobile services. They modified their mobile services to offer official service content from Japanese mobile carriers, au of KDDI in 2006 and DoCoMo and Softbank in 2007. They also started to offer their own mobile game content that users could buy to get more fun from their game play. The subsequent mobile content sales were an immediate windfall for GREE, and it went on to make an initial public offering in December 2008. Currently, virtual content sales account for 77% of its annual revenue (Jan-Dec 2009); the rest comes from advertising.

The GREE case shows that a strategic shift in business domains was the critical factor in a dramatic revitalization. In particular, GREE's shifting priority from a PC-based SNS to a mobile SNS driven by game content was the key to transforming its business models and changing the nature of its business as a whole.

Table 3. The evolution of GREE's business

	2004-2006	**2007 -**
Core business domains	- PC-based SNS	-PC-based SNS + -*Mobile SNS*
Revenue models	- Display ads [AD] - Content-match ads [AD]	-Display ads [AD] -Content-match ads [AD] + -*Virtual content sales in mobile game services [SA]*

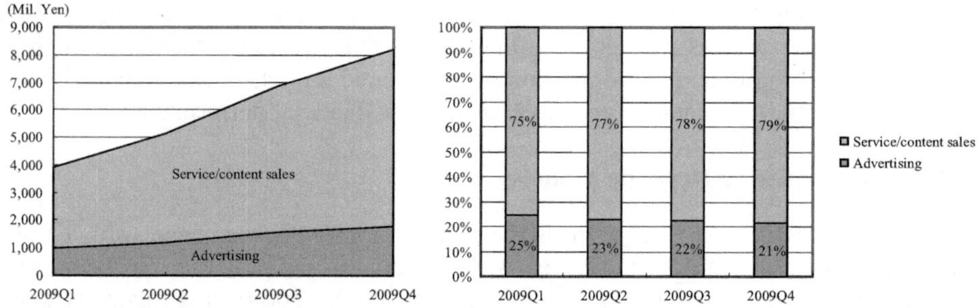

Fig. 5. Rapid change in GREE's revenue models

6 Concluding Remarks

We discussed the dynamic nature of business models by looking at the dynamic revenue models of two Japanese online service businesses.

Due to the limited paper length, we could not consider cases from other countries. However, we believe there must be many more good examples of dynamic revenue model design in the U.S. and Europe. Furthermore, we know there are other business fields that are as fast-moving and turbulent as the online services business is. For example, the apparel business is a fast-moving one where firms businesses are always trying to predict ever-changing customer tastes in fashion. We did not discuss the generalizability or applicability of dynamic revenue model design in other business settings. These issues will be theoretically and empirically addressed in our future work.

References

1. Al-Debei, M.M., El-Haddadeh, R., Avison, D.: Defining the Business Model in the New World of Digital Business. In: Proceedings of the 14th Americas Conference on Information Systems (AMCIS 2008), Toronto, Canada (2008)

2. Alt, R., Zimmermann, H.-D.: Introduction to Special Edition: Business Models. Electronic Markets 11(1), 3–9 (2001)
3. Barney, J.B.: Firm Resources and Sustained Competitive Advantage. Journal of Management 17(1), 99–120 (1991)
4. Battelle, J.: The Search: How Google and its Rivals Rewrote the Rules of Business and Transformed Our Culture. Portfolio, New York (2005)
5. Boudreau, K.J., Hagiu, A.: Platform Rules: Multi-Sided Platforms as Regulators. In: Gawer, A. (ed.) Platforms, Markets and Innovation, pp. 163–189. Edward Elgar Publishing (2009)
6. Bower, J.L., Christensen, C.M.: Disruptive Technologies: Catching the Wave. Harvard Business Review (January-February 1995)
7. Bouwman, H., MacInnes, I.: Dynamic Business Model Framework for Value Webs. In: Proceedings of the 39th Hawaii International Conference on System Sciences (HICSS-39), Hawaii, U.S.A (2006)
8. Brandenburger, A.M., Nalebuff, B.J.: Co-opetition. Doubleday, New York (1996)
9. Christensen, C.M., Overdorf, M.: Meeting the Challenge of Disruptive Change. Harvard Business Review (March-April 2000)
10. Chun, S.Y., Hahn, M.: Network Externality and Future Usage of Internet Services. Internet Research 17(2), 156–168 (2006)
11. de Reuver, M., Bouwman, H., MacInnes, I.: Business Model Dynamics: A Case Survey. Journal of Theoretical and Applied Electronic Commerce Research 4(1), 1–11 (2009)
12. Eisenhardt, K., Martin, J.: Dynamic Capabilities: What Are They? Strategic Management Journal 21(10-11), 1105–1122 (2000)
13. Eisenmann, T., Parker, G., Van Alstyne, M.W.: Strategies for Two-Sided Markets. Harvard Business Review 84(10), 92–101 (2006)
14. Grant, R.M.: The Resource-Based Theory of Competitive Advantage: Implications for Strategy Formulation. California Management Review 33(3), 114–135 (1991)
15. GREE (2010). Investor Relations Reports. (Only in Japanese), `http://www.gree.co.jp/ir/` (Access: April 20, 2010)
16. Kakihara, M.: Japan as the Leading Mobile Market at the Crossroad. In: Yoo, Y., et al. (eds.) Trends in Mobile Technology and Business in the Asia-pacific Region, pp. 87–107. Chandos Publishing, Oxford (2008)
17. Lindgardt, Z., Reeves, M., Stalk, G., Deimler, M.S.: Business Model Innovation: When the Game Gets Tough, Change the Game. In: The Boston Consulting Group Report (2009), `http://www.bcg.com/documents/file36456.pdf` (Access: April 20, 2010)
18. Lyons, K., Playford, C., Messinger, P.R., Niu, R.H., Stroulia, E.: Business Models in Emerging Online Services. In: Proceedings of the 15th Americas Conference on Information Systems (AMCIS 2009), San Francisco, U.S.A. (2009)
19. MacInnes, I.: Dynamic Business Model Framework for Emerging Technologies. International Journal of Services Technology and Management 6(1), 3–19 (2005)
20. Magretta, J.: Why Business Models Matter. Harvard Business Review 80(5), 86–92 (2002)
21. OECD, Information Technology Outlook 2008 (2008), `http://www.oecd.org/document/20/0,3343,en_2649_33757_41892820_1_1_1_1,00.html (Access: April 20, 2010)`
22. Porter, M.E.: Competitive Strategy. Free Press, New York (1980)
23. Porter, M.E.: Competitive Advantage: Creating and Sustaining Superior Performance. Free Press, New York (1985)

24. Rappa, M.: Managing the Digital Enterprise (2000), http://digitalenterprise.org/ (Access: April 20, 2010)
25. Timmers, P.: Business Models for Electronic Commerce. Electronic Markets 8(2), 3–8 (1998)
26. Weill, P., Malone, T.W., D'Urso, V.T., Herman, G., Woerner, S.L.: Do Some Business Models Perform Better than Others? A Study of the 1000 Largest US Firms. MIT Center for Coordination Science Working Paper No. 266 (2005)
27. Yahoo! JAPAN, Annual Report 2008 (2009), http://ir.yahoo.co.jp/en/archives/nenji/ (Access: April 20, 2010)

Pricing of Content Services – An Empirical Investigation of Music as a Service

Jonathan Doerr, Alexander Benlian, Johannes Vetter, and Thomas Hess

Ludwig-Maximilians-University
Munich School of Management
Institute for Information Systems and New Media
{doerr,benlian,vetter,thess}@bwl.lmu.de

Abstract. In the last years new concepts of digital music distribution have been developed. One of them is Music as a Service, which provides music streaming over the internet as a service - without transferring ownership for the content. This differentiates Music as a Service from Download to Own, which is used by music download platforms predominantly and is the most widely studied concept in academic research. The aim of this paper is to receive first research implications about customers' attitudes towards MaaS.

Based on an empirical survey of 132 Music as a Service users, this research explores the effects of product configurations on consumers' utility and their willingness to pay (WTP) for premium offers. We can show that next to price, contract duration and music quality as the most important product attributes, there is a high WTP for overcoming insufficient mobile internet coverage.

Keywords: Music as a Service, Content as a Service, music streaming, digital distribution, willingness to pay, pricing, business model.

1 Introduction

It seems that the market for legal music downloads is about to establish itself. In 2009, 27 per cent of industry's revenue was generated in digital channels through over 400 licensed music services worldwide. However, in the time from 2004-2009, the music industry's global sales fell by 30% (IFPI 2010). There are two main reasons for that, which have been empirically demonstrated. First, there is significant revenue lost, due to 29.8 million frequent users of file-sharing services in the top five EU markets alone (Zentner 2006). Second, the digitization of music allows the unbundling of albums and in the digital world customers download singles increasingly. This means that the downloads are not as rewarding as previous CD sales were (Elberse 2010). To address these two problems, there are a number of new distribution concepts, one of which is Music as a Service (MaaS). The first music platforms, which use MaaS, e.g. Spotify, Grooveshark, Deezer and Steereo, already started their business.

The current revenue source of MaaS is a combination of ad-based financing and a model referred to as "freemium". In the freemium model, services can be used both for free or with a paid subscription to obtain premium content. In the case of MaaS the free version is also financed by advertising. Other popular services in the Internet

M.L. Nelson et al. (Eds.): Sustainable e-Business Management, LNBIP 58, pp. 13–24, 2010.

such as Flickr, LinkedIn and Skype already use the freemium model. Here, users who are willing to pay for additional services are clearly outnumbered and move usually at five per cent (Anderson 2009). According to estimates, there are only four per cent premium subscribers on the MaaS platform Spotify, as well (Jackson and Mitton 2010). But what is behind MaaS and where is it located on the research map?

There are new opportunities for content distribution in the Internet. One of these new distribution concepts is Content as a Service (CaaS), whose technical foundation is referred to as data-streaming and which is analog to the concept of the much discussed Software as a Service (SaaS). CaaS describes a type of business model which provides content over the internet as a service - without transferring ownership. This differentiates CaaS from "rent or buy models" in the internet. MaaS represents the CaaS concept on music platforms.

CaaS as a new form of content distribution has not yet been explored and therefore requires, in addition to the technological investigation, a scientific investigation of economic issues. One of these issues is the design of viable business models for providers of such services. MaaS, which is represented with first offers on the market, is therefore a suitable subject of study. The premium offer, as an important revenue stream of the current business models, stands in the center of attention. This paper examines from a customer perspective, the importance of the different features of premium offers. It shows the preferred features and the WTP for the different product attributes. The results will specifically shed light on current business models in the field of MaaS, but will be transferable to CaaS as a whole.

The structure of the paper is as follows. In the next section, a review of the relevant literature on the configuration and the WTP for digital music offers is presented, pointing out a research gap in empirically testing these questions for MaaS. Subsequently we illustrate the state of the art of MaaS by showing the characteristics and business models of these services and close this chapter with the research questions and framework. We then proceed by describing the methodological approach to measure consumer utility and WTP. The empirical results of the study are shown in the following chapter. Thereafter, we discuss our results and suggest implications for other researchers and the music industry. The paper closes with an assessment of the limitations of our study and future research in this area.

2 Literature Review

As mentioned before music streaming platforms can be seen as a service. In contrast to the Download-to-Own (DtO) business model, the customer doesn't buy the song and therefore doesn't acquire any property rights. Instead, the customer uses a service which is specified by the characteristics immateriality and the uno-actu-priciple, which means that production and consumption happen simultaneously. This is due to the integration of the user (as an external factor) into the production process (Chesbrough and Spohrer 2006; Rai and Sambamurthy 2006). In case of MaaS, immateriality doesn't stand for the digital good itself but the service of provision. Production and consumption don't stand for the real production of a song in the studio but rather for the process of listening to music. Due to the music streaming, the consumer is included in the production process which wouldn't happen without him.

For the MaaS user the payment method changes as well. Instead of paying for each song separately as it is common in the Pay-per-Download (PpD) business models, the user pays periodic fees for a subscription. These subscription or rental fees, are also often used on SaaS solutions (Cusumano 2007). Usually this monthly fee is well below the one-time payment for the license. Contrary to SaaS the content supply with MaaS increases due to the release of new songs without an increase of the monthly fee. The assessment base for the fee in current services is independent of the usage and builds on the flat-rate principle.

Current research on the design of services and the WTP in the area of digital music distribution is mostly based on PpD-models of DtO. Using a conjoint measurement of music downloads, Bamert et al. argue that the price is the most important attribute for the purchase decision of consumers (Bamert, Meier-Bickel and Rüdt 2005). The study of Buxmann et al. shows that the willingness to pay for current hits, older songs, rarities and newcomer differs (Buxmann et al. 2005). Also based on a conjoint measurement Breidert and Hahsler investigate the WTP for different product configurations of music downloads. They used the attributes price, package (number of songs in the subscription), sound quality, distribution channel and booklet. Price and package were by far the most important attributes for the subjects. Furthermore they showed that the WTP per title decreases with larger package sizes, which is an argument against a linear pricing strategy for flat-rate models (Breidert and Hahsler 2006). In 2007 Buxmann et al. conducted an empirical investigation with internet users that showed that a better part of consumers evaluate the price for music downloads as to high. Furthermore, they argued that price reductions could seriously increase the revenues in the market segment of online music (Buxmann, Strube and Pohl 2007). An alternative form of payment in DtO-offers was analyzed by Regner und Barria. They investigated the payment behavior on a platform were customers may pay what they want for albums, as long as the payment is within a given price range. They concluded that the fact that consumers do pay voluntarily, can be explained with a sufficiently high level of social preferences (Regner and Barria 2009). Chiang and Assane explored the influential factors on the WTP for digital music and concluded with the indication of consumer acceptance of fee-based music services (Chiang and Assane 2009). Current research analyzes the effect of the disappearance of digital rights management (DRM) on the price. The results confirm earlier studies and show that the WTP rises with the disappearance of DRM (Sinha, Machado and Sellman 2010).

Some publications indicate that there are plenty of pricing strategies for digital goods that partially suit online music very well. Especially, consumers show different WTP that could be perfectly exploited with new pricing strategies and alternative licensing procedures (Bhattacharjee et al. 2006). Nonetheless, the mentioned studies almost exclusively focus on PpD for DtO. Hence, there is a research gap concerning the design of music streaming services or rather fee-based services as well as the WTP for these services. This research gap will be covered in the paper at hand.

3 Business Model and Characteristics of Music as a Service

The technical concept of streaming music is not new and is used in lots of services like e.g. last.fm. Such services usually show the characteristics of radio stations. They do not offer the possibility to listen directly and on-demand to the music. The central point of MaaS is not the sale or lending of music, but the service of making all the music available all the time. Offerings like Spotify, Grooveshark, Deezer and Steereo are the first providers using the concept of MaaS.

Because the music is on demand accessible, MaaS follows the concept of classical DtO offers. For a first classification of MaaS, a comparison of these two is therefore obvious. This classification is based on a content analysis of the current music platform providers. The differences between the two distribution concepts are presented in Table 1.

Table 1. Comparison of Download to Own- und Music as a Service-platforms

Characteristics	Download to Own platforms (e.g. iTunes)	Music as a Service platforms (e.g. Spotify)
Payment	Pay per Download	Free (advertising-based) and flat rate
Consumption	Download to Own / Offline	Streaming / Online
Server environment	Client-server model	Client-server model and Peer-to-Peer model
Device synchronization	Synchronization after download	Streaming with mobile application
Ownership	Ownership (without DRM)	Without ownership (with DRM)
Community features	Not available	Available, e.g. Playlist sharing
User registration	Required	Required for subscription model only

The biggest difference between DtO and MaaS is the payment. The concept of the DTO adopted the sales model of physical music distribution. The customer pays an amount per song or album, mostly US$ 0.99 or US$ 9.99. In the case of MaaS, the customer uses the platform entirely free or she pays a monthly subscription fee, mostly US$ 9.99. In contrast to downloads, MaaS users have to be online to receive their music by streaming. To reduce the transmission costs, MaaS platforms use both client-server and the peer-to-peer concepts. For mobile consumption, the user of DtO has to synchronize the music with his mobile device. In the case of the MaaS the music gets streamed to the mobile device with the help of a mobile application. Some of these applications allow the offline availability of selected titles, as well. They are stored in the cache of the device.

With the help of community features, MaaS users have the ability to share their playlists and favorite tracks for example on social networks. Some MaaS providers require the users registration only when signing a contract for a premium product. Other characteristics such as music quality, music recommendation, search functions, etc., are the same or similar for both distribution concepts and will be not discussed at this point.

4 Research Framework: Determinants of Customer Value

Previous research models of customer value of digital goods have traditionally included price, quality, distribution channel, DRM and related attributes (Breidert and Hahsler 2006; Mann et al. 2008). In terms of MaaS we also use price, quality and the distribution channel as attributes. Regarding a subscription fee, the attribute price is to be extended by the contract duration that we also add as an attribute. The attribute music quality is operationalized as in the reference papers. The distribution channel focuses on the MaaS provider's choice to offer its service via an internet browser on a website or via special software. Furthermore, we add four attributes to our research framework which are regarded as additional features in a premium offer: application for mobile devices, offline access, community features to share playlists or favorites with friends in social networks and personalized music recommendations, generated for example trough collaborative filtering. Figure 1 depicts the attributes and their influence on the customer value, which in turn influence the WTP, and thus determines the pricing.

On the basis of our framework, we formulated three research questions. They all deal with the issues discussed in the introduction of this paper and aim on the one hand at receiving first research implications about customers' attitudes towards MaaS, and on the other hand at getting information for MaaS providers about a proper product configuration.

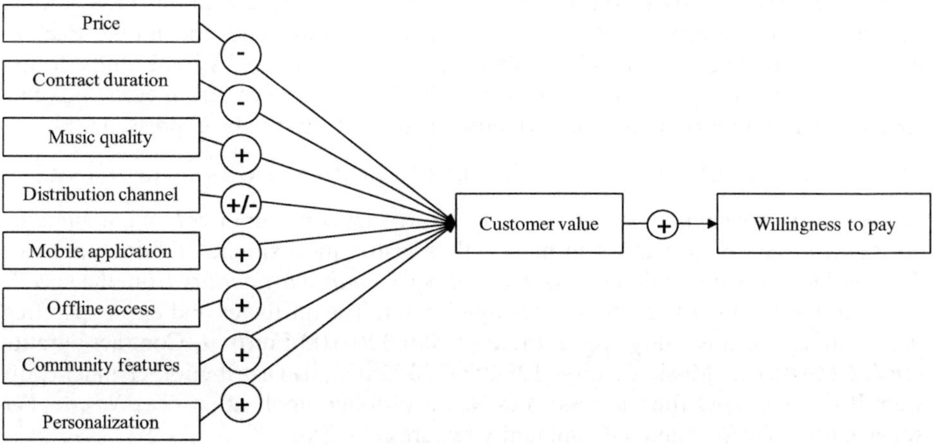

Fig. 1. Research framework: Determinants of customer value

The first research question concerns the relative importance of each attribute in customers' estimation of total utility.

RQ1: How important is each attribute in customers' estimation of total utility of MaaS premium offers?

The second research question investigates the specifications of the attributes. For example, which distribution channel is preferred (Browser or Software) and how does it influence the buying decision?

RQ2: Which attribute levels are preferred and how does it influence the buying decision?

In terms of sensitivity analysis, the third research question clarifies the customers' WTP for each attribute of a MaaS premium offer.

RQ3: How much would customers' WTP for MaaS premium offers rise or fall with changing attribute levels?

5 Research Methodology and Analysis

5.1 Adaptive Conjoint Analysis

The Conjoint analysis (CA) is a method for the measurement of costumer value and preferences for so-called multi-attribute objects. These are goods that are composed of certain product attributes, which each have specific attribute levels. In our study, the adaptive conjoint analysis (ACA) was used. This represents a hybrid model in which the holistic to be evaluated alternative product configurations will be generated due to the previously queried the relevance and importance of individual attributes and attribute levels (Vriens 1995). ACA is an advancement of the classical full profile CA, because it incorporates the advantages of letting respondents evaluate complete product configurations, but does not require every possible combination to be presented and thus significantly reduces complexity and drop-outs (Johnson 1987).

ACA in general is based on four assumptions: First, products, in this case, a MaaS premium offer, are bundles of attributes, which in turn are sales incentives. Each attribute has a number of possible attribute levels. An individual's total utility from a product configuration is equal to the sum of the utilities received from each one of the specifications comprised therein. Formally, the total utility can be expressed as:

(1) $$u_{it} = u_i(a_1) + u_i(a_2) + u_i(a_3) + u_i(a_4) + u_i(a_5) + u_i(a_6) + u_i(a_7) + u_i(a_8)$$

Let u_{it} denote consumer *i*'s *total utility* from product configuration *t*. We assume the attributes to be compensatory in nature, thus justifying a simple addition approach. The *total utility* is a function of $u_i(k_t)$, consumer *i*'s *part worth utility* from the specification of the attribute *k* in product configuration *t*. The attributes and exact specifications defined for this study are: a_1 Price (2.00/6.00/10.00 Euro), a_2 Contract duration (1/6/12 Month), a_3 Music quality (128/256/320 kbit/s), a_4 Distribution channel (Software/Browser), a_5 Offline access (Yes/No), a_6 Mobile application *(Yes/No)*, a_7 Personalization (Yes/No) and a_8 Community features (Yes/No).

The second assumption of the ACA is that preferences for the incentives given vary by those interviewed. The different preferences are described by the term part worth utilities. The third assumption is that the sum of the part worth utilities from an offer configuration is equal to customers' total utility who have subscribed to this service. The fourth assumption is that adoption of third can also be applied conversely. If there is information about references to different products, then, we could get the part worth utilities derived for each attribute (Johnson 1987).

The ACA is divided in four steps. The aim of the first step is to find out the preferences of respondents for specific attribute levels. Subsequently, the investigation of the attributes importance occurs. Respondents must specify for each attribute how important the difference between the least and the most preferred attribute level is. In the next step, respondents are faced with paired comparisons to find the better product configuration. The last step is the calibration. The respondent states his purchase intention as a percentage value for different product configurations, which consist of the most important attributes. The results are the calibrated part worth utilities that reflect the utility of each attribute level. Critical to the importance of an attribute is the total interval and not the absolute level of the part worth utility. It is a measure of attribute importance to the preference change (Johnson 1987).

5.2 Deriving Willingness to Pay from Conjoint Data

As the price is included in our conjoint measurement we can calculate the WTP for each possible product configuration using the following method. The method developed by Kohli and Mahajan has already been used in other research papers (Mann et al. 2008; Strube, Pohl and Buxmann 2008). The total utility of a certain product configuration is compared with a reference product. The WTP for the fictitious product is equal with that of the reference product when the worth utility is equal or bigger. The related utilities can be expressed as follows:

(2) $$u_{it|\text{-}p} + u_i(p_{it}) = u_{ir|\text{-}p} + u_{ir}(p_{ir}) + \varepsilon_i$$

As the total utility of a product is defined as the sum of its part worth utility it can be disjointed as follows: $u_{it|\text{-}p}$ is an individual i's total utility of any product configuration t without the price attribute. $u_i(p_t)$ is the individual's part worth utility of a specification of the price attribute. $u_{ir|\text{-}p}$ is the individual's total utility of the reference product r without the price attribute, $u_{ir}(p_{ir})$ is the individual's part worth utility of a specification of the price attribute of the reference product, ε_i is any small positive number.

With the ACA we investigated three price points. Using a linear interpolation we could also calculate the utility values $u_i(p_t)$ for additional price points (Kohli and Mahajan 1991; Mann et al. 2008; Strube, Pohl and Buxmann 2008). We conducted the interpolation in steps of 25 cents. If the equation is satisfied, p_{it} reflects the individual's WTP for product configuration t. In the first place, for each consumer a WTP of zero is assumed for the product configuration t. This WTP increases step by step as long as ε_i reaches a minimum or 0. In our analysis only one attribute at a time is changed in its level to ascribe the change of the WTP to this attribute. The reference product can either be an individual's most strongly preferred product or a status quo product (Wübker and Mahajan 1999). In this study we used a product that is currently commercially available as the status quo product. This reference product is mostly bought from the provider Steereo.

5.3 Data Collection and Analysis

Our data was collected using a quantitative standardized online survey from the 1st to the 31st December 2009 on the website of the German MaaS platform Steereo. Steereo is the only MaaS provider in Germany and a typical service comparable to the French Deezer. The only difference between those two and other MaaS platforms is the browser as the distribution channel. The data set of respondents was therefore a passively recruited sample that is subject to self-selection bias and therefore exhibits limited external validity. We used Globalpark's EFS Survey Center 7.0 with the Conjoint Extension 2.0, which facilitated the software assisted adaptive conjoint analysis. The survey was subjected to a pretest, after which the wording and structure of multiple questions were refined. In order to stimulate the response rate, an incentive sweepstake for 50 free trial subscriptions was included. The questionnaire starts with the phases of conjoint analysis. Following the participants were asked to give socio-demographic information and to answer questions about their music consumption habits. Analyses of the exported data were performed using SPSS version 17.0.

6 Results

6.1 Sample Description

A total of 134 participants filled out the questionnaire completely. Two data sets had to be excluded from further analysis because of inconsistent response behavior, so that the adjusted sample consists of 132 participants. The average processing time was 9 minutes and 42 seconds. Among the participants were 98 men and 34 women. 63 per cent were 20 to 29-year-old, followed by the 30 to 39-year-old with approximately 21 per cent. The average age was 28 years, with the youngest participant 16 and the oldest 63 years old. We have 46 per cent employees and 34 per cent students in our data set. Nearly 61 per cent of respondents own a smartphone. The subjects also specified that they daily (13%), several times a week (36%), several times a month (18%) and occasionally (34%) use Steereo. In addition to the use of Steereo, 48 per cent of respondents purchase music on DtO services. Half of these users cannot imagine giving up downloading completely.

6.2 Part Worth Utilities of the Attribute Levels and Importance of the Attributes

The coefficient of determination of the regression of utilities and WTP (R^2) is 0.745. First, the relative importance and then the part worth utilities of the attributes presented, summarized in Table 2.

Table 2. Part worth utilities of the attribute levels and importance of the attributes

Price (20%)	Utility mean	Std. Dev.	**Contract duration (16%)**	Utility mean	Std. Dev.	**Music quality (14%)**	Utility mean	Std. Dev.
2.00 Euro	0.59	0.39	1 Month	0.36	0.30	320 kbit/s	0.26	0.43
6.00 Euro	-0.15	0.18	6 Month	-0.07	0.21	256 kbit/s	-0.02	0.20
10.00 Euro	-0.78	0.31	12 Month	-0.63	0.30	128 kbit/s	-0.59	0.38
Offline access (12%)	Utility mean	Std. Dev.	**Distribution channel (11%)**	Utility mean	Std. Dev.	**Personalization (10%)**	Utility mean	Std. Dev.
Online & Offline	0.29	0.37	Browser	0.14	0.34	Yes	0.14	0.36
Online	-0.52	0.38	Software	-0.37	.037	No	-0.37	0.34
Mobile application (9%)	Utility mean	Std. Dev.	**Community features (7%)**	Utility mean	Std. Dev.	$R^2 = 0.745$		
Yes	0.18	0.32	Yes	0.04	0.31	**Legend**		
No	-0.42	0.29	No	-0.27	0.31	Price (20%) = Relative importance of the attribute		

To answer RQ1 the following section addresses attribute importance. For the volunteers, especially the attribute price (20%), followed by the subscription period (16%), music quality (14%), offline access (12%), distribution channel (11%), personalized recommendations of music (10%), mobile application (9%) and access to various community features (7%).

Based on the part worth utilities of the attribute levels, the preferred product configuration can be read and answered thus RQ2. Because almost all attribute levels have a clear utility direction the optimal product is fairly intuitive. Only the decision on the distribution channel could not be answered in advance. The respondents prefer the browser usage. It should be noted, that the platform Steereo offers its service through the browser. The part worth utilities show, in contrast to the relative importance, significant differences in the impact of product utilities. For example, the product price of 2.00 Euro (0.59) increases the value of total utility by a multiple greater than an existing community feature (0.04).

6.3 Willingness to Pay for Changing Attributes Levels

To answer RQ3 as the reference product for the calculation of WTP, we have opted for a typical configuration of the provider Steereo. It costs 5.00 Euro per month, has contract duration of 6 months, is delivered via the browser and additionally has community features. There is no personalization, no mobile application and no offline access delivered. For the calculation in each case, one attribute was changed and thus determine the WTP for individual attributes, which are summarized in Table 3.

The prices represent the additional monthly WTP of the customer, if the particular attribute is changed in its level. For example, the user would pay 3.25 Euro more per month for a mobile application. If the product has contract duration of 12 months, the provider would have to lower the price 3.00 Euros, to create the same utility for the customer. The results show that the contract duration (5.25 Euro), the music quality (4.50 Euro) and the possibility of offline access (4.50 euro) increase the price most.

Table 3. Willingness to pay for changing the attributes levels per Month

Product attribute	Changing attribute level from	WTP for changing the attribute level
Contract duration #1	12 to 1 Month	Δ 5.25 Euro/Month
Contract duration #2	12 to 6 Month	Δ 3.00 Euro/Month
Music quality #1	128 to 320 kbit/s	Δ 4.50 Euro/Month
Music quality #2	128 to 256 kbit/s	Δ 3.00 Euro/Month
Offline Access	Online to Online&Offline	Δ 4.50 Euro/Month
Distribution	Software to Browser	Δ 2.75 Euro/Month
Mobile application	No to Yes	Δ 3.25 Euro/Month
Personalization	No to Yes	Δ 2.75 Euro/Month
Community features	No to Yes	Δ 1.50 Euro/Month

Compared to the results of the relative importance in this analysis, the value of the mobile application is drawn clearly (3.25 Euro). The low WTP for personalization (2.75 Euro) and community features (1.50 Euro) point to the use of MaaS as an on-demand service.

7 Discussion and Implications

In this study we explored the importance and the WTP for attributes of MaaS premium offers. This is a first empirical investigation of a new distribution model. In comparison to the relative importance, the results concerning the WTP offer a concrete assessment of the different attributes possible. Hence, the combination of the two results allows a sophisticated interpretation of customer needs.

Similar to the empirical investigations of PpD offers with DtO our results show, that the price is by far the most important attribute of premium offers (Bamert, Meier-Bickel and Rüdt 2005). This is strengthened by the contract duration which is also very important for customers. Beside the mobile application the quality of music and offline access are important levers for the pricing of a MaaS premium offer. As distribution channel for the service, the customers favored the browser over the software. As personalization and community features are not important for the purchase decision and also show a low WTP our assumptions are confirmed that MaaS is rather used as a demand service and therefore lines up next to DtO offers.

But the results also show that MaaS falls short of its opportunities due to technical limitations. The subjects give offline access a high relative importance while they give the mobile application a low one. This could invert in the future due to a higher mobile broadband coverage. All things considered this means that the speed of stationary internet is sufficient for CaaS but other technical limitations like insufficient mobile broadband coverage could thwart the CaaS distribution concept. The multiplicity of technical devices and the consumers need to fully exploit their capabilities especially in a mobile context give CaaS a good chance to fully deploy its capabilities. Thereto the internet cloud around the consumer and its devices has to improve.

8 Limitations and Future Research

A significant limitation of the present study lies in its restriction to the German MaaS platform Steereo. While its configuration can be compared with other platforms, future studies should try to investigate the whole MaaS market. The findings of this study may be transferable to other platforms and provide first indications of the configuration and WTP for premium offers.

The recent studies on digital music often took place among established download platforms. In contrast, MaaS is a new distribution concept, and users belong to the group of early adopters. Consequently this study is only a snapshot in time that needs to be replicated in the future. It remains to be explored, how especially the diffusion of mobile Internet sets a different focus in the assessment of premium offers.

Because of the novelty of the topic there are a lot of research gaps and questions for the future. Regarding MaaS, piracy was always a topic which has been heavily discussed in scientific context. All indications are that some users stop illegal downloading while using MaaS platforms (IFPI 2010). Here arise the questions, what influences this decision and how big the impact will be.

For the new form of content distribution, the question arises, from what theoretical perspective, the topic can be examined. First of all, the literature on the Service Science can be applied (Chesbrough and Spohrer 2006; Ostrom et al. 2010). For example the property rights theory could be used, to examine the changes in property rights under MaaS in comparison to the DtO-model. But first it is vitally important to do a precise classification and definition of CaaS in the research area of Service Science.

References

1. Anderson, C.: Free - The Future of a Radical Price. Random House, London (2009)
2. Bamert, T., Meier-Bickel, T.S., Rüdt, C.: Pricing music downloads: A conjoint study. In: Proceedings of the European Academy of Management Annual Conference, pp. 409–416. TUM Business School, Munich (2005)
3. Bhattacharjee, S., Gopal, R.D., Lertwachara, K., Marsden, J.R.: Consumer Search and Retailer Strategies in the Presence of Online Music Sharing. Journal of Management Information Systems 23(1), 129–159 (2006)
4. Breidert, C., Hahsler, M.: Adaptive conjoint analysis for pricing music downloads. In: Proceedings of the 30th Annual Conference of the Gesellschaft für Klassifikation e.V., pp. 1–8. Freie Universität, Berlin (2006)
5. Buxmann, P., Pohl, G., Johnscher, P., Strube, J., Groffmann, H.-D.: Strategies for Digital Music Markets: Pricing and the Effectiveness of Measures against Pirate Copies - Results of an Empirical Study. In: Proceedings of 13th European Conference on Information Systems, Regensburg, pp. 1–12 (2005)
6. Buxmann, P., Strube, J., Pohl, G.: Cooperative Pricing in Digital Value Chains - the Case of Online Music. Journal of Electronic Commerce Research 8(1), 32–40 (2007)
7. Chesbrough, H., Spohrer, J.: A research manifesto for services science. Communications of the ACM 49(7), 35–40 (2006)
8. Chiang, E.P., Assane, D.: Estimating The Willingness To Pay For Digital Music. Contemporary Economic Policy 27(4), 512–522 (2009)
9. Cusumano, M.A.: The changing labyrinth of software pricing. Communications of the ACM 50(7), 19–22 (2007)
10. Elberse, A.: Bye Bye Bundles: The Unbundling of Music in Digital Channels. Journal of Marketing (forthcoming), 1–39 (2010)
11. IFPI, IFPI Digital Music Report, - Music how, when, where you want it, London (2010)
12. Jackson, J., Mitton, G.: Only 4% of Spotify users pay to listen (2010), `http://digitalmedia.strategyeye.com/article/fe34f088af/2010/01/22/Only_4_of_Spotify_users_pay_to_listen/` (last viewed on 02/03/2010)
13. Johnson, R.M.: Adaptive Conjoint Analysis. In: Sawtooth Software Conference on Perceptual Mapping. Conjoint Analysis, and Computer Interview, Ketchum, ID, pp. 253–265 (1987)
14. Kohli, R., Mahajan, V.: A Reservation-Price Model for Optimal Pricing of Multiattribute Products in Conjoint Analysis. Journal of Marketing Research 28(3), 347–354 (1991)

15. Mann, F., Ahrens, S., Benlian, A., Hess, T.: Timing is money - evaluating the effects of early availability of feature films via video on demand. In: Proceedings of the International Conference on Information Systems (ICIS) 2008, Paris, pp. 1–18 (2008)
16. Ostrom, A.L., Bitner, M.J., Brown, S.W., Burkhard, K.A., Goul, M., Smith-Daniels, V., Demirkan, H., Rabinovich, E.: Moving Forward and Making a Difference: Research Priorities for the Science of Service. Journal of Service Research 13(1), 4–36 (2010)
17. Rai, A., Sambamurthy, V.: Editorial Notes - The Growth of Interest in Service Management: Opportunities for Information Systems Scholars. Information Systems Research 17(4), 327–331 (2006)
18. Regner, T., Barria, J.A.: Do consumers pay voluntarily? The case of online music. Journal of Economic Behavior & Organization 71, 395–406 (2009)
19. Sinha, R.K., Machado, F.S., Sellman, C.: Don't Think Twice, It's All Right: Music Piracy and Pricing in a DRM-Free Environment. Journal of Marketing 74(2), 40–54 (2010)
20. Strube, J., Pohl, G., Buxmann, P.: Der Einfluss von Digital Rights Management auf die Zahlungsbereitschaften für Online-Musik - Untersuchung auf Basis einer Conjointanalyse. In: Proceedings of the MKWI, Munich, pp. 1043–1058 (2008)
21. Vriens, M.C.: Conjoint Analysis in Marketing. Developments in Stimulus Representation and Segmentation Methods, University of Groningen (1995)
22. Wübker, G., Mahajan, V.: A conjoint analysis-based procedure to measure reservation price and to optimally price product bundles. In: Füderer, R., Herrmann, A., Wübker, G. (eds.) Optimal bundling: Marketing strategies for improving economic performance, Berlin, pp. 157–174 (1999)
23. Zentner, A.: Measuring the Effect of File Sharing on Music Purchases. Journal of Law and Economics 49(4), 63–90 (2006)

Informational Determinants of Customer Acquisition and eTailer Revenue

Amitava Dutta and Nirup M. Menon

George Mason University
{adutta,nmenon}@gmu.edu

Abstract. Firms have leveraged the Internet in innumerable ways to derive business value from this technology. However, one class of firm that is distinctively dependent on this platform is the online retailer or eTailer. One aspect of this distinctiveness is that eTailers depend on their Web portals to attract customers, engage them in purchase activities, and execute transactions connected with a purchase ultimately leading to revenue generation. In this study, we wish to examine the informational determinants of this customer interaction and their relationship to eTailer revenue. We propose a two-phase path model of customer acquisition leading to revenue generation. Informational determinants are included in the path structure. The model is empirically tested using a dataset of 500 eTailers. The results indicate that the model is able to explain a large proportion of the variability in financial performance of these eTailers. We find that the type of information made available on the eTailer's website, along with transactional capabilities and customizability, significantly correlate with customer acquisition. Analytical capability correlated significantly with the transition to phase two – which we refer to as conversion. These findings have implications for information technology governance within firms as they manage their IT investments to deliver maximum value.

Keywords: Online retailer, customer acquisition, portal functionality, financial performance.

1 Introduction

Organizations continue to make ever more widespread use of the Internet to carry out common business activities with customers, suppliers, and other business partners. While the nature and extent of Internet use varies across organizations, one class of organization is especially dependent on this technology. These are the so called Internet retailers or eTailers. A distinctive characteristic of these companies is that their Web portals and the Internet is the primary platform for them to ply their wares, solicit customers, execute purchases and otherwise maintain relationships with their customers. These are the activities that, ultimately, lead to revenue generation. It therefore stands to reason that the information-based functionalities of their Web portals will play an important role in these customer interactions and revenue generation. There is an extensive body of research that examines a variety of consumer behaviors at eTailer websites. It is not possible to enumerate all the different types of studies,

M.L. Nelson et al. (Eds.): Sustainable e-Business Management, LNBIP 58, pp. 25–35, 2010.

but some examples will illustrate the variety. Some studies, for instance, use the technology acceptance model to explain consumer's use of a portal (e.g. Chen et al., 2002). Others have examined the effect of portal layout on customer behavior (e.g., Vrechopoulos and Atherinos, 2009; Kim et al., 2007; Jiang and Benbasat, 2007). Sia et al (2009) establish the importance of incorporating cultural factors into website design, and the effectiveness of recommender systems has been investigated in Xiao and Benbasat (2007). A few relationships between website features – informational and transactional – have been studied (Mithas et al., 2006), but other important features and relationships are yet to be studied. To include a broader set of features and relationships, we take a process view of revenue generation by an eTailer, which consists of customer acquisition, conversion to a purchase, followed by retention of the customer for multiple future purchases. With this process in mind, we wish to examine the relative impact of different information-based functionalities of the eTailer's portal on this revenue generation process. We test the model empirically and, based on the results, discuss implications for the design and implementation of such Internet based systems by eTailers.

A small example would be helpful in setting the stage for our investigation. 1-800-flowers is a quintessential eTailer – its Internet portal is the focal site for customer interactions and revenue generation. The portal for 1-800-Flowers, pictured in Figure 1, shows that a lot of the content is information in that it tells the consumer about products and services provided by this company. Some of this information is static, such as pictures of flower arrangements. Other content is dynamic, such as an audio or video clip from a famous personality promoting 1-800-flowers, or the status of a customer order. Other content clearly involves a two-way interaction between the customer and 1-800-Flowers, such as various payment functions and the functions 'Catalog quick order', and 'Flower Blog' in Figure 2. The website offers search capability, as in determining the availability of a certain type of flower arrangement for a specific day and occasion and at a specific location. Affiliates programs are particularly popular with eTailers given the ease with which electronic links can be established between the two entities. On the other hand, there are no sophisticated recommender systems on this portal as there are on, say, Amazon.com. For example,

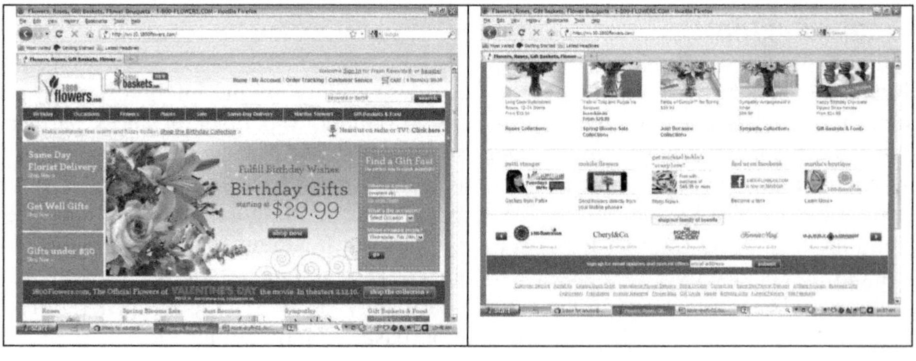

Fig. 1. Web Portal of 1-800-Flowers

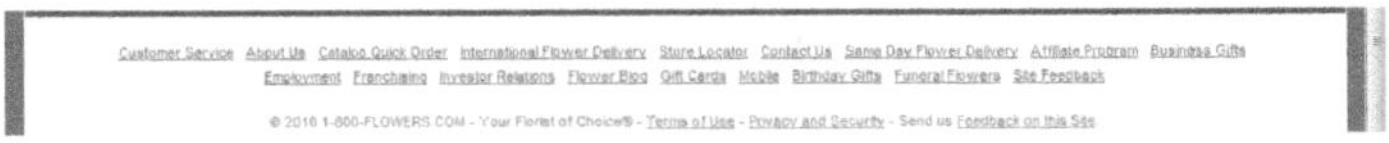

Fig. 2. Specific Functions Available at 1-800-Flowers Website

on the latter portal, when you buy a book, the system offers recommendations about other books bought by customers who also bought the book you just bought. Moreover, a visitor to 1-800-Flowers cannot customize their experience at the portal. By comparison, at Amazon.com, when a registered customer logs in with their username and password, the system comes back with recommendations based on the user's profile and preferences and provides your recent browsing history at the portal.

In short, there are different types of information based functionalities manifested in the web portals of eTailers. With the help of these functionalities, the firm goes about acquiring customers and getting them to convert to revenue generating entities. We wish to examine this linkage between the functionalities, the customer acquisition process and revenue generation. By doing so, we hope to get a better understanding of which aspects of the content architecture of these portals have a significant impact on customer acquisition and revenue generation.

2 Model

Our conceptual model of eTailer customer acquisition and revenue generation is shown in Figure 3. We first present the constructs of the model, linkages among these constructs, and how they are measured in the dataset. The theoretical basis for the model follows thereafter. Our model hypothesizes that, for an eTailer, revenue generation is realized through a multiphase interaction with customers. The first phase, which we name Acquisition Capability, occurs when new customers visit the eTailer's site. The ability of an eTailer to attract traffic to its website is known as the Acquisition Capability. While there would be many drivers of this capability, we are specifically interested in the information based functionalities in the portal that would drive this construct. We hypothesize that there are four such constructs, which we name Information Capability, Transaction Capability, Customization Capability and Analytical Capability respectively. Our conceptual model looks to extend prior literature in two ways. First, we extend the model of information technology infrastructure, e-commerce capability and financial performance (Zhu 2004) to include additional capabilities. The model proposed by Zhu (2004) directly related e-commerce capability (comprised of information, transaction, customization, and backend integration capabilities) to financial performance. It does not delve into the details of how financial performance is realized from the business processes. We add such details in this paper. The second way in which we extend prior literature is that we extend the process-oriented view of business value generated by information technology investments such as (Barua et al., 2004) with customer-based capabilities of a firm. The model proposed by Barua et al. (2004) associates customer-based information capabilities to financial performance. We extend their model by proposing a phased approach to the association between customer-based capabilities and financial performance.

Information refers to a variety of static and dynamic content that is available to a customer when they visit the website. The distinguishing feature of this capability is that this is primarily one-way communication from the eTailer to the online customer. eTailers provide product comparisons, product reviews, customer self-help portal, etc., that enable customers to inform themselves. Such ancillary services on a website play an important role in affecting customer purchasing behavior (Cenfetelli et al., 2008; Wang and Benbasat, 2007). It was also found that website presentation flaws affect user perceptions of website quality and, ultimately, their intention to purchase (Everard and Galletta, 2005). Transaction refers to a two-way electronic interaction between the eTailer and the customer. The purpose of website features such as express checkout and mapping is to enable a purchase transaction, either electronically or physically. Payments must be made and goods/services ordered and delivered. Customization is measured in our model by the ability of the eTailer's portal to allow the customer to both personalize what they see on the website and to articulate customized needs. On 1-800-Flowers, for example, one can ask for flower arrangements for a particular occasion, such as birthdays. Analytical Capability refers to the eTailer's ability to analyze enterprise data to facilitate various business objectives, including the acquisition of new customers. This capability increases by the use of customer relationship management and web traffic analysis. After all, one must have the customer-centric data to analyze as well as the technical capacity to actually carry out the analysis.

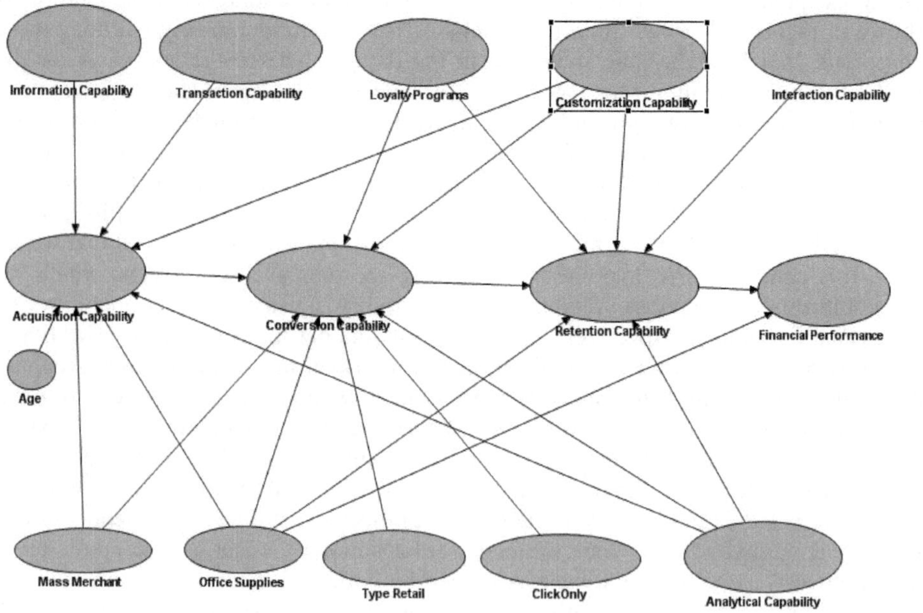

Fig. 3. A Path Model of Customer Acquisition and Revenue Generation

The phase following Acquisition is named Conversion Capability. Usually, only a small fraction of the visitors to a portal actually engage in revenue generating activity. Conversion captures the transition for a customer from being a mere visitor to becoming a first time revenue generator. Of course, one of the major determinants of Conversion Capability, per our process view of revenue generation, is Acquisition Capability. We hypothesize that, in addition to Acquisition Capability, loyalty programs available on the portal, Customization Capability, and Analytical Capability drive Conversion Capability. Users have been found to be receptive to personalized content on the websites of online retailers and find it useful as a decision aid (Tam and Ho, 2006). This can contribute to getting a visitor to actually buy after visiting the portal. In our conceptual model, Conversion Capability is followed by a phase, which we name Retention Capability, which captures repeat customers and their revenue generating activities. It is measured by the number of customers who return to the portal. In addition to Conversion Capability, we hypothesize that the other major drivers of Retention Capability are the Customization Capability, the Analytical Capability, and a third construct which we have named Interactivity Capability. This latter construct is measured by the presence/absence of social media functionalities on the eTailer's portal, and the presence/absence of recommender and rating software agents. The rationale for this construct is to capture IT based mechanisms by which the eTailer stays engaged with the revenue generating customer on an ongoing basis in order to encourage and sustain continued revenue generation. Interactivity of product presentations has been shown to affect customers intentions to return to an online site and purchase (Jiang and Benbasat, 2007). Customer generated feedback can be very useful in building trust and ultimately generating revenue producing transactions. This kind of information or interactive capability should therefore have a positive influence with conversion and loyalty (Pavlou and Dimoka, 2006). Our final dependent variable is the revenue generated (Financial Performance) and is measured by eTailer's sales. There are a number of control variables in the model, as shown in Figure 3. These control variables are age of the company (year launched), the type of products sold (mass merchant or office supplies), and eTailer selling model (retailer and pure click).

3 Data

The data for this research was obtained from the publication called the Internet Retailer Top 500 2008 edition, published by Vertical Web Media. This company surveys the top 500 retailers by revenues on the features of information systems and characteristics of the company. The broad categories of data are customer service features, payment features, vendor used, website features, website summary, and operational, marketing and financial performance. There is a total of 109 data items in these eight categories. Most items in the customer service features, payment features, and website features are binary items; the item was coded 1 if the feature is present, otherwise it was coded 0. All binary items were used as-is. A few variables that were multinomial were converted into binary variables. Two items, conversion rate and return shoppers, were present in data in percentage terms. An item, the Number of Converted Shoppers, was created by multiplying the conversion rate by the number of unique monthly visitors. Another item, the Number of Return Shoppers, was created by multiplying return shoppers by the Number of Converted Shoppers. These transformations were done because the Acquisition Capability and the Financial Performance constructs were weighted by items that were measured in number of customers and sales dollars, rather than as percentages.

We mapped the 109 items into the constructs of our model. Since there is no apriori reason to believe if the items mapped to a construct would covary, each latent construct was defined as a formative (rather than reflective) construct following the norm in this type of research. Next, we dropped items that had a skewed distribution in the data, i.e., over 80% was 1 or 0. The reason for dropping items with a skewed distribution is that these items would not help much in explaining the variance of the outcome variables – for e.g., almost all companies had a toll free 800 number. Other examples of dropped items are presence of frequently asked questions, keyword search, wiki, order management, etc. In all, we dropped 27 items. The only item retained from items with more than 80% distribution on one value was Web Analytics because there is currently a great deal of interest in practice on analytics based capabilities of firms. Thereafter, we ran the partial least squares (PLS) analysis for our model using the SmartPLS software (Ringle et al., 2005). One of the problems that can affect the performance of a PLS result is a high correlation between an item and the construct to which it is mapped as well as between the item and other constructs to which it is not mapped. Similarly, a low correlation of an item on the construct that it is mapped to, as well as to other constructs, indicates that the item is not contributing to the model's explanatory powers as we surmised it would. We used a cutoff of 0.4 to decide whether or not a correlation was high. Items that suffered from high cross-loading on other constructs or low correlation with all constructs were dropped from the further analysis. We were left finally with 29 items for the ten constructs of the model.

Finally, we also dropped observations with missing data. For example, over 150 observations were missing data on the percentage of return shoppers. After dropping missing variables, the data contained 341 observations. The mean and standard deviation of the items are presented in Table 1, Descriptive Statistics.

4 Results

After the PLS model was finalized, we ran it once more for the results that are presented on Table 2 and Table 3. To obtain the significance of the estimates, a bootstrapping method was used. We set the number of observations to 500 (thereby allowing sampling with replacement of the original 342 observations) and the number of samples to 200. Table 2 shows that the regression weights of Account Status Feature, Comparison Feature, Coupon Feature, and Syndicated Content Feature are significant and positive, highlighting that the Information Capability is primarily about customers being aware of the amount that they currently owe, which products are better, whether discounts are possible, and does a third party provide valuable information.

Table 1. Descriptive Statistics of Items

Item	Mean	Standard Deviation
Account Status Feature	0.542	0.027
Comparison Feature	0.240	0.023
Coupon Feature	0.686	0.025
Customer Relationship Management Feature	0.583	0.026
Product Customization Feature	0.340	0.025
Customer Review Feature	0.436	0.026
Express Checkout Feature	0.741	0.023
Frequent Buyer Feature	0.328	0.025
Mapping Feature	0.407	0.026
Monthly Email Campaigns	7.296	0.424
Monthly Email Incentives	4.882	0.332
Monthly Unique Visitors	2299296	259250
Monthly Visits	5185230	870448
Outlet Store Feature	0.624	0.026
Payment Processor Feature	0.706	0.024
Personalization Feature	0.598	0.026
Customer Ratings Feature	0.448	0.026
Recommendation Feature	0.700	0.024
Sales Volume in 2007	285995	54589
Number of Converted Shoppers	68139	8032
Number of Return Shoppers	28783	5878
Social Media Feature	0.252	0.023
Buy at Store Feature	0.554	0.026
Syndicated Content Feature	0.243	0.023
Value Card Feature	0.340	0.025
Video Feature	0.217	0.022
Web Analysis Feature	0.906	0.015
Web Hosted Feature	0.697	0.024
Web Performance Feature	0.686	0.025

The regression weight of Monthly Unique Visitors with Acquisition Capability is positive and significant, but that of Monthly Visits is negative. This means that Acquisition Capability is primarily a representation of new visitors. Transaction Capability is represented by express checkout, mapping, and value card features. The presence of a store or use of it does not contribute to this capability positively. Analytical capability is made up of customer relationship management and web performance. Finally, Interaction Capability is made up of social media features of the eTailer.

The results of the path model in Figure 2 show that the R^2 for the four dependent variables, Acquisition Capability, Conversion Capability, Retention Capability, and Financial Performance are respectively 0.29, 0.63, 0.80, and 0.81. The high R^2 indicate a good overall performance of the model. The results in Table 3 reveal that Acquisition Capability increases with Information, Transaction, and Customization capabilities. The impacts of Information and Transaction capabilities are not very different from each other, and the impact of Customization is small compared to the impact of these two capabilities. Conversion Capability increases with Acquisition, Loyalty and Analytical capabilities. Loyalty and Analytical capabilities show similar impacts on Conversion. Retention Capability increases with Conversion Capability and Interaction Capability. However, it decreases with Customization Capability. Finally, Financial Performance increases with Retention Capability.

Among control variables, we see that mass merchants and office supplies retailers possess higher Acquisition and Conversion capabilities. Office supplies retailers do not have an average positive Retention Capability, but have enjoyed an average positive financial performance. Results also show that younger firms have a better Acquisition Capability than older firms. Both retail only and pure click retailers have an average negative Conversion Capability.

Table 2. Regression Weight of Indicator Variables on Main Constructs based on Partial Least Squares†

Constructs	Indicator Variables	Coefficient Estimate	Standard Error
Information Capability	Account Status Feature	0.563	0.08***
	Comparison Feature	0.258	0.11**
	Coupon Feature	0.236	0.07***
	Customer Review Feature	0.123	0.10
	Syndicated Content Feature	0.286	0.12**
	Video Feature	0.124	0.13
Acquisition Capability	Monthly Unique Visitors	1.922	0.31***
	Monthly Visits	-1.063	0.36***
Transaction Capability	Express Checkout Feature	0.281	0.16*
	Mapping Feature	0.605	0.18***
	Monthly Email Campaigns	-0.149	0.13
	Monthly Email Incentives	0.312	0.18
	Outlet Store Feature	-0.287	0.16*
	Buy at Store Feature	-0.415	0.21*
	Value Card Feature	0.627	0.17***
Conversion Capability	Number of Shoppers	1.000	0.00
Loyalty Capability	Frequent Buyer Feature	1.000	0.00
Customization Capability	Product Customization Feature	-0.042	0.20
	Personalization Feature	0.977	0.03***
Analytical Capability	Customer Relationship Management Feature	0.558	0.16***
	Payment Processor Feature	-0.010	0.25
	Web Analysis Feature	0.255	0.24
	Web Hosted Feature	-0.176	0.32
	Web Performance Feature	0.502	0.16***
Interaction Capability	Recommendation Feature	0.332	0.23
	Social Media Feature	0.697	0.16***
	Customer Ratings Feature	0.300	0.22
Retention Capability	Number of Return Shoppers	1.000	0.00
Financial Performance	Sales Volume in 2007	1.000	0.00

*: $p<0.05$; **: $p<0.01$; ***: $p<0.001$; single-tailed.

†: All constructs that are control variables in our model have single-indicators. They are not reported in this table, because their regression weights on their respective constructs will be 1.

5 Discussion

Our results show that information systems features and website features together create value for an eTailer. Results also validate the phases of value creation from acquisition of the customer to financial performance, via conversion and retention. The results highlight the importance of different capabilities at each phase. Based on the results, we suggest some possible implications for the design and implementation of the Internet platforms on which the eTailers depend for revenue generation. Since analytical capability was significantly associated with only the conversion phase of the path model, it suggests that the business intelligence capabilities of an eTailer is relatively more influential in generating the first purchase compared to repeat purchases. This finding is somewhat surprising in that one could expect analytical capability to play a major role in customer retention. After all, once a customer is acquired, the retailer probably has some information on the customer's identity and can therefore proceed to collect relevant information on them, which can then be subjected to analysis for the purpose of generating potential repeat purchases. Among the other informational drivers, we find that Customization ability was significantly associated with acquisition and retention, but not with conversion. Customization includes both the ability of the customer to express specific custom requirements for a good or service, as well as the ability to customize the portals appearance and content to ones one's tastes and preferences. We conjecture that the first ability is relevant for acquisition, while the second is more relevant for customer retention.

Table 3. Partial Least Squares Estimates of Regression Coefficients for the Path Model

Dependent Variable	Explanatory Variable	Coefficient Estimate	Standard Error
Acquisition Capability	Information Ability	0.265	0.04^{***}
	Transaction Ability	0.203	0.06^{***}
	Analytical Ability	-0.061	0.06
	Customization Ability	0.082	0.03^{**}
Conversion Capability	Acquisition Capability	0.707	0.05^{***}
	Customization Ability	0.003	0.02
	Loyalty Ability	0.088	0.02^{***}
	Analytical Ability	0.067	0.03^{**}
Retention Capability	Conversion Capability	0.952	0.03^{***}
	Customization Ability	-0.031	0.01^{**}
	Analytical Ability	-0.022	0.02
	Interaction Ability	0.032	0.01^{*}
	Loyalty Ability	-0.012	0.01
Financial Performance	Retention Capability	0.776	0.15^{***}
	Control Variables		
Acquisition Capability	Age	0.063	0.02^{***}
	Mass Merchant	0.313	0.07^{***}
	Office Supplies	0.032	0.01^{*}
Conversion Capability	Mass Merchant	0.080	0.03^{**}
	Office Supplies	0.230	0.08^{**}
	Retail Only	-0.110	0.02^{***}
	Pure Click	-0.081	0.04^{*}
Retention Capability	Office Supplies	-0.257	0.11^{**}
Financial Performance	Office Supplies	0.368	0.14^{**}

*: p<0.05; **: p<0.01; ***:p<0.001; single-tailed.

Information technology governance has become an important and established function in many organizations. Effective information technology governance helps ensure that information systems supports business goals, optimizes business investment in information systems and appropriately manages information systems-related risks and opportunities (Luftman and Brier, 1999). In recent surveys of CxOs, alignment of information systems investments with business objectives ranked among the top three information systems priorities of organizations (the other two were control and compliance). Like other businesses, eTailers need to know where they are likely to get the most return for their information technology dollars. Our investigation can shed some light on that connection, and guide the information systems-business objective alignment process, by identifying the relationship between information functionalities of the web Portals used by eTailers and the revenue generation process.

6 Limitations and Conclusions

In this paper, we presented and validated a model of value creation in the context of eTailers. The data for validating the model was obtained from the field. The results validated the phases of value creation and highlighted the importance of different information systems capabilities, analytical, information, customization and interaction. For each of these capabilities, we were able to identify the information system feature or website feature that enables the building of the capability.

As with any empirical study one must be cautious in interpreting the results in light of limitations of the data which were discussed earlier. One major limitation is that there is no data on the eTailer's back end operations. Thus we do not know what information infrastructure is used to communicate and coordinate activities with suppliers. Moreover, we do not have cost data. Our performance metric is revenue and would be useful to determine if the associations uncovered in our analysis hold when the performance metric includes costs in some realistic manner. Also, many variables had to be coded as 0/1 which is not completely realistic. For instance, two eTailers could both have CRM systems and yet one could be using it much more effectively than the other. Our data set does not reflect intensity of usage of different software components, or the effectiveness of internal procedures and organizational structures. Nevertheless, the results can be used to provide guidance to managers with design prescriptions for building information systems capabilities, as we have done in the discussion section. The empirical model contributes to theory by elucidating the phases of value creation for eTailers.

References

1. Barua, A., Konana, P., Whinston, A.B., Yin, F.: An Empirical Investigation Of Net-Enabled Business Value. MIS Quarterly 28(4), 585–620 (2004)
2. Cenfetelli, R., Benbasat, I., Al-Natour, S.: Addressing the What and How of Online Services: Positioning Supporting-Services Functionality and Service Quality for Business-to-Consumer Success. Information Systems Research 19(2), 161–181 (2008)
3. Chen, L., Gillenson, M.L., Sherrell, D.L.: Enticing online consumers: An extended technology acceptance perspective. Information & Management 39(8), 705–719 (2002)

4. Everard, A., Galletta, D.F.: How Presentation Flaws Affect Perceived Site Quality, Trust, and Intention to Purchase from an Online Store. Journal of Management Information Systems 22(3), 55–95 (2006)
5. Jiang, Z., Benbasat, I.: Investigating the Influence of the Functional Mechanisms of Online Product Presentations. Information Systems Research 18(4), 454–472 (2007)
6. Jiang, Z., Benbasat, I.: The Effects of Presentation Formats and Task Complexity on Online Consumers' Product Understanding. MIS Quarterly 31(3), 475–500 (2007)
7. Kim, J.H., Kim, M., Lennon, S.J.: Information components of apparel retail web sites: task relevance approach. Journal of Fashion Marketing and Management 11(4), 494–510 (2007)
8. Luftman, J., Brier, T.: Achieving and Sustaining Business-IT Alignment. California Management Review 42(1), 109–122 (1999)
9. Mithas, S., Ramasubbu, N., Krishnan, M.S., Fornell, C.: Designing Web Sites for Customer Loyalty Across Business Domains: A Multilevel Analysis. Journal of Management Information Systems 23(3), 97–127 (2007)
10. Pavlou, P.A., Dimoka, A.: The Nature and Role of Feedback Text Comments in Online Marketplaces: Implications for Trust Building, Price Premiums, and Seller Differentiation. Information Systems Research 17(4), 392–414 (2006)
11. Ringle, C.M., Wende, S., Will, A.: SmartPLS 2.0 (beta) Hamburg (2005), `http://www.smartpls.de`
12. Sia, C., Lim, K., Leung, K., Lee, M., Huang, W., Benbasat, I.: Web Strategies To Promote Internet Shopping: Is Cultural-Customization Needed? MIS Quarterly 33(3), 491–511 (2009)
13. Vrechopoulos, A., Atherinos, E.: Web banking layout effects on consumer behavioural intentions. The International Journal of Bank Marketing 27(7), 524–546 (2009)
14. Wang, W., Benbasat, I.: Recommendation Agents for Electronic Commerce: Effects of Explanation Facilities on Trusting Beliefs. Journal of Management Information Systems 23(4), 217–246 (2007)
15. Xiao, B., Benbasat, I.: E-Commerce Product Recommendation Agents: Use, Characteristics, and Impact. MIS Quarterly 31(1), 137–185 (2007)
16. Zhu, K.: The Complementarity of Information Technology Infrastructure and E-Commerce Capability: A Resource-Based Assessment of Their Business Value. Journal of Management Information Systems 21(1), 167–202 (2004)

Adoption of a Centralised Post-Trade Processing Market Infrastructure after the Credit Crisis

Olga Lewandowska

Goethe-University Frankfurt, Chair of Economics, esp. Information Systems, Frankfurt am Main, Germany
Lewandowska@econ.uni-frankfurt.de

Abstract. The recent credit crisis has heightened the awareness of credit risk among financial markets' regulators and participants. However, despite the public discussion on centralized processing systems for the off-exchange traded (Over-The-Counter, OTC) transactions no research has been conducted on the factors that could explain their adoption among market participants. With this study, an attempt is made to cover this gap, in parallel opening the space for further scientific investigation on centralized clearing for OTC derivatives. Based on the Diffusion of Innovation Theory, this first empirical study in the OTC clearing area introduces a model aimed at identifying the drivers and inhibitors for the adoption of an IT-enabled innovation in the form of centralized clearing by the financial organizations. The partial least squares structural equation modeling technique was applied to analyze the results of the survey with the Heads of Clearing/ Operations in various international financial institutions.

Keywords: Diffusion of Innovation, IS in Financial Markets, IT-enabled Innovation, Clearing, OTC Derivatives.

1 Introduction

Encouraged by increasing use of electronic trading systems in recent years, centralized clearing has established itself as a standard risk mitigation mechanism in the on-exchange traded financial markets. Clearing is understood as the process of calculating the mutual obligations of market participants, usually on a net basis, for the exchange of securities and money (Bank for International Settlements, 2004). In the recent years of its tremendous growth preceding the credit crisis, the OTC market of privately negotiated derivatives has developed a decentralized, bilateral clearing arrangement characterized by low automation and limited transparency (Bliss and Steigerwald, 2006). Regulators and policy makers have recognized the potential benefits of centralized clearing for the Over-the-Counter (OTC) derivatives which were blamed for the recent credit crisis and are pushing to clear the privately negotiated transactions through central clearing facilities.

Central counterparty (CCP) clearing is a service performed by a central clearing house. CCP is an entity that interposes itself between counterparties to the financial contracts, becoming the buyer to every seller and seller to every buyer. In this way, the original counterparties to the trade are not exposed to counterparty credit risk of

M.L. Nelson et al. (Eds.): Sustainable e-Business Management, LNBIP 58, pp. 36–47, 2010.

the other party (risk of loss if the counterparty to the trade defaults) but to that of the CCP. Moreover, as the CCP stands between the trading counterparties, multilateral position offsetting is possible (Cecchetti, Gyntelberg, Hollanders, 2009).

Central counterparties are structured to manage and mitigate the credit risk of counterparties during the lifetime of the contract (Ripatti, 2004). The CCP calculates the change in value of the positions of its members on regular basis in order to determine the collateral the members have to post (margin requirement).

A clearing house with its increasing informational and calculative capacity requirement strongly relies on the Information and Communication Technology (Millo, Muniesa, Panurgias and Scott, 2005). In this context, pricing and calculation of margin requirements for relatively complex OTC derivatives is particularly challenging.

The main focus of this study regards the factors affecting adoption of CCP clearing for OTC derivatives as perceived by sell-side[1] market participants. The notion that CCP clearing process is indeed an IT-enabled innovation in the context of the OTC market is the starting point of this study. Mahnke, Overby and Oscan (2006) define IT-enabled innovation as something that "blends hardware and/or software assets with business capabilities to generate a novel process, product or service". Up until now most authors have regarded CCP clearing merely as a risk mitigation mechanism. This study sets out to investigate OTC CCP as an IT-enabled innovation, considering this type of post-trade processing system from multiple perspectives.

The study is broken down in three sections: 1) theory and model development, 2) methodology employed to empirically validate the model 3) discussion of the research findings and their implications.

2 Theory and Model Development

The conceptual background of the presented model creates the Diffusion of Innovation (DOI) theory with the innovation attributes as factors that facilitate or hinder innovation adoption (Figure 1). In Rogers' theory (Rogers, 1995) an innovation is defined as "an idea, practice, or object that is perceived as new by an individual or other unit of adoption". According to Roger's classification, a CCP is considered as preventive innovation, "a new idea that requires action at one point in time in order to avoid unwanted consequences at some future time" (Rogers, 2002). The role of a CCP clearing arrangement is to minimize the losses to its members after a participant's default using a predefined loss-sharing mechanism (Wendt, 2006).

One of the main focuses of DOI are the characteristics of an innovation which may influence its adoption. Whereas in the original work of Rogers five such attributes are identified as to significantly influence the adoption decision, other authors expanded the list by further characteristics (e.g. Benbasat, 1991). Nevertheless, Tornatzky and Klein's (1982) meta-analysis of 75 studies showed that from several identified innovation attributes, only three: relative advantage, compatibility, and complexity had in the most cases the significant relationship to innovation adoption. Therefore, in this study the set of constructs from DOI related to innovation characteristics will be limited to three.

---

[1] Sell-side encompasses financial institutions (mostly banks) offering trading services to asset managers, hedge funds etc. (Harris, 2003)

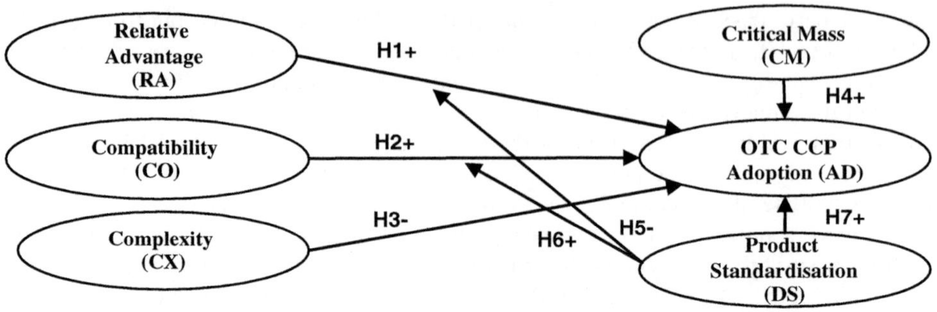

Fig. 1. Research model

2.1 Conceptualization of the Innovation Attributes

"Relative advantage" in the presented model is in accordance with existing DOI literature and refers to: the "degree to which an innovation is perceived as being better than the idea it supersedes'" (Rogers, 2002). In case of CCP clearing for OTC derivatives the comparison base is the bilateral clearing process. Relative advantage is conceptualized as multidimensional aggregate second order construct with three subconstructs referring to different aspects of CCP's potential advantages: processing efficiency, capital efficiency and counterparty credit risk mitigation.

H1 A higher level of perceived relative advantage (measured by processing-, capital- and risk mitigation efficiency) leads to a stronger adoption of CCP clearing for OTC derivatives.

The conceptualizations of compatibility in this study takes into account its operational aspects understood as fit with existing practices, routines and infrastructure rather than individual values. This approach corresponds to reality of new process implementation within an institution. As the integration of OTC CCP may require substantial changes in the internal processes, operational compatibility may play a significant role in taking adoption decisions.

H2 A higher level of perceived compatibility leads to a stronger adoption of CCP clearing for OTC derivatives.

A productive system is complex if it consists of numerous elements and those elements interact with one another richly (Rivkin, 2001). Complexity refers in this study to CCP specific processes spurred by daily margining and their cost (Wendt, 2006).

H3 A higher level of perceived complexity leads to a weaker adoption of CCP clearing for OTC derivatives.

2.2 Conceptualization of Context Variables

Although DOI has proven to be a viable framework for examining adoption of innovation (Dwivedi, Williams, Lal, Schwarz, 2008), it is necessary to incorporate additional factors that help in explaining contextual effects.

Critical mass construct is an extension to traditional framework of DOI. Fichman (1992) recognizes lacking consideration of adopters' interdependencies as a substantial limitation of classic diffusion model. When an innovation is subject to network externalities, like in case of clearing (Pirrong, 2009), achieving critical mass of market participants who want to adopt the innovation becomes crucial. If critical mass is achieved the innovation is likely to be universally adopted, otherwise it will be probably abandoned (Markus, 1987).

H4 Achieving critical mass of market participant willing to support implementation of OTC CCP influences positively the adoption of CCP clearing for OTC derivatives.

In case of CCP the key moderator is product standardization. According to Chin, Marcolin and Newsted (1996): "The moderator affects the direction and/or strength of the relation between an independent or predictor variable and a dependent or criterion variable". In case of product standardization the moderating effect is expected to influence the relation between endogenous variable- CCP adoption- and its predictors- relative advantage and compatibility.

Due to the recent improvements in automation of the post-trade infrastructure for electronic eligible OTC derivatives, the relative advantage of CCP innovation may be conceived to be higher for highly customized rather than standardized products. Therefore, it is argued that for the standardized products, the influence of the relative advantage on OTC CCP adoption is weakening.

H5 The higher a degree of product standardization the weaker the influence of relative advantage on adoption of CCP clearing for OTC derivatives.

Conversely, a strengthening effect of product standardization on relation between compatibility and adoption is hypothesized. Some elements of existing global infrastructure (electronic trade confirmation platforms, trade information warehouse) may still be utilized as complementary to OTC CCP process which may ease the implementation efforts.

H6 The higher a degree of product standardization the stronger the influence of compatibility on adoption of CCP clearing for OTC derivatives.

The instrument standardization level is defined by three product group features based on existing literature: 1) market commonality of instrument terms and conditions (Bank for International Settlements, 2007), 2) existence of valuation model accepted by majority of market participants (ibidem), 3) level of profit margins for dealers the product group brings (Tabb and Iati, 2009).

Moreover, the positive direct influence of product standardization on adoption is hypothesized as the standardization is a basic requirement for centralized trade processing within a clearing house.

H7 The higher a degree of product standardization the stronger the adoption of CCP clearing for OTC derivatives (direct influence).

2.3 Adoption Construct

The traditional DOI framework has its limitation. It tends to neglect the realities of implementing technological innovations within organizations, where the decision to adopt the new technology is made at the organization or division level rather than by the individual user. Sullivan (2006) refers to these conditions of non-voluntary adoption as to a "contingent authority adoption decision" meaning that "an authority makes initial decision to adopt and mandates adoption/use of new technology by the targeted users".

The endogenous variable was adjusted in order to cater for the organizational character of this research. For the purpose of evaluating the construct both actual usage and intention of the future usage of OTC CCP by organizations have been employed. Adopters may make a binary decision to adopt or reject, or may choose differing levels of CCP usage (Bayer and Melone, 1989). Concerning adoption alone, a binary variable is applied based on whether an organization uses/is a member of OTC CCP or not. Moreover, the intensity measure defined as percentage of eligible trades cleared centrally is used.

3 Research Method

Due to lack of sources on factors affecting adoption of clearing arrangements, the items were developed by the author and tested in interviews with four clearing experts. The objective was to verify the convergent and discriminant validity of the scales by examining how the items were sorted into various construct categories (Davis, 1989). The judges were asked to rank how well the items fit the construct definitions and then asked to assign items to specific constructs. Moreover, they were requested to assess the item's wording. Based on expert assessment of the items' wording and content, in several cases, item formulation was improved and one item shifted between constructs.

The scale was developed as reflective since it was assumed that for all items "a change in the latent variable causes variation in all measures simultaneously; furthermore, all measures in a reflective measurement model are positively intercorrelated" (Diamantopoulos, Riefler, Roth, 2008).

3.1 Data Collection and Analysis

Survey data was collected by means of an e-mail questionnaire. In order to assess and refine the form, the instrument was pre-tested with a mail pilot with 20 Heads of Clearing/ Operations from the sell-side institutions. Questions were rearranged to reduce the potential ceiling and floor effect that may induce monotonous responses from participants. Moreover, the scale consists of some items that are worded in opposite directions to alleviate response biases; prior to statistical data analysis the reverse scored items were recoded.

In total, the sample of 256 respondents was approached by phone to participate via e-mail and promised a copy of the results. The sample encompassed the largest international sell-side institutions active in the OTC market and was derived from Capital Market Association database and personal contacts. For organizational perspective of this research (only) one of the following respondents within each company was invited to take part in the survey: Head of (OTC) Operations or Head of Clearing. The respondents who agreed in a phone call to take part in a survey received an e-mail questionnaire. Despite the pre-selection, 8 of the contacted persons admitted to have no experience with CCPs and, therefore, were not able to answer the questionnaire. Four weeks after the initial mailing the non-respondents were sent a follow up e-mail. A resulting sample of 248 respondents was collected, all of which had enough knowledge regarding the specific questions on OTC CCP subject. Overall, 53 completed questionnaires were received, which corresponds to 21 % response rate. Addressing the questionnaire to management level professionals with experience in OTC clearing has made it difficult to reach a higher response rate as, in most companies only one contact person was available. However, the sample size fulfilled the requirements imposed by model specification. Early and late respondent analysis was conducted (Armstrong and Overton, 1977). T-test for independent samples of early and late respondents provided evidence that non-response bias does not affect significantly the study results.

The partial least squares (PLS) approach was employed to estimate both the measurement and the structural parameters in the structural equation modeling approach. The PLS is considered to be the most appropriate analysis technique for the current study as it supports exploratory research and places minimum requirements on sample size (Chin, 1998).

Missing values represent a challenge if they substantially reduce the number of available cases. According to Schafer and Graham (2002), "If a missing-data problem can be resolved by discarding only a small part of the sample, then the method (case deletion) can be quite effective". In this study, missing data represented only 0.9 % of responses and for the reasons outlined above casewise deletion was used to handle them.

The research model (figure 1) was tested using SmartPLS software Version 2.0 (Ringle, Wende, Will, 2005). As the software allows to measure latent multidimensional variables by repeated indicators and maximizes variance explained it considered to fit the nature of this study. The indicators presented in table 1 were used to measure the latent variables. The Lickert type 5 item scale with a neutral middle was employed and adapted for the current context. Additionally, a binary variable was used to measure two items of adoption. All indicators and constructs were operationalized using a reflective mode. The dimensions of relative advantage i.e. processing efficiency, counterparty risk mitigation and capital efficiency were aggregated to second order constructs.

The results will be interpreted in two stages: first, the measurement model and then the structural model. Evaluation of the measurement model is based on evaluation of the item loadings, reliability of scales and the constructs' discriminant validity.

Table 1. Indicators (5-item Lickert scale used: 1- I strongly agree to 5- I strongly disagree - if not stated otherwise; reverse scored items indicated)

Item	Question
AD1	We use CCP clearing for eligible OTC derivatives trades. (binary)
AD2	We are members of CCP clearing facility for OTC derivatives. (binary)
AD3	What percentage of eligible OTC derivatives trades do you clear centrally by CCP? (1-"100-85%" to 5-"15-0%")
AD4	Given that OTC CCP facility is available I would recommend the executives in our company to use CCP clearing for OTC derivatives we trade.
AD5	I intend to actively support implementation of CCP facility for OTC derivatives in my organization.
AD6	Assuming that my company can have access to the CCP clearing for OTC derivatives I think that we should use it.
CX1	Overall collateral requirement of OTC CCP has to be higher than that while clearing on bilateral basis.
CX2	The margin requirement of OTC CCP is ... in comparison to average collateral paid in the OTC market. (1-"very high" to 5-"very low")
CM1	Our company would support creation of OTC CCP clearing only if other large market participants support it too.
CM2	Our company would support creation of OTC CCP clearing only after most active derivatives dealers had expressed their commitment to do it.
CM3	Due to their large trading volume, the dealer support is mandatory to create OTC CCP.
CO1	OTC CCP clearing is not compatible with our work practice (reverse scored).
CO2	I think that it would be easy to integrate CCP process in the internal processes in our company.
CO3	Usage of OTC CCP is consistent with our experience for on-exchange trades.
DS1	The most eligible OTC derivatives products for CCP clearing are ...a) those for which a broadly accepted valuation models exist.
DS2	b)... those with relative low profit margins for dealers.
DS3	c)... those with relative highly standardized terms and conditions.
DS4	CCP clearing is not applicable for exotic OTC derivatives due to relative low standardization of their terms and conditions.
DS5	Using CCP for clearing standardized OTC trades is more reasonable than for exotic trades.
RC1	CCP clearing will enable us to employ our capital for higher margin products.
RC2	Usage of OTC CCP would enable us to enlarge our business as it frees up credit lines.
RM1	OTC CCP clearing could decrease counterparty credit risk exposure more than other bilateral OTC risk mitigation mechanisms.
RM2	In case of default of an OTC market participant we trade with... a) OTC CCP minimizes the loss for our company.
RM3	b)... the close out of the position will be faster probably through CCP than bilaterally.
RP1	Compared to bilateral processing, ...a) CCP clearing for OTC trades has a potential to reduce errors.
RP2	b)...OTC CCP has a potential to reduce the need for resolving position and valuation discrepancies (portfolio reconciliation).
RP3	c)...OTC CCP has a potential to improve correctness and completeness of data.

3.2 Measurement Model Evaluation

According to Chin (1998), each factor loading should be greater than 0.707 in order to share more variance with the component score than with error variance. However, loadings of 0.60 are also acceptable in the early stage of measures development and if additional indicators exist in the block for comparison basis (Hulland, 1999). In this research only one indicator (CX3) loaded under 0.6 and was dropped. Two items of adoption constructs loaded under 0.707 but still with high and acceptable values of 0.701 and were kept in the model (eliminating these indicators might change the domain of the adoption construct). The individual item loadings for the rest of the constructs exceeded 0.707 (table 2). In case of multi item constructs (which is the case in this study) the composite reliability should be tested (Hulland, 1999). All the reflective constructs had a composite reliability above 0.89. Hence, they were above the recommended 0.70 level (Chin et al., 1996) suggesting internal consistency. The convergent validity for the reflective constructs was also confirmed, as the average variance extracted (AVE) was

Table 2. Parameters of the measurement model (significance: *p≤ 0.1; **p ≤ 0.05; *** p≤ 0.01)

Construct	Indicator	Loading	T-value	AVE	Composite reliability
AD	AD1	0,701	12.026609***	0,733	0,942
	AD2	0,701	12.026609***		
	AD3	0,932	88.455616***		
	AD4	0,938	94.967297***		
	AD5	0,907	57.19231***		
	AD6	0,919	73.818836***		
CX	CX1	0,923	3.638199***	0,712	0,972
	CX2	0,756	3.032265***		
CM	CM1	0,966	70.539003***	0,897	0,963
	CM2	0,963	69.215425***		
	CM3	0,911	34.619182***		
RA-CO	CO1	0,861	21.738284***	0,736	0,893
	CO2	0,824	17.583526***		
	CO3	0,888	53.440538***		
DS	DS1	0,745	3.631701***	0,624	0,892
	DS2	0,747	3.764646***		
	DS3	0,715	3.452306***		
	DS4	0,807	5.76155***		
	DS5	0,919	7.295528***		
RA-CE	RC1	0,972	108.178949***	0,946	0,972
	RC2	0,973	142.851766***		
RA-RM	RM1	0,801	29.288031***	0,863	0,950
	RM2	0,837	102.801703***		
	RM3	0,814	41.115627***		
RA-PE	RP1	0,949	12.554148***	0,853	0,946
	RP2	0,902	10.067567***		
	RP3	0,919	11.46152***		

above the guideline of 0.5 (Chin, 1998). Barclay et al. (1995) suggest that no manifest variable should load higher on other constructs than on the construct it intends to measure. Results of the cross-loading analysis showed that all items load higher on their respective intended latent variable compared to other latent variables.[2] Therefore, discriminant validity at the indicator level is ensured.

3.3 Structural Model Evaluation

Figure 2 shows all the path coefficients, significance levels and variance explained in the research model. The requirements regarding paths coefficients in the structural model of more than 0.1 (Sellin and Keeves, 1994) are fulfilled for all structural relationships except the relationship between complexity and adoption construct. Bootstrap method with 500 samples was used to assess the statistical significance of the path coefficients. The paths between complexity and adoption as well as moderating effect of product standardization on relation between compatibility and adoption lack the significance. Further paths were significant. The R-squared value for the dependent variable indicates that the model explained variance accounts for 52,5 % which is seen as an average (Chin et al., 1996). The Stone-Geisser's Q^2 was calculated using the blindfolding cross-validation method. The test criterion values exceed zero which confirms predictive relevance of the model (Chin, 1998). Discriminate validity of the model has been confirmed as the diagonal elements (square root of AVE) are significantly higher than off the diagonal values (representing correlation between constructs) in the corresponding rows and columns.

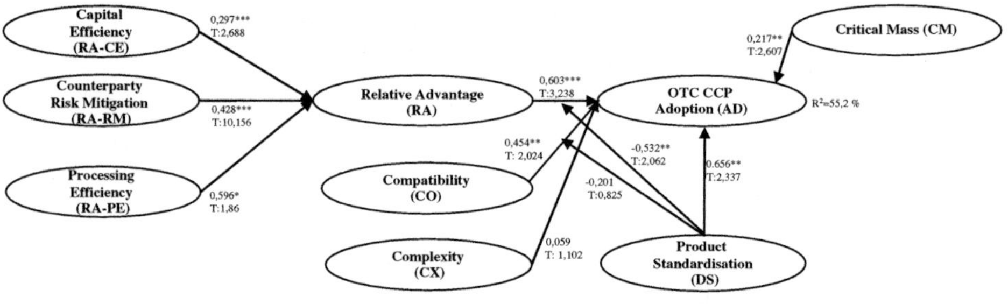

Fig. 2. Estimated parameters of the structural model

The hypotheses of the influence of complexity on adoption was rejected as well as the moderating effect of product standardization on relation between compatibility and adoption. The linkages corresponding to rejected hypotheses were dropped, and the PLS model was re-estimated. The analysis revealed that the beta coefficients and t-values of the remaining model were strong and significant. In addition, the R-squared value changed only slightly (54,5%), which manifests the statistical validity of the remaining linkages.

---

[2] Due to limited length of this paper, full test results will not be displayed but are available upon request.

4 Discussion of Research Findings and Implications

Based on DOI framework, this study explored the adoption of Central Counterparty clearing as an innovative IT-enabled system in the OTC market and identified the influential and impeding factors.

The empirical analysis confirmed that perceived relative advantage of the OTC CCP and compatibility with existing post- trade processes contribute substantially to adoption of centralized clearing for OTC derivatives, whereas complexity does not appear to be an important predictor. All three dimensions of relative advantage as well as aggregate second order construct exhibit strong influence on OTC CCP adoption. Critical mass was confirmed as having strong direct influence on OTC CCP adoption. Product standardization was found to have both strong direct influence on OTC CCP adoption as well as to moderate the relationship between relative advantage and adoption. However, the strengthening effect of the latter on the linkage between compatibility and adoption was not significant.

The findings are in line with the observations on the CCPs' diffusion in the OTC derivatives market. As the market participants had made high investments in the post-trade processing solutions and connections to global infrastructure in the past years, the operational compatibility between current processing of OTC derivatives and CCP service seems essential. An accelerated OTC CCP adoption has been observed after the turmoil caused by the sub-prime crisis. This may be explained by an increase in perceived relative advantage of OTC CCP- mostly on counterparty credit risk level. The complexity of the OTC CCP was not found in this study to influence the adoption willingness as expected. The explanation may be a perceived relative low margin requirement within CCP resulting from increasing competition within clearing sector or/and increasing use of collateral in the bilateral post-trade processing. Critical mass was found to directly influence CCP adoption. Due to economies of scale existent in clearing, achieving critical mass of market participants and volumes cleared makes the OTC CCP adoption dependent on the largest derivatives dealers. Product customization impedes automation of post-trade processing; lack of a commonly accepted valuation model makes risk management difficult. Therefore, standardization is a requirement for effective CCP clearing.

This study adds to the base of knowledge concerning clearing arrangements and provides several groups of stakeholders (including clearing houses and regulatory bodies) with valuable information about the factors influencing adoption of OTC CCPs. Despite the public discussion on CCP clearing for OTC derivatives no empirical research has been conducted on the factors that might explain CCP adoption among market participants. With this study, an attempt is made to cover this gap, in parallel opening the space for further scientific research on OTC CCPs.

Some limitations of the presented study will be highlighted below in order to formulate implications for future research. The used sample size of 53 is adequate for an exploratory investigation as in the presented study, but larger sized samples are required for future confirmatory research. The development of a more rigorous model with formative scales (focusing on causes of CCP efficiency) might further improve the variance explained.

This research raises several fields of interest for further investigation. This work is the first that empirically explores the OTC CCP process adoption. Up until now most authors have regarded CCP merely as a risk mitigation mechanism, ignoring the potential impact of this post-trade system on operational risk as well its capital efficiency implications. It is suggested that these factors be considered in future research and their meaning for the effective development of a market infrastructure investigated. As the focus of the study lies at perceptions of sell-side market participants regarding OTC CCP adoption, the public cost/benefit perspective was neglected. However, one possible research direction is to investigate the regulatory pressure as one of the factors influencing OTC CCP adoption if considered in a public context.

References

1. Armstrong, J.S., Overton, T.S.: Estimating nonresponse bias in mail surveys. Journal of Marketing Research 16, 396–402 (1977)
2. Bayer, J., Melone, N.: A critique of diffusion theory as a managerial framework for understanding adoption of software engineering innovations. Journal of Systems and Software, 161–166 (1989)
3. Barclay, D., Higgins, C., Thompson, R.: The Partial Least Squares (PLS) Approach to Causal Modeling: Personal Computer Adoption and Use as an Illustration. Technology Studies 2, 285–309 (1995)
4. Bank for International Settlements: New developments in clearing and settlement arrangements for OTC derivatives (2007), `http://www.bis.org`
5. Bliss, R., Steigerwald, R.S.: Derivatives clearing and settlement: A comparison of central counterparties and alternative structures. Economic Perspective 30 (2006)
6. Cecchetti, S., Gyntelberg, J., Hollanders, M.: Central counterparties for over-the-counter derivatives. Bank for International Settlements. BIS Quarterly Review (September 2009)
7. Chin, W.W.: The Partial Least Squares Approach to Structural Equation Modeling. In: Marcoulides, G.A. (ed.) Modern Methods for Business Research. Lawrence Erlbaum Associates, Mahwah (1998)
8. Chin, W.W., Marcolin, B.L., Newsted, P.R.: A Partial Least Squares Latent Variable Modeling Approach for Measuring Interaction Effects: Results from a Monte Carlo Simulation Study and Voice Mail Emotion/Adoption Study. Information Systems Research 14, 2 (1996)
9. Davis, F.D.: Perceived usefulness, perceived ease of use, and user acceptance of information technology. MIS Quarterly 13, 319–340 (1989)
10. Diamantopoulos, A., Rieflerl, P., Roth, K.: Advancing formative measurement models. Journal of Business Research 61(12), 1203–1218 (2007)
11. Dwivedi, Y.K., Williams, M.D., Lal, B., Schwarz, A.: Profiling Adoption, Acceptance and Diffusion Research in the Information Systems Discipline. In: 16th European Conference on Information Systems, Galway, Ireland, pp. 1204–1215 (2008)
12. Fichman, R.: Information Technology Diffusion: A review of Empirical Research. In: Proceedings of the Thirteenth International Conference on Information Systems (1992)
13. Harris, L.: Trading and Exchanges: Market Microstructure for Practitioners. Oxford University Press, US (2003)
14. Hulland, J.S.: Use of Partial Least Squares (PLS) in Strategic Management Research: A Review of Four Recent Studies. Strategic Management Journal, 195–204 (1999)
15. Mahnke, V., Overby, M., Oscan, S.: Outsourcing innovative capabilities for IT-enabled services. Industry and Innovation, 189–207 (2006)

16. Markus, M.L.: Toward a 'Critical Mass' Theory of Interactive Media: Universal Access, Interdependence and Diffusion. Communications Research 14, 491–511 (1987)
17. Millo, Y., Muniesa, F., Panourgias, N.S., Scott, S.V.: Organised detachment: Clearinghouse mechanisms in financial markets. Information and Organization 15(3), 229–246 (2005)
18. Moore, G.C., Benbasat, I.: Development of an instrument to measure the perceptions of adopting an information technology innovation. Information Systems Research 2(3) (1991)
19. Pirrong, C.: The Economics of Clearing in Derivatives Markets: Netting, Asymmetric Information, and the Sharing of Default Risks Through a Central Counterparty, University of Houston (2009)
20. Ringle, C.M., Wende, S., Will, S.: SmartPLS 2.0 (M3) Beta (2005), `http://www.smartpls.de`
21. Ripatti, K.: Central Counterparty Clearing: Constructing a Framework for Evaluation of Risks and Benefits, Bank of Finland Discussion Papers (2004)
22. Rivkin, J.W.: Reproducing Knowledge: Replication Without Imitation at Moderate Complexity. Organization Science 12, 274–293 (2001)
23. Rogers, E.M.: Diffusion of preventive innovations. Addictive Behaviors 27(6), 989–993 (2002)
24. Rogers, E.: Diffusion of Innovations, 4th edn. Free Press, New York (1995)
25. Schafer, J., Graham, J.W.: Missing Data: Our View of the State of the Art. Psychological Methods 7(2), 147–177 (2002)
26. Sellin, N., Keeves, J.P.: Path analysis with latent variables. In: Husen, T., Neville Postlethwaite, T. (eds.) International encyclopedia of education. Elsevier Publishers, London (1994)
27. Tabb, L., Iati, R.: Global Credit Default Swap clearing: Getting the model right, TABB Group (2009)
28. Tornatzky, L.G., Klein, K.J.: Innovation Characteristics and Innovation Adoption-Implementation: A Meta-Analysis of Findings. IEEE Transactions on Engineering Management, 29 (1982)
29. Wendt, F.: Intraday Margining of Central Counterparties: EU Practice and a Theoretical Evaluation of Benefits and Costs Oversight. DNB Working Papers, Netherlands Central Bank (2006)

The Impact of Information Technology on European Post-Trading

Torsten Schaper and Michael Chlistalla

Chair of e-Finance, Goethe-University Frankfurt
{schaper,chlistalla}@wiwi.uni-frankfurt.de

Abstract. The European post-trading landscape is recently changing fundamentally due to regulatory actions, the financial crisis, and the strong linkage of the global financial markets. The systemic importance of post-trading infrastructures underlines the industry's significant dependence on safe and efficient processes and thus the importance of reliable IT-systems. Using the Delphi methodology in a study among a multitude of experts from different areas of post-trading, we develop a joint and coherent view of the most important issues relating to IT the post-trading system has to cope with.

Keywords: Post-Trading, Delphi Study, Financial Market Infrastructures.

1 Introduction and Objective of the Study

The value of share trading on European securities markets has doubled in the last decade (WFE 2009). Investments in Europe are becoming more and more international as 37% of stocks are held by foreign investors (FESE 2008). A growing proportion of trades are in foreign shares or by foreign investors, meaning that not only more transactions need to be settled, but more of these transactions require cross-border settlement. Moreover, the complexity of settlement rises with the increasing use of complex derivatives composed of one or more underlying assets from different trading venues. Trading activity, market liquidity, and capital market growth depend on safe and efficient trading and post-trading systems.

In the light of the 2007-2009 financial crisis, the importance of appropriate post-trading arrangements has gained even more weight and the focus of regulators is on ensuring their integrity, efficiency, and robustness. The European Commission's plans for future policy actions, for instance, are bound to change the European post-trading landscape fundamentally (European Commission 2009). It is therefore relevant and guiding information both for policy makers and market participants to understand how the future post-trading industry might look like in five or ten years from now and to assess the implications for information technologies (IT). Challenges for the IT at providers of post-trading services result from regulatory intervention as likewise from the need to establish seamless cross-border processes. Although an important driver for managing these challenges efficiently, IT in this context has not been discussed systematically yet; the post-trading industry is still missing a clear vision of how the role of IT is evolving and how the regulatory changes affect the IT-landscape. The objective of

M.L. Nelson et al. (Eds.): Sustainable e-Business Management, LNBIP 58, pp. 48–62, 2010.

this paper is to develop this vision; by means of a Delphi study, we ask a broad variety of experts to provide their opinion on the research question "What are the most important IT/ IS issues the European post-trading system needs to cope with?"

2 Previous Research

As interest in international securities trading has grown over the last years, so has the awareness of academics in researching these markets. Research topics cover a wide range from market microstructure theory and transaction cost analysis to the investigation of competitive markets and of network effects.

In contrast to the vast amount of academic research focusing on the trading level, research with regard to the post-trading sector is rather sparse. Existing research on clearing, settlement, and custody issues or on the parties involved in these businesses regularly only addresses isolated factors or individual institutions within this industry:

Schmiedel, Malkamäki, and Tarkka (2006) investigate the existence of economies of scale in depository and settlement systems. The evidence from 16 settlement institutions for the years 1993-2000 indicates the existence of significant economies of scale depending on size of the institution and region. Small settlement service providers reveal a high potential of economies of scale, larger institutions show an increasing trend towards cost effectiveness. For clearing and settlement systems in countries in Europe and Asia substantially larger economies of scale are reported than those in the US system.

Serifsoy (2007) analyzes technical efficiency and factor productivity of exchanges by investigating 28 stock exchanges from 1999-2003. His findings suggest that exchanges which diversify into related activities are mostly less efficient than exchanges that remain focused on the cash market. Moreover, his findings show no evidence that vertically integrated exchanges are more efficient than non-integrated exchanges.

A first study concerning the usage of IT in securities settlement is Gomber and Schaper (2007). The survey shows the diversity of the analyzed players and highlights differences in their settlement processes and their usage of IT. Most providers of settlement services still see IT as a core competence, and most of them have a dedicated Chief Information Officer (CIO) and an own IT-division.

Pirrong (2008) combines the economics of securities trading, clearing, and settlement in a micro-analytic analysis. He discusses the existence of economies of scale in trading and post-trading applying theoretical models. He demonstrates that in clearing particularly strong scope economies exist, and illustrates the impact of economies of scale and scope on the organization of these services. As a central result, the paper reveals that the integration of trading and post-trading is the modal form of organization in financial markets.

Chlistalla and Schaper (2009) were the first to investigate the impact of increasing competition and regulatory changes on intra-organizational performance measurement in post-trading; they modify the concept of the Balanced Scorecard to the specifics of a network industry and develop a framework for the modification of the traditional Balanced Scorecard to fit the needs of clearing and settlement institutions. They emphasize the importance to include risk management and IT into the business strategy.

By providing a study on the prices, costs, and volumes for trading and post-trading of securities in the EU, Oxera (2009) gives a detailed description of how the European capital markets are operating in terms of market dynamics as well as customer and supplier behavior. According to the paper, the costs of cross-border transactions in Europe are still between two and six times higher than domestic transactions. At the same time, using infrastructure providers has become cheaper, by up to 80% over two years. This reflects significant price reductions as competition increases.

3 The European Post-Trading Industry

The securities trading value chain consists of the complete set of relationships from investors to custody service providers, including the provision of all trading and post-trading activities. Post-trading services, in particular clearing and settlement, are required after two parties have decided to transfer the ownership of a security. The purpose of clearing is the efficient handling of risks inherent to concluded, but still unfulfilled contracts. Clearing confirms the legal obligations from the trade. It involves the calculation of the mutual obligations of market participants and determines what each counterpart receives and what each counterpart has to deliver. Central counterparties (CCPs) can be included in the process of clearing. A CCP is an entity that interposes itself between the transactions of the counterparties in order to assume their rights and obligations, acting as a buyer to every seller and as a seller to every buyer. The original legal relationship between the buyer and the seller is thus replaced by two new legal relationships. The CCP thereby absorbs the counterparty risk and guarantees clearing and settlement of the trade (Wendt 2006). Subsequent to the clearing stage, the second operation is settling a trade. Settlement is the exchange of cash or assets in return for other assets or cash and transference of ownership. A CSD is the organization that performs these functions (European Commission 2006).

3.1 Network and Scale Effects in Clearing and Settlement

Clearing and settlement are subject to network effects. Network effects arise in clearing because the greater the number of transaction counterparties that use the services of a CCP, the greater the probability that a transaction by a given party will be accepted by the CCP, and therefore the greater the utility for that party from buying the CCP services (European Commission 2006). Through multilateral netting the costs of collateral can be reduced. Network effects in settlement are existent in analogy to the telecommunication sector as settlement is a particular form of a telecommunications service (Knieps 2006): The greater the number of custodians connected to the CSD, the greater the network and therefore the utility for all users.

Economies of scale occur when firms achieve cost savings per unit by producing more units of a good or service. Such effects arise when it is possible to spread fixed costs over a higher output. The providers of trading, clearing, and settlement can achieve significant economies of scale, as the set-up costs for a transaction platform have a substantial portion of fixed costs and thus the average costs fall with an increasing transaction volume (Serifsoy and Weiß 2007). For the provision of a trading and post-trading infrastructure, high investments in IT infrastructure are necessary, which are largely independent from the number of transactions (Schmiedel, Malkamäki, and Tarkka 2006).

Economies of scope occur when firms achieve cost savings by increasing the variety of goods and services they produce (joint production). Strong scope economies influence the efficient organization of trading, clearing, and settlement. These services require similar IT/IS infrastructures (e.g. datacenters, bandwidth, or connectivity) which provide potential for synergies. Scope economies may also originate from processing multiple products. For instance, if multiple asset classes are cleared within one clearing house the gains and losses can be netted across the customer's positions (Pirrong 2008). This cross-collateralization improves collateral efficiency and increases liquidity (European Commission 2009b).

3.2 Regulation and Market Initiatives in European Post-Trading

Compared with the US, the clearing and settlement industry in Europe is fragmented. Settlement in Europe has its origins in a patchwork of national systems. At the national level, consolidation has taken place and in most countries only one CSD has prevailed (Giovannini Group 2001). Domestic settlement systems are efficient within their national boundaries. The costs per transaction in domestic settlement are similar to the costs in the US, but European CSDs realize higher margins (NERA 2004). In contrast, the settlement of cross-border transactions in Europe is not efficient because of various barriers (Giovannini Group 2001; Schmiedel, Malkamäki, and Tarkka 2006). The main reason for the fragmented European settlement industry is that historically securities were traded nationally, partly as a result of the existence of different currencies. In consequence, several CSDs at continue to coexist and only recently consolidation has taken place.

The European post-trading industry is currently affected by regulatory initiatives (e.g., MiFID), market initiatives (e.g., Link Up Markets, SSE), and initiatives started by the European Commission or the Eurosystem (e.g., Code of Conduct, T2S). They are briefly portrayed in the following.

The **Markets in Financial Instruments Directive (MiFID)** is a European Union law which provides a homogeneous regulatory regime for investment services across the European Economic Area (European Commission 2004). The main objective of the directive is to increase competition and consumer protection in investment services. By abolishing concentration rules, in which member states required investment firms to execute client orders on regulated markets only, MiFID allows new execution venues alongside established exchanges. In Article 34, MiFID regulates access to central counterparty, clearing and settlement facilities for investment firms and regulated markets. Chi-X, BATS, and Turquoise are examples of new trading platforms designed to rival incumbent exchanges. These new platforms bring competition into European securities trading and thus also into the clearing and settlement of cross-border transactions.

The **European Code of Conduct for Clearing and Settlement** (FESE, EACH, and ECSDA 2006) is a voluntary self-commitment of trading venues, CCPs, and CSDs in Europe stipulating a number of principles on the provision of post-trading services for cash equities. The intention is to establish a strong European capital market and to allow investors the choice to trade any European security within a consistent, coherent, and efficient European framework. The Code of Conduct intends to offer market participants the freedom to choose their preferred provider of services separately at each layer of the securities trading value chain. "Access and interoperability", the second implementation phase, is currently affecting the post-trade industry as the guidelines defined for access and interoperability provide the basis for the development of links between respective service providers. In total, more than 80 such requests can be counted. Progress has recently been considerable, with the Link Up Markets initiative on the settlement side (see below) and the arrival of EuroCCP and the European Multilateral Clearing Facility (EMCF) on the clearing side, providing new clearing facilities and fuelling competition among clearinghouses.

TARGET2-Securities (T2S) is the Eurosystem's proposal to European CSDs to transfer their securities accounts to a common technical platform. The main benefit of T2S would be the reduction of settlement engines and therefore the reduction of costs for CSD infrastructure and for custodians' back offices. Background of T2S is the technical debate about the best way to synchronize delivery of securities with the cash payment. The settlement of securities and cash would be realized within one single European platform. In July 2009, 27 CSDs from 25 countries, including the CSDs in all euro area countries as well as nine non-euro area CSDs, and the Eurosystem signed the T2S Memorandum of Understanding (European Central Bank 2009). Details of T2S, like supervision of the platform, governance, questions on competition, the effects on the private enterprise infrastructure, and alternatives to integrate the different national infrastructures remain to be clarified in the near future (LIBA, ESF, and ICMA 2007).

Link Up Markets is a joint venture by nine CSD aiming to create a technical platform which links together multiple CSD markets. The idea is to overcome hurdles and inefficiencies in cross-border equities business by establishing a single cross-border operating organization. Link Up Markets plans to deliver a central linkage to the national systems. While CSDs will still provide the single point of access for customers for domestic and cross-border business (Link Up Markets 2009) and all domestic institutions and infrastructure will remain unchanged, savings are expected as only one organization needs to implement and to manage the cross-border network. The need to maintain several different access points will recede for market participants. Reduced interconnection costs are expected regarding negotiations, link processing, interfaces, synchronization of systems, data formats, link contracts, liquidity requirements, and effective use of collateral. In addition, Link Up Markets targets to achieve network externalities leading to further cost savings shared by the whole community, as a centralized linkage of domestic systems can help standardize processes and practices (Link Up Markets 2009) and catalyze common technical standards, harmonized rules and regulations, and identical tax treatment. The first markets went live in March 2009 with six CSDs connected as of December 2009.

The **Single Settlement Engine (SSE)** is an integration project of the Euroclear Group. Instead of achieving interoperability of the different national systems, Euroclear is implementing an integrated platform for securities settlement in Belgium, France, the Netherlands, Ireland, and the UK. The SSE provides integrated cash and securities settlement, merging five settlement platforms into one and thus harmonizing services on a consolidated processing platform. Users of the SSE operate as if they acted in a domestic market. The next step towards a single platform is the launch of Euroclear's Settlement for Euronext-zone Securities (ESES). Using the SSE as its foundation, ESES will serve as a single processing solution to process both domestic and cross-border fixed-income and equity transactions in the Belgian, Dutch, and French markets as if they were a single market. The final consolidation of the platforms is aimed for 2010 (Euroclear 2002).

3.3 Impact of the Financial Crisis on European Post-Trading

In the course of the financial crisis some of the financial infrastructures had to handle enormous peaks in volumes (Gomber 2009): for instance, the settlement system of the UK, Euroclear, had to handle 1.6 million transactions on a single day, double the average monthly volume (Francotte 2009). Moreover, the crisis has brought over-the-counter (OTC) derivatives at the forefront of regulatory attention. OTC derivatives, in particular Credit Default Swaps (CDS), played a significant role as originators of the crisis. The financial market turbulence illustrated that the absence of an adequate post-trading infrastructure contributed to the weaknesses in operational and counterparty risk management. A lack of transparency and oversight in OTC derivatives markets with negative implications for overall financial market functioning and financial stability was observed. OTC derivatives markets seem to have acted as a contagion channel during the crisis, because of a lack of information about where risks related to OTC derivatives arose and how they were distributed through the financial system.

OTC derivatives markets are large in size and closely linked to the cash markets (European Central Bank 2009b). In order to improve financial stability in derivatives markets, the European Commission has called for concrete proposals how to mitigate the risks associated with credit derivatives. Key priority was given to the effective implementation and usage of CCPs for CDS within the euro area. As a result, CDS dealers committed to start clearing eligible CDS through European CCPs starting 31st July 2009 (European Commission 2009). The development of post-trading infrastructures for OTC derivative markets should be accompanied by enhanced cross-border cooperation among authorities in order to achieve a consistent regulatory framework for different infrastructures (European Central Bank 2009b).

4 Study Setup

4.1 The Delphi Methodology

The Delphi methodology is a group facilitation technique in the form of an iterative multi-stage process designed to transform individual opinions into group consensus. It is a flexible approach commonly used within the social sciences (Hasson, Keeney, and McKeena 2000). This technique seeks to obtain the opinions of experts through a series of structured questionnaires (referred to as "rounds") or interviews. The initial questionnaire may also collect qualitative comments. After each of these rounds and following statistical analysis regarding group collective opinion, the results are fed back in a structured questionnaire to the previous round's participants who are then asked to reassess these results. This process is ongoing until consensus is obtained or diminishing returns can be observed (Brancheau, Janz, and Wetherbe 1996).

One of the most significant benefits of the Delphi methodology is the fact that participants retain the opportunity to change their opinions in later rounds when realizing from the collective opinion that they may have missed items or thought them unimportant

(Couper 1984). Yet, participants cannot influence each other directly. Controversial debate rages over the use of the term "expert" and how to identify a professional as an expert. Hasson, Keeney, and McKeena 2000 point out the importance of a fine balance among the expert panel. In order to avoid biased opinions of participants distorting the overall picture, responses are clustered by interest group where appropriate. Our research question required a broad set of opinions from true subject-matter experts to be collected. As due to the competitive and regulatory sensitivity of the issues under scrutiny the number of experts in this field is limited and potential interview partners or study participants are extremely reluctant to share their knowledge and expertise, we decided in favor of the Delphi methodology.

4.2 Setup of the Delphi Study on European Post-Trading

In order to define the scale and scope of the Delphi study as a first step an industry analysis was performed. Stakeholders that are involved within the securities trading value chain were considered, i.e. in trading, clearing, settlement or in adjacent services such as custody and transaction banking. Two attributes can be defined to identify stakeholders: power to influence the firm and the legitimate claim or interest in the firm (Freeman 1984). Dominant stakeholders are both powerful and have a legitimate claim or interest in the firm. These stakeholders are the key stakeholders that actually draw the attention of the management. They are important for managers, because their claims or interest in the firm are justified by the legitimacy of their relationship with the firm. In addition, they have the capacity to force the firm to take account of their claims (Mitchell, Agle, and Wood 1997). Seven categories of expert groups were identified for the Delphi study: five stakeholder groups plus experts from academics and associations. These are (1) financial infrastructures (clearing houses, CSDs, and International CSDs), (2) regulated markets and MTFs, (3) custodian banks and users of financial infrastructures, (4) supervisory authorities (e.g. central banks), (5) suppliers (e.g. consultancies and technical infrastructures), (6) academics and researchers, and (7) associations (including issuer and investor associations).

For the composition of the study's participant panel, we identified between 15 and 25 industry experts per above-mentioned category. The interviewees were selected from participant lists of relevant institutionalized groups such as the Code of Conduct Monitoring Group (MOG), the T2S Advisory Group and its various sub-groups, or the European Commission's Clearing and Settlement Advisory and Monitoring Expert groups (CESAME and CESAME2) as found on the relevant websites. In case of multiple potential interviewees, participants were selected according to their hierarchy within their institution and according to their assumed expertise in terms of securities trading and/or post-trading. Moreover, we identified a number of experts by reviewing academic as well as practitioners' publications and presentations on post-trading. Potential participants finally summed up to 158.

The study consisted of three consecutive rounds. The objective of round one was to generate the hypotheses for assessment in the subsequent rounds. As in a classical Delphi study, round one began with an open-ended question that generated ideas and allowed participants complete freedom in their responses. This helped to identify issues which would be addressed in subsequent rounds (Gibson 1998). Participants were encouraged to contribute with as many opinions as possible so as to maximize the chance of covering the most important opinions and issues (Hasson, Keeney, and McKeena 2000). Round two was made up of the analysis of the results of round one; the answers from the first round were analyzed and transformed into hypotheses, which were then presented to the experts in round two. Data analysis involves the analysis and careful management of qualitative and quantitative data (Hasson, Keeney, and McKeena 2000). In our case, the outcome of the first round amounted to 83 hypotheses and 3000 words. During the analysis process, duplicate answers were eliminated and similar items were grouped together according to a coding scheme developed during the process. In order not to influence the participants, this coding scheme was not communicated to the panel. As Hasson, Keeney, and McKeena (2000) propose, no items should be added during analysis and the wording used by participants, with minor editing, should be used as much as possible for round two. No items were added and only very few statements were dropped, where either the meaning was entirely unclear or where apparently sentences had been left incomplete by the study participant. Where different terms were used for what appeared to be the same issue, they were grouped together to provide unambiguous descriptions. Finally, 20 hypotheses were derived in total.

For their assessment, a 5-item Likert scale was provided with the following attributes: "strongly agree", "rather agree", "neutral", "rather disagree" and "strongly disagree" plus an additional option "no answer" to be ticked in case the individual intentionally did not want to provide an opinion regarding a certain statement. For the purpose of providing mean and standard deviation (STD), each attribute was assigned a value ranging from 1 for "strongly agree" to 5 for "strongly disagree". "No answer" was assigned the value zero and was not considered for the statistical analysis. Additionally, the participants were given the possibility to comment their answers within text fields provided for remarks or comments.

In round three, the participants were provided the results of the analysis of round two's responses with corresponding statistical information (mean and STD) presented to indicate first trends towards collective opinion.

Before starting each round, a series of pre-tests with selected participants of the study was conducted in order to assure intuitiveness of the online tool and comprehensibility of the questions and hypotheses. Per round, the feedback from three pretests was incorporated.

We asked the participants whether we were allowed to report individuals' participation in the study, which was agreed by 20 panelists. Apart from that, we guaranteed full anonymity and confidentiality.

The Delphi study was designed as an online survey. Registration for participation in the study was open beginning April 28th 2009. The experts were initially given a period of three weeks per round to answer the questions, which was extended by another two weeks per round to account for holiday season and other absences. The Delphi survey was finally closed on September 25th 2009.

The following Table 1 shows the number of participants per round and per expert group. Upon their registration, the participants were requested to provide details on their affiliation, position, and the number of years of industry expertise. They were also asked to select from a list of categories the perspective from which they would be answering the questionnaire. The mean industry expertise of the panel is 12.5 years. 94 percent of the hypotheses were assessed by the participants.

Of the 158 experts contacted in round one, 42 from 15 European countries took part. In rounds two and three, all participants of the first round were included. Some participants deliberately missed out on round two and re-joined the study for the final round. This explains e.g. the drop from 14 to 9 in the "Financial Infrastructures" group between round one and round two and the rise from 9 to 12 participants between round two and round three. The response rates of the last two rounds were above 80 percent of the sample.

Table 1. Participants and Response Rates

	Round 1 (N=158)	Round 2 (N=45)	Round 3 (N=45)
Financial Infrastructures	14	9	12
Custodian Banks / Users	7	5	6
Supervisory Authorities	5	6	6
Academics	4	5	6
Suppliers (Consultancies / Technical Infrastructures)	4	4	3
Associations	4	4	4
Regulated Markets / MTFs	4	3	3
Total	**42**	**36**	**40**
Response rate	**27%**	**80%**	**89%**

5 Results: Most Important IT/IS Issues the Post-Trading System Needs to Cope with

When asked whether the post-trading system was efficient, the expert opinion turned out to be dichotomous (Chlistalla, Gomber, and Schaper 2010): On the one hand, Europe's post-trading system is regarded efficient at the national level, for reasons such as high settlement rates, technical reliability and effective risk mitigation tools provided by financial infrastructures. On the other hand, the experts judge the European post-trading system to be rather inefficient at the cross-border level. In sum, the experts stated that – in particular in light of the global crisis – the financial infrastructures have been very robust during the crisis. Still, a number of areas of improvement remain.

Our objective was to develop a coherent and well-grounded picture of significant IT/IS issues in the changing European post-trading system. In this section, an analysis of the study's results will be presented. The focus is on the final assessments, i.e. on the results from round three.

According to relevant literature, consideration must be given to the level of consensus to be employed. A universally agreed proportion does not exist for the Delphi methodology (Hasson, Keeney, and McKeena 2000). Details are therefore provided according to the following criteria:

- The focus of the analysis lies on the mean. Those hypotheses with agreement (mean ≤ 2.0) and disagreement (mean ≥ 4.0) will be described in detail and incorporated in

the formation of the coherent views. All items with a mean ≤ 2.0 or ≥ 4.0 will be highlighted in light grey color in the result tables.
- In addition, hypotheses will be analyzed that are fundamental for the post-trading system (e.g. due to the frequency of similar answers in the first round or the status in public discussions).

Most experts rather disagree [mean = 3.78 in the 5-item Likert scale] that IT-systems are not a competitive factor in the post-trading landscape anymore, and only three experts rather agree to this thesis. The rest of the panel emphasizes that IT-systems are still a competitive factor in the post-trading industry. Risk due to the concentration in the post-trade industry does not seem to be an IT issue as the majority of the experts are neutral towards this proposition [2.95] (see Table 2).

Table 2. General Statements

The most important IT/ IS issues the post-trading system needs to cope with are:	**Mean**	**STD**	**n (N=40)**
IT-systems are not a competitive factor in the post-trading landscape anymore.	3.78	0.89	37
Risk due to the concentration in the post-trading industry.	2.95	0.78	37

Important IT issues in post-trading are the establishment of links from legacy systems to T2S and CCBM2 (Collateral Central Bank Management) [2.12], the consolidation of IT platforms [2.12], and the increasing IT investments due to the dynamics in the post-trading markets [2.11]. The experts are afraid that these projects might lead to a scarcity of resources when IT-systems need to be upgraded in all parts of the post-trading area at the same time [2.03] (see Table 3).

Table 3. IT Projects

The most important IT/ IS issues the post-trading system needs to cope with are:	**Mean**	**STD**	**n (N=40)**
Scarcity of resources (staff and IT) when IT-systems need to be upgraded in all parts of the post-trading area at the same time (e.g. due to T2S).	2.03	0.87	34
Increasing IT investments due to dynamics on post-trading markets.	2.11	0.84	37
Consolidation of IT platforms.	2.12	0.77	34
To establish links from legacy systems to T2S and CCBM2.	2.12	0.98	34

Experts agree that IT-systems in the post-trading industry need to achieve a real straight-through-processing (STP) environment to keep manual intervention low [1.72]. Further important requirements are flexibility and modularity to meet new requirements [1.83]. Achieving access and interoperability analog to the European Code of Conduct for Clearing and Settlement is also an important IT/IS issue [1.89]. Interestingly outsourcing in the area of post-trading seems not to be an issue. The experts are neutral towards the theses on outsourcing (see Table 4).

Table 4. IT-System Provisioning

The most important IT/ IS issues the post-trading system needs to cope with are:	**Mean**	**STD**	**n (N=40)**
IT-systems need to achieve a real STP environment in order to reduce manual intervention.	1.72	0.61	36
Flexibility / modularity of systems to meet new regulatory and product-related requirements.	1.83	0.51	36
Access and Interoperability (analog to the Code of Conduct).	1.89	0.82	36
Scalability (capacity to deal with peak volumes).	2.08	0.77	36
Availability.	2.51	0.98	35
Outsourcing of IT infrastructure (or services).	2.63	1.00	35
Outsourcing of IT infrastructure (or services) outside the EU.	3.09	0.95	35

The harmonization of protocols and communication standards is another important IT issue [1.69]: Examples are the implementation of SWIFT / ISO [2.26] and the establishment of secure internet connectivity for messaging [2.39] (Table 5).

Table 5. Communication

The most important IT/ IS issues the post-trading system needs to cope with are:	**Mean**	**STD**	**n (N=40)**
Harmonization of protocols and communication standards.	1.69	0.82	36
Establishment and implementation of SWIFT / ISO as standard for messaging.	2.26	0.85	35
Establishment of secure internet connectivity for messaging.	2.39	1.02	36
Establishment and implementation of FIX as standard for messaging.	3.09	1.15	32
Availability of old message formats for user convenience.	3.37	0.97	35

Other important IT/IS issues in post-trading that the experts emphasize are: the need for real-time or event-triggered risk management [1.84] and the interaction between clearing houses and customers and between linked clearing houses [1.89] (see Table 6).

Table 6. Others

The most important IT/ IS issues the post-trading system needs to cope with are:	**Mean**	**STD**	**n (N=40)**
Real-time or event-triggered risk management.	1.84	0.76	37
Interaction between clearing houses and customers (for margin payments or collateral provision) and between linked clearing houses.	1.89	0.67	36

6 Conclusion and Outlook

The post-trading industry is facing challenges from regulation, the financial crisis, and competition. In context of the global financial crisis, these challenges show that the IT-platforms need to be adapted to the new situation. E.g. real-time risk management is becoming very important as risk positions need to be monitored on a continuous basis to be able to react to changing environments. Moreover, the multitude of initiatives is affecting the post-trading industry fundamentally as many changes in the legacy systems need to be implemented at the same time.

Until now, a systematic assessment of the European post-trading industry is missing in academic literature. So far, this industry has only been analyzed in terms of single infrastructures and financial intermediaries. Our Delphi study supplies a comprehensive picture of IT issues in the post-trading industry in the current challenging environment. This contributes not only to practitioners' notions of this industry; the insights from the Delphi study mirror those developments that have an impact on the future industry structure and therefore on scale effects, risk management and eventually on transaction costs for the end-customer.

The participants of our study believe that IT-systems can still be a competitive factor in the post-trading industry. Important IT/IS issues are the flexibility of the systems to meet the new regulatory and product-related requirements, the harmonization of protocols and communication standards, and the access to and interoperability of the systems. Moreover, IT-systems need to achieve real STP environments in order to reduce manual interventions.

The experts are afraid that the high number of currently ongoing major projects (such as T2S for instance) might end up in a scarcity of resources when the IT-systems need to be upgraded in all parts of the post-trading area at the same time. Further requirements concerning IT in post-trading are real-time or event-triggered risk management and the interactions between clearing houses due to new market situations such as competitive clearing, which changes the processes in this area essentially.

One of the panelists bemoans the "avalanche of regulatory changes [that] has spurred a lot of mandatory IT work", claiming that "not all of it is productive, as regulators are not always able to deal with the mass of data they require". He adds that a "major issue that has come up with MiFID and the Lehman default is that the local legal frameworks [are] often organized along different lines in different countries". He states that "as long as politicians do not take this up seriously and prefer their local influence over and above a true European community, it will remain very difficult to achieve a true single European market".

In terms of future research we intend to repeat the study to consider the new market developments in the area of market failures in OTC-derivatives markets, regulatory requirements for pre- and post-trade transparency for equities, the switch of supervisory authorities' focus from efficiency and competition to stability and integrity, and the consolidation of supervisory powers and the resulting mass reporting data. Specifically, the impacts of these developments on IT and IS in post-trading will be assessed.

Acknowledgements

The authors gratefully acknowledge the support from Dominik Adler (Association of German Banks), Marc Bayle (European Central Bank), Wilfried Blaschke (Commerzbank AG), Andrew Douglas (SWIFT scrl), Georg Fink (Oesterreichische Kontrollbank AG), Dorien Fransens (EuropeanIssuers), Kerstin Höltje (Eurex Clearing AG), Tomas Kindler (Link Up Markets), Mogens Kruse (VP Securities A/S), Vivian Mitropoulou (Hellenic Exchanges S.A.), Maik Neubauer (European Commodity Clearing AG), Ilse Peeters (Euroclear S.A.), Rafael Plata (Federation of European Securities Exchanges), Hilmar Schwarz (Deutsche WertpapierService Bank AG), Baris Serifsoy, Micha Sigloch (Consileon Business Consultancy GmbH), Meike Ströter (European Central Bank), Diego Valiante (Centre for European Policy Studies), Susanne Trimbath (STP Advisory Services LLC), and Geert Vanderbeeke (Fortis Bank Nederland NV), but to the same extent also from the many other participants who chose to remain anonymous.

References

1. Brancheau, J.C., Janz, B.D., Wetherbe, J.C.: Key Issues in Information Systems Management: 1994-1995 SIM Delphi Results. MIS Quarterly 20(2), 225–242 (1996)
2. Chlistalla, M., Gomber, P., Schaper, T.: The Future of the European Post-Trading System - A Delphi Study on the Future of the European Post-Trading System in the Light of Globalization and the Financial Crisis. Ibidem-Verlag, Hannover (2010)
3. Chlistalla, M., Schaper, T.: Modifying the Balanced Scorecard for a Network Industry - The Case of the Clearing Industry. In: Godart, C., Gronau, N., Sharma, S., Canals, G. (eds.) Software Services for e-Business and e-Society, Nancy, pp. 255–271 (2009)
4. Couper, M.R.: The Delphi Technique: characteristics and sequence model. Advances in Nursing Science 7, 72–77 (1984)
5. Euroclear, Delivering a Domestic Market for Europe (July 2002)
6. European Central Bank, T2S Online. Quarterly Review 1/2009 (2009)

7. European Central Bank, OTC Derivatives and Post-Trading Infrastructures (2009b)
8. European Commission Directive 2004/39/EC of the European Parliament and of the Council of April 21, 2004 on markets in financial instruments amending Council Directives 85/611/EEC and 93/6/EEC and Directive 2000/12/EC of the European Parliament and of the Council and repealing Council Directive 93/22/EEC (2004)
9. European Commission, Draft working document on Post-Trading (2006)
10. European Commission, COM(2009) 332 Ensuring efficient, safe and sound derivatives markets (2009)
11. European Commission, SEC (2009) 905 Staff Working Paper (2009b)
12. FESE Share Ownership Structure in Europe (December 2008), http://www.fese.be/_lib/files/Share_Ownership_Survey_2007_Final.pdf (retrieved November 4, 2009)
13. FESE, EACH, and ECSDA, The European Code of Conduct for Clearing and Settlement (2006)
14. Francotte, P.: Rising to the challenge of the crisis and change. The view from the CEO of Euroclear (14), 1–8 (2009)
15. Freeman, R.E.: Strategic Management: A Stakeholder Approach, Pitman (1984)
16. Gomber, P.: The transformed environment of the derivatives industry after recent market turmoil, Focus No. 193, World Federation of Exchanges (2009)
17. Gomber, P., Schaper, T.: Impact of Information Technology on Settlement Services for Equities. Market Study (2007)
18. Gibson, J.M.E.: Using the Delphi to identify the content and context of nurses continuing professional development needs. Journal of Clinical Nursing 7, 451–459 (1998)
19. Giovannini Group, Cross-Border Clearing and Settlement Arrangements in the EU (2001)
20. Hasson, F., Keeney, S., McKeena, H.: Research Guidelines for the Delphi survey technique. Journal of Advanced Nursing 32(4), 1008–1015 (2000)
21. Knieps, G.: Competition in the Post-Trade Markets: A Network Economic Analysis of the Securities Business. Journal of Industry, Competition and Trade 6(1), 45–60 (2006)
22. LIBA, ESF, and ICMA, Letter to the ECB on Securities Sector Representation in T2S Committees (2007), http://www.icma-group.org/market_practice/Advocacy/clearing_and_settlement/target2-securities.html (accessed April 27, 2007)
23. Link Up Markets, Link Up Markets (2009), http://www.linkupmarkets.com/pdf/LinkUpMarkets_August2009.pdf (retrieved October 20, 2009)
24. Mitchell, R.K., Agle, B.R., Wood, D.J.: Toward a Theory of Stakeholder Identification and Salience: Defining the Principle of Who and What really Counts. Academy of Management Review 22(4), 853–886 (1997)
25. NERA, The direct costs of clearing and settlement: an EU-US comparison, Corporation of London City Research Series, No. 1 (2004)
26. Oxera, Monitoring prices, cost and volumes of trading and post-trading services, Report prepared for the European Commission (2009)
27. Pirrong, C.: The Industrial Organization of Execution, Clearing and Settlement in Financial Markets. In: CFS, DBAG and EFL Research Conference, Frankfurt, June 13-14 (2008)
28. Schmiedel, H., Malkamäki, M., Tarkka, J.: Economies of scale and technological development in securities depository and settlement systems. Journal of Banking & Finance 30, 1783–1806 (2006)

29. Serifsoy, B.: Stock exchange business models and their operative performance. Journal of Banking & Finance 31, 2978–3012 (2007)
30. Serifsoy, B., Weiß, M.: Settling for efficiency – A framework for the European securities transaction industry. Journal of Banking & Finance 31, 3034–3057 (2007)
31. Wendt, F.: Intraday Margining of Central Counterparties: EU Practice and a Theoretical Evaluation of Benefits and Costs. Netherlands Central Bank, Amsterdam (2006)
32. WFE, Report on Total Value of Share Trading (2009), `http://www.world-exchanges.org/statistics/time-series/value-share-trading` (retrieved October 22, 2009)

Privately Waiting – A Usability Analysis of the Tor Anonymity Network

Benjamin Fabian, Florian Goertz, Steffen Kunz, Sebastian Müller, and Mathias Nitzsche

Institute of Information Systems
Humboldt-Universität zu Berlin
bfabian@wiwi.hu-berlin.de,
goertzfl@cms.hu-berlin.de,
steffen.kunz@wiwi.hu-berlin.de,
sebastian.mueller.4@hu-berlin.de,
mathias.nitzsche@student.hu-berlin.de

Abstract. As the Internet is increasingly absorbing information from the real world it becomes more important to prevent unauthorized collection and abuse of personalized information. At the same time, democratic societies should establish an environment helping not only their own people but also people who face repressive censorship to access public information without being identified or traced. Internet anonymization tools such as Tor offer functionalities to meet this demand.

In practice, anonymization of Internet access can only be achieved by accepting higher latency, i.e., a longer waiting time before a Web site is displayed in the browser, and therefore reducing its usability significantly. Since many users may not be willing to accept this loss of usability, they may refrain from or stop using Tor – at the same time decreasing the anonymity of other users, which depends on shared resources in the Tor user community. In this paper[1], we quantify the loss of usability by measuring the additional latency of the Tor software and combine our measurements with metrics of the existing Web usability and performance literature. Our findings indicate that there is still a major usability gap induced by Tor, leading to its possible disuse accompanied by a higher risk exposure of Internet users.

Keywords (Required): Usability, Latency, Security, Privacy, Anonymity, Tor.

1 Introduction

Today, information technology allows data analysis to a degree which was unconceivable a few years ago. Simultaneously to the increasing amount and availability of information on the Internet, new information retrieval, data mining, and further technologies allow to automatically collect, filter, and analyze personal information and draw conclusions based on this process. In repressive political regimes, where personal rights, the freedom

[1] This research was funded by the German Federal Ministry of Education and Research under grant number 01IA08001E as part of the Aletheia project (http://www.aletheia-projekt.de/). The responsibility for this publication lies with the authors.

M.L. Nelson et al. (Eds.): Sustainable e-Business Management, LNBIP 58, pp. 63–75, 2010.

of speech, and in particular free access to information is restricted, these possibilities of modern data collection can lead to persecution of individuals if their identity is unveiled. Another restraint is censorship, which is used by repressive political regimes to restrict access to unwanted information (Amnesty International 2006).

By using anonymization tools such as the Tor onion routing network (Tor Project 2010a), Internet users can conceal their virtual tracks, leading to a non-personalized Internet access. With Tor, application messages are not directly routed to the receiver, but are encrypted and forwarded through ephemeral paths of an overlay network, using more complicated routes that are hard to analyze for an adversary. The more users participate, the harder it is to correlate senders and receivers. The anonymity provided within the Tor network attracts many different groups of users like journalists and activists or business, governmental, military, and private users (Palme and Berglund 2002; Vitone 2008). A recent study showed significant growth in Tor users in China as the governmental censorship increased and also in Iran when the riots after the presidential election took place (Loesing et al. 2009).

Besides one-time installation and configuration efforts, the main usability costs for using an anonymization tool such as Tor consist of an increase in Web latency. Several authors already discussed technically why Tor is slow and proposed how to improve the performance (Dingledine and Murdoch 2009; Loesing 2009; Loesing et al. 2009). In this paper, we compare requests via Tor to direct requests (without Tor) in order to discuss the impact of latency problems and the associated expected user cancelation rate, the percentage of users who abandon the wait during a certain time interval. This metric is an indicator how easy it would be to keep existing users and to attract new, "average" Web users to Tor for increasing their own anonymity as well as the anonymity of the whole user community.

The rest of this paper is structured as follows. In the following section, we focus on the influence of usability in security. Next, we introduce two forms of latency, core and average (technical) latency, which we use as the major usability factor for Web anonymity, followed by a description of our experimental setup. Additionally, we describe the execution and the results of our experiment. Finally, we discuss our major findings as well as related and future work.

2 Usability of Security

With the increasing need for human rights enforcement in a globalized world, the topic of security has recently gained momentum on the Internet. Security can generally be understood as the prevention of adversary attacks and can be divided in local (system) and communication security (Wright 2004). Local security is well-debated in public as a necessary precondition for privacy. However, the same is also true for communication security, though most Internet users are not aware of the attacks threatening their daily communication links. One potential countermeasure against the adversary attacks on communication security is anonymization (Wright 2004). In our case, the Tor security software provides privacy for Internet users by fundamentally enhancing their anonymity when using the Internet.

The problem associated with most of today's security and privacy solutions is not that the level of security they provide is insufficient, but rather their lack of usability.

If the usability for certain security features is too low, end users are not willing to apply them, increasing the users' personal risk exposure to adversary attacks. Recent studies show that too complex security features are not applied if they are not obligatory, see Mannan and van Oorschot (2008) for usage of security in a banking scenario. The amount of time or money users are willing to spend for more security is restricted and differs individually.

There exist two ways to foster a broader application of security mechanisms: either (i) to increase the awareness of security risks in order to raise the willingness to pay money or time, or (ii) to increase the usability of the security features. In the case of Tor, our main hypothesis is that due to its poor usability, i.e., its additional latency, Tor is not frequently and intensively used.

3 Latency as Usability Factor

In the area of e-commerce, there is a common understanding that waiting time impedes increasing online commerce (Nielson 1999; Rose et al. 1999; Ryan and Valverde 2003; Stockport et al. 2001), although the authors do not agree on concrete metrics. Due to the fact that in our Tor usability experiment latency has to be classified and finally quantified, we need to define metrics to measure when users cancel their Web page request or in other words, how long users tolerate waiting for a request. Table 1 summarizes the existing literature about critical latency thresholds for Internet users, providing different classifications (e.g., response time below x seconds is acceptable, but response time higher than x seconds is not).

According to these works, we assume that user tolerance for waiting for Web page requests decreases after 2s; it falls sharply within the interval between 7s and 15s, and ends with 50s when the user stops waiting. In our opinion, the research conducted by Nah (2004) is best suited for our experiment due to its empirical grounding and most recent data compared to the other studies. In particular, we apply the results presented in Figure 1 referencing Nah's (2004) *first attempt waiting scenario* in which the user is confronted with a broken link while not getting any feedback from the Web browser. Here, an important metric is introduced: the percentage of users who abandoned the wait during the time interval specified. We label and adopt this *cancelation rate* as a good indicator for the user's waiting tolerance in our setting.

In our experiment, we focus on technical latency, i.e., the latency that can be measured while providing reproducible results. In particular, we examine the *core latency*, which is the duration of a single HTTP request without downloading the complete content of the Web page. This latency also entails the time for the Domain Name System (DNS) request which will be discussed later. The *average latency*, on the other hand, refers to the time for downloading the complete content necessary to display the whole page in the Web browser. We do not focus on perceived latency, i.e., how individual users perceive the waiting time, since this metric strongly depends on soft social, cultural, and further context factors as well as individual browser and operating system settings that are difficult to quantify and pose interesting research challenges for future work. Further, at this stage of our research, we have not investigated how much additional latency a user is willing to accept for anonymous browsing. This will be part of future research.

Table 1. Classification of Tolerable Waiting Time

Author	Critical Latency	Description	Year	Source
Nah	2s	For simple information retrieval tasks	2004	Journal
AccountingWEB	8s	Optimal Web page waiting time	2000	Practical advise
Bhatti	8.57s	Tolerable delay by users	2000	Conference
Selvidge	10s	Tolerable delay by users	1999	Practical advise
Nielson	10s	Optimal Web page waiting time	1999	Practical advise
Galetta	12s	Start of significant decrease in user satisfaction	2004	Journal
Nah	15s	Free user from physical and mental captivity	2004	Journal
Ramsay	41s	Suggestion as cut-off for long delays	1998	Journal

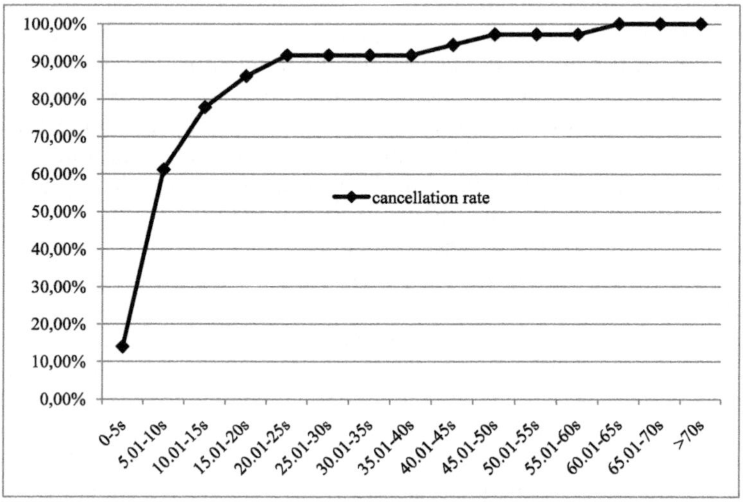

Fig. 1. Cancelation Rate of *waiting for broken link in first attempt* (Nah, 2004, p.159)

4 Experiment

The experiment was conducted from a standard Internet user's point of view, i.e., the behavior of a user is simulated and modeled as follows: The user is accessing the Internet from his home location via DSL (situated in Europe), requesting different Web sites over a certain period of time. The 50 Web sites, we sent requests to, were taken from SEOMOZ[2], which provides a list of the 500 most linked Web pages on the Internet. For collecting the empirical data, Perl scripts that simulate user requests were developed. In order to prevent distortion of the results, competing traffic during the experiment was omitted. The experiment itself was conducted within a period of 3

[2] http://www.seomoz.org/

days and the tests took place during different times of the day. Table 2 shows the hardware and software we used for our experiment.

4.1 Core Latency

For measuring the *core latency* – the duration of a single HTTP request without downloading the complete content of the Web page –, the time needed for each of altogether 50 *GET* requests to each of the target Web sites was measured. A Perl script using the *LWP library* (Aas 2010) was used to perform these HTTP requests automatically. This library provides methods to dispatch *GET* requests. In each request, only a single HTML Web source was demanded. Additional data or media, like images, videos, or java scripts were not transferred. The Perl script iterated a list of targets, which stores the 50 most linked Web sites. Each target was requested once with Tor and once without Tor in an alternating sequence. All Tor requests were directed over Socks protocol proxy "Privoxy" (Privoxy 2010), which then forwarded the request over the Tor network. After having processed one target, one run was complete. Altogether, 50 runs were executed. Date and time, request duration, and received bytes were logged for each request.

Figure 2 and Figure 3 compare the duration of HTTP requests with and without Tor. All results gained by completing 50 runs are visualized. The 50 different Web sites are shown on the x-axis. Each vertical line displays the maximum and minimum time of the core latency and the 0.25- and 0.75-quantile included as bar. Further analysis showed that 50% of all HTTP requests of the direct connection take between 0.79s and 1.95s, while 50% of all HTTP request with Tor are between 3.9s and 12.4s. This indicates that the core latency of Tor-based requests has a larger deviation. Further, we calculated the median of core latency across all 50 sites for both access methods. The median value was chosen because a high deviation and peak values can distort the arithmetic average. Tor's median of 6.98s compared to 1.37s for direct connection indicates a five times higher core latency.

Table 2. Hardware Deployment for Experiments

PC	IBM Lenovo X61s Intel Core 2 Duo 1.60 GHz 2GB memory
Operation System	Windows XP SP3
Software	TorPortable 1.3.1 Privoxy 3.0.12 Vidalia 0.1.15 Strawberry Portable 5.10.0.6 TorDNS v1.7 WiresharkPortable 1.2.5 GNU Wget tool LWP library
Internet Access	ADSL 16 Mbit/s Download, 1 Mbit/s Upload

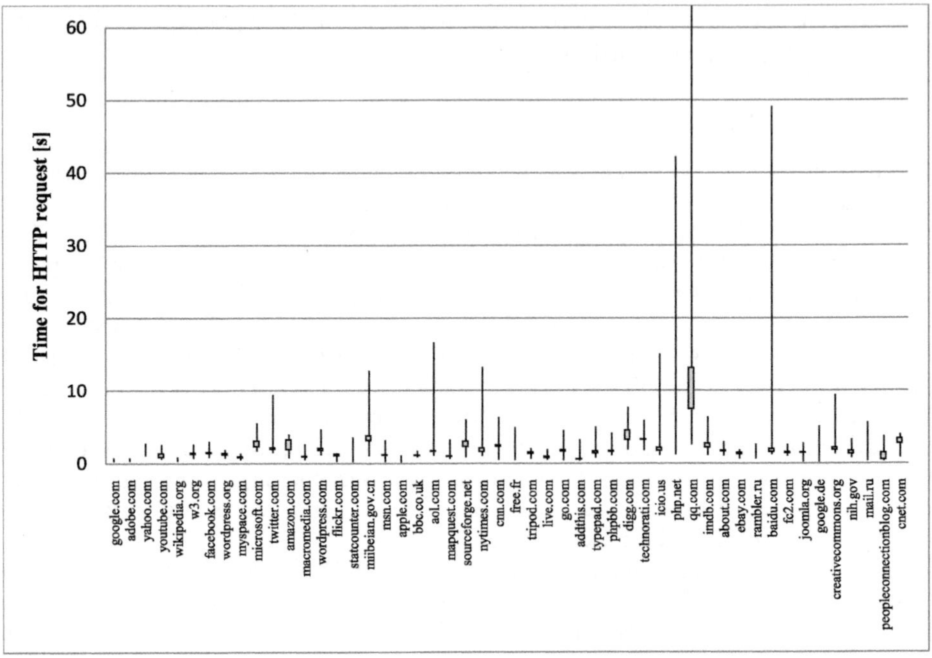

Fig. 2. Core Latency for Direct Access (in Seconds)

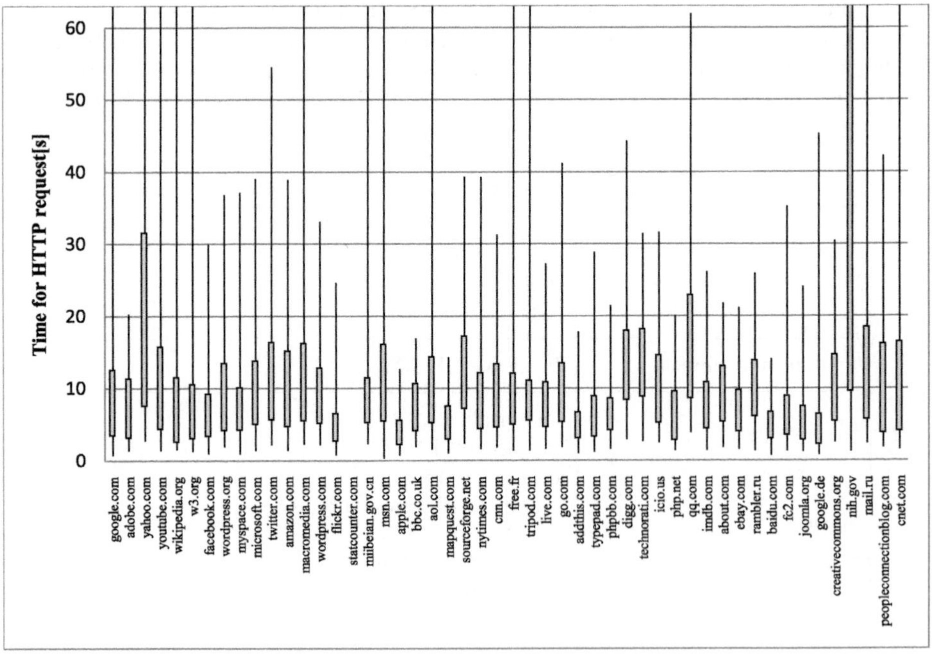

Fig. 3. Core Latency with Tor (in Seconds)

4.2 DNS Request as a Part of the HTTP Request

In order to break down the core latency, we further investigated the DNS latency of the HTTP request by applying a Perl script that looped over the 50 most linked Web sites and conducted alternating DNS requests with and without Tor using the *dig* command line tool. Instead of the standard DNS Server of the Internet service provider, for direct requests, Google's public DNS server (with IP 8.8.8.8) was used via the User Datagram Protocol (UDP), to make the experiment outcome reproducible for later experiments. For request over the Tor network, a local DNS proxy was used to forward UDP-based DNS requests to Tor as Transmission Control Protocol (TCP) based requests that are currently necessary for Tor. The Tor-DNS-Tool v1.7, which is recommended on the Tor homepage, was used for this purpose.

Figure 4 shows the (rounded) median and the 0.25- and 0.75-quantile included as bar. It reveals that the Tor DNS request in our experiments was around 45 times slower with a much larger span of values compared to a direct DNS request.

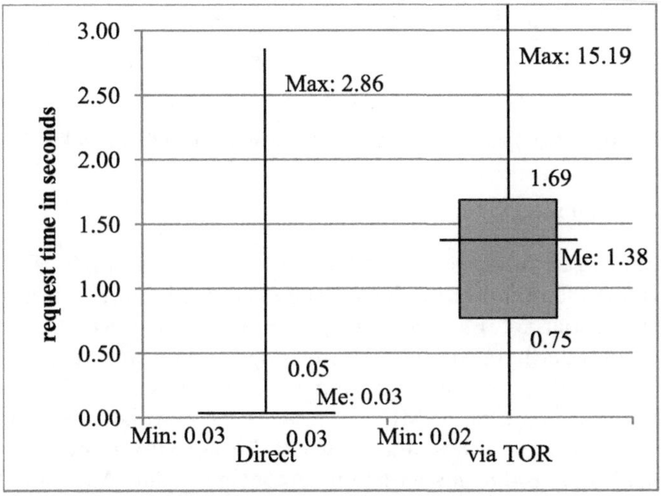

Fig. 4. Direct and Tor-Based DNS Requests (in Seconds)

Figure 5 shows the proportion of DNS latency compared to the average latency. We applied the median value for this comparison. It can be noticed that the latency portion of the DNS request was always under 35% and it is therefore not dominant for the whole request time. However, it can also be recognized that the proportion of the Tor DNS latency, as part of the core latency, was disproportionally higher than for direct requests. One possible reason could be that Tor is currently sending DNS requests via the TCP stack instead of using UDP. In future releases, Tor may be able to use the UDP stack for DNS requests.

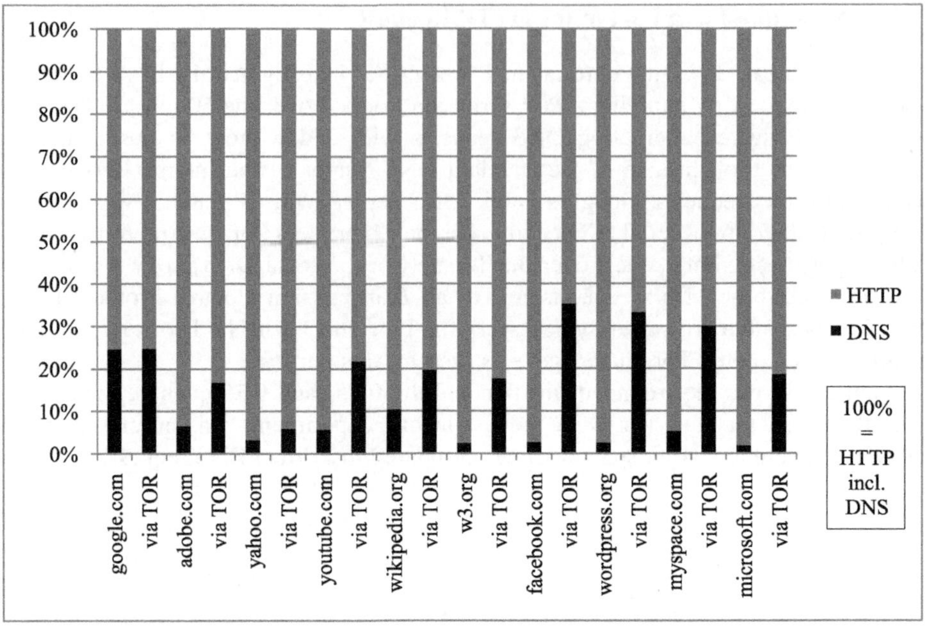

Fig. 5. Comparison of Latency Proportions of HTTP and DNS

4.3 Average Latency

In the preceding paragraphs, we referred to the latency for a single HTTP request. In order to determine the usability, we have to take the waiting time for a complete Web site into consideration, i.e., to download all the content necessary to display a complete Web site. In order to do so, we tested the top 50 Web sites (the same ones as for the core and DNS latency setting) and found out that downloading a complete Web page, instead of only the first HTML page, raises the core latency by the factor 2.4. We repeated our test three times and the result did not vary more than 15% (upside and downside). We consider this variation as nonsignificant. Accordingly, using this *average latency* as an indicator for downloading entire Web sites, we extrapolate the downloading time of one page by the factor 2.4.

We have to note that this approach, though most suited for our experimental setting, has some limitations: (i) The results vary between different Web sites, while extrapolating does not cover this issue. We do not consider this as crucial due to the fact that we focus on average latency. (ii) When downloading the complete Web page, additional variations in terms of time and coverage for different browsers and individual browser settings may be experienced. In order to provide a most reproducible and browser independent benchmark for the average latency factor, we decided to do the request via the *GNU Wget* tool for downloading Web sites from the command line. Our comparison is based on the *wget* and *wget –p* command, with *wget –p* as estimator for retrieving entire Web sites (including inline images, sounds, and referenced style-sheets). Some parallel control experiments using the *Yslow* plug-in for

Firefox[3] indicated that this approach provides a good estimation in the average case for our set of Web sites.

The extrapolation by the identified factor 2.4 increases the median of the HTTP Tor request from 7.08s to 16.99s. The median of the HTTP requests without Tor increases from 1.37s to 3.29s. Figure 6 shows the results of our comparison. The extrapolated average latency is referenced by *AVG*, the core latency by *CORE* and the latency of the DNS request by *DNS*, while requests directed via the Tor network are referenced by *TOR* and the direct requests by *Direct*. The bars show the difference between the 0.25-quantile and the 0.75-quantile of the requests' latency. In every bar, there is an additional indicator for the median latency. The 0.75-quantile of the extrapolated download time of whole Web sites via Tor is 30.26 seconds, the median 16.99 seconds, and the 0.25-quantile 9.60 seconds. It can be recognized that every 0.25-quantile of Tor requests is higher than the 0.75-quantile of direct requests of the same request type. Hence, at least 75% of all direct requests are faster than 75% of all Tor requests. Figure 6 also implicates that the variance of different Tor requests is much higher than for direct requests.

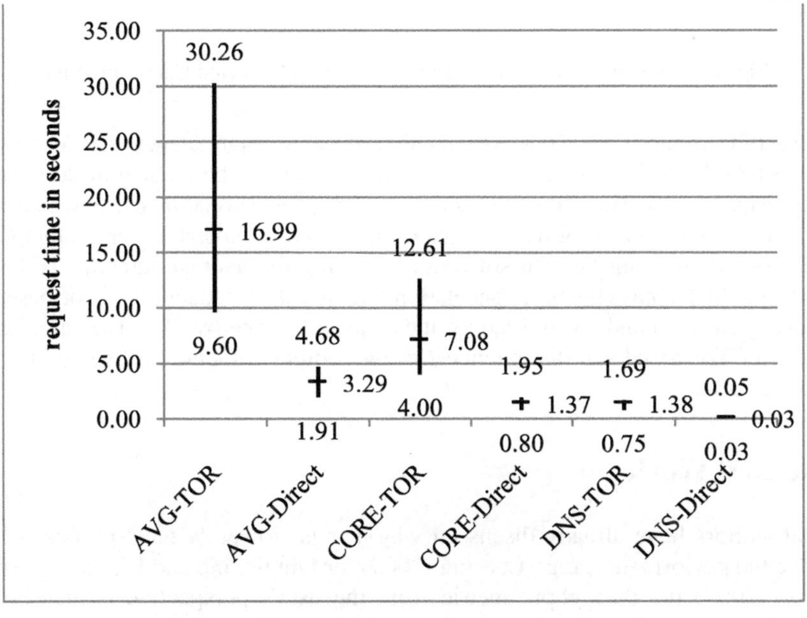

Fig. 6. Comparison of Request Times (in Seconds)

4.4 Cancelation Rate for Average and Core Latency

In Figure 7, we map our technical latency results to the user cancelation rate of Figure 1. This mapping shows direct and Tor-based core and average latency and the respective cancelation rate. This indicates an expected disproportionate increase in user cancelation

[3] http://developer.yahoo.com/yslow/

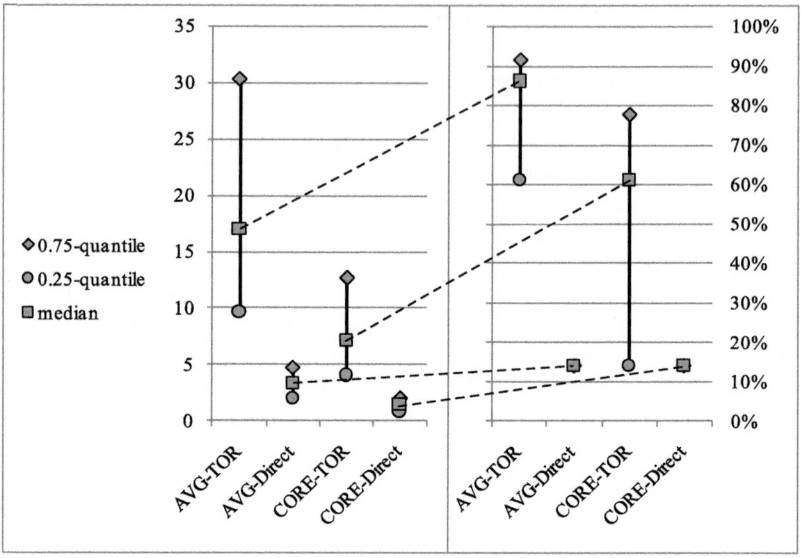

Fig. 7. Mapping of Core and Average Latency to Expected Cancelation Rate

when sending requests via TOR. The median of the average latency via Tor maps to a median of 88% cancelation rate, while user frustration for the median of direct average latency maps to 14% cancelation. This expected disproportional increase, which we aim to support by our own set of user studies in future work, indicates a crucial gap in user cancelation when using the Tor software. Lowering the average latency via Tor by 2 seconds would decrease the user cancelation rate by 8%. A reduction of Tor-based average latency by 7 seconds would reduce the cancelation rate by 25% The same cancelation rate for Tor-based and direct request would require reducing the average latency of Tor by 12 seconds.

5 Related Work

Several authors have already discussed why Tor is slower or have proposed how to improve the performance, e.g., Loesing (2009), or Dingledine and Murdoch (2009). In Loesing (2009) the throughput metric from the user's perspective is measured and analyzed. Other research approaches have conducted demographic studies, e.g., number and countries of exit nodes or estimation of user numbers and origin (Loesing et al. 2009). These approaches differ from our approach as this paper focuses on a comparison of performance. In the Tor Metrics subproject (Tor Project 2010b) different users have provided long-term data of the Tor performance. Their results indicate that the performance of Tor is volatile over time, but they do not discuss the latency gap compared to a direct connection. In our paper, we aim to close this research gap by a comparison of Internet access with and without the application of Tor.

In the existing security literature there are other security related technologies that generate additional latency: Fathi et al. (2005) discuss the latency of WLAN security mechanisms, while Zia et al. (2007) focus on the latency of security mechanisms in wireless sensor networks. Lyu and Lau (2000) measure the latency of various firewall security levels. Dinev and Hu (2007) discuss the user behavior toward protective technologies. They mention that awareness of the threats posed by attacks (negative technologies) has a strong impact on the user behavioral intention for using protective technologies.

6 Discussion and Future Work

In our experimental setting, we focused on the 50 most linked Web sites on the Internet. In future work less optimized and less country-specific Web sites should also be taken into consideration. We assume that the average latency between direct and Tor-based requests will even increase in such settings. In addition, a larger number of Web sites could be taken into account. The approach that could reflect a real user's browsing behavior best would be to provide a Tor exit node by ourselves and use the requested Web sites of the exit node for our experiment. We focused on the usability losses, i.e., the costs for gaining anonymity on the Internet. This paper may provide a good starting point for future research focusing on the reasons for high latency caused by Tor – compared to direct requests. Future experimental setups should include a long-term analysis as well as an examination of different user locations, e.g., on different continents. Changing the Internet connection speed from a private DSL connection to a corporate or University Internet connection could also provide interesting data for a sensitivity analysis.

We focused on clear-cut technical metrics that can be measured via automated requests. In the real world, the perceived latency of the user depends on various other aspects. Additional studies about influence factors for perceived latency, e.g., cultural issues, the task at hand, or individual user settings of the browser or operating system could provide valuable information about how latency is experienced by users and what countermeasures could be applied, e.g., introducing a loading progress bar for Tor users. In future work, we plan a set of user studies on capturing those further, more individual or subjective aspects of latency acceptance and influence factors for user willingness to tolerate more latency for anonymity. These studies will be evaluated with the help of structural equation models.

7 Conclusion

In this paper, we addressed an important facet of the general topic of "costs" of security and privacy, i.e., the loss of usability in exchange for improved anonymity while browsing the Web via Tor. In particular, we compared the DNS, core and average technical latency for direct as well as Tor-based HTTP requests for the 50 most linked Web sites on the Internet. In terms of the Tor core latency, the median of all requests was five times higher than the median of the direct connection. Furthermore, the results revealed that Tor HTTP requests seem to be less constant, i.e., the actual duration of the Tor HTTP request is hard to anticipate for the user. As far as the DNS requests are concerned, the Tor response was almost 40 times slower than direct DNS requests. The overall latency that a user finally experiences is approximated by the average latency, simulating the download of a complete Web page. Our results indicate that at least 75% of all direct requests are faster than 75% of all Tor request.

Based on the results of our experiments, we provided a mapping that measures the expected increase in average Web user cancelation rate while using Tor. Comparing the average latency between Tor-based and direct requests, there is a difference of 74% in expected cancelation rate. This is a strong indicator for potentially high user frustration when using the Tor anonymization network. We suggest that a usability improvement in terms of reducing latency will significantly increase the adoption of the Tor anonymization network by new users, and thereby increase the anonymity of current users as well.

References

1. Aas, G.: libwww-perl (2010), `http://search.cpan.org/dist/libwww-perl/`
2. AccountingWEB, Is Your Web Site Too Big? (2000), `http://www.accountingweb.com/item/29331`
3. Amnesty International, Undermining Freedom of Expression in China – The Role of Yahoo!, Microsoft and Google (2006), `http://irrepressible.info/static/pdf/FOE-in-china-2006-lores.pdf`
4. Bhatti, N., Bouch, A., Kuchinsky, A.: Integrating User-perceived Quality into Web Server Design. In: Computer Networks, Amsterdam, Netherlands, vol. 33, pp. 1–16 (1999)
5. Dinev, T., Hu, Q.: The Centrality of Awareness in the Formation of User Behavioral Intention toward Protective Information Technologies. Journal of the Association for Information Systems 8(7), 386–408 (2007)
6. Dingledine, R., Murdoch, S.J.: Performance Improvements on Tor – or, why Tor is Slow and What we're Going to do about it (2009), `http://www.torproject.org/press/presskit/2009-03-11-performance.pdf`
7. Fathi, H., Kobara, K., Chakraborty, S.S., Imai, H., Prasad, R.: On the Impact of Security on Latency in WLAN 802.11b. In: Proceedings of the IEEE Global Telecommunications Conference, vol. 3 (2005)
8. Galletta, D.F., Henry, R., McCoy, S., Polak, P.: Web Site Delays: How Tolerant are Users? Journal of the Association for Information Systems 5 (2004), `http://aisel.aisnet.org/jais/vol5/iss1/1`
9. Loesing, K., Murdoch, S.J., Dingledine, R.: A Case Study on Measuring Statistical Data in the Tor Anonymity Network. In: Proceedings of the Workshop on Ethics in Computer Security Research, WECSR 2010 (2010), `http://www.cl.cam.ac.uk/~sjm217/papers/wecsr10measuring.pdf`
10. Loesing, K.: Measuring the Tor Network from Public Directory Information. In: 2nd Hot Topics in Privacy Enhancing Technologies, HotPETs (2009), `http://www.freehaven.net/~karsten/metrics/measuring-tor-public-dir-info-final.pdf`
11. Lyu, M.R., Lau, L.K.Y.: Firewall Security: Policies, Testing and Performance Evaluation. In: COMPSAC, pp. 116–121 (2000)

12. Mannan, M., van Oorschot, P.C.: Security and Usability: The Gap in Real-world Online Banking. In: Proceedings of the 2007 Workshop on New Security Paradigms, pp. 1–14 (2008)
13. Nah, F.F.: A study on Tolerable Waiting Time: How Long are Web Users Willing to Wait? Behaviour & Information Technology 23(3), 153–163 (2004)
14. Nielson, J.: Top Ten Mistakes. Revisited Three Years Later, Alertbox (May 1999), `http://www.useit.com/alertbox/990502.html`
15. Palme, J., Berglund, M.: Anonymity on the Internet (2002), `http://people.dsv.su.se/~jpalme/society/anonymity.pdf`
16. Privoxy, Privoxy Home Page (2010), `http://www.privoxy.org/`
17. Ramsay, J., Barbesi, A., Preece, J.: A Psychological Investigation of Long Retrieval Times on the World Wide Web. Interacting with Computers 10, 77–86 (1998)
18. Rose, G., Khoo, H., Straub, D.W.: Current Technological Impediments to Business-to-Consumer Electronic Commerce. Communications of the AIS 1(5), 1 (1999)
19. Ryan, G., Valverde, M.: Waiting Online: a Review and Research Agenda. Internet Research: Electronic Networking Applications and Policy 13, 195–205 (2003)
20. Selvidge, P.: How Long is Too Long to Wait for a Website to Load? Usability News 1, 2 (1999), `http://www.surl.org/usabilitynews/12/time_delay.asp`
21. Stockport, G.J., Kunnath, G., Sedick, R.: Boo.com – The Path to Failure. Journal of Interactive Marketing 15, 56–70 (2001)
22. Tor Project, Tor: Anonymity (2010a), `http://www.torproject.org/`
23. Tor Project, Tor Metrics Portal (2010b), `http://metrics.torproject.org/`
24. Vitone, D.: Anonymous Networks (2008), `http://blag.cerebralmind.net/wp-content/uploads/2008/05/tor.pdf`
25. Wright, T.: Security, Privacy, and Anonymity. Crossroads 11(2), 5 (2004)
26. Zia, T., Zomaya, A., Ababneh, N.: Evaluation of Overheads in Security Mechanisms in Wireless Sensor Networks. In: Proceedings of the 2007 International Conference on Sensor Technologies and Applications, pp. 181–185 (2007)

E-Commerce Readiness in Ethiopia: A Macro-Level Assessment

Elizabeth Ayalew[1], Lemma Lessa[1], and Mariye Yigzaw[2]

[1] Information Systems Track of the IT-PhD Program
Addis Ababa University
Addis Ababa, Ethiopia
{liza.ayalew,lemmalessa}@gmail.com
[2] Information Systems Track of the IT-PhD Program
Addis Ababa, Ethiopia
myfa1992@yahoo.com

Abstract. This study is a work in progress that intends to measure the readiness for e-commerce of an aggressively developing economy in East Africa – Ethiopia – a nation that has a significant historical and geo-political status at the horn and is competing in the global information economy. The paper initially embarks on explaining the distinction among the fundamental concepts of e-commerce, e-readiness and e-commerce readiness. It then reviews some of the major e-commerce readiness studies conducted and models developed both at the regional and international level. From among such models, the Asia-Pacific Economic Cooperation (APEC) self-assessment tool is selected as an appropriate instrument for adoption and development of a measure for e-commerce readiness in Ethiopia. Apart from identifying the nation's standing regarding its e-commerce readiness, customizing existing instruments and developing a new version, is believed to add value to the contemporary knowledge capital in the specific domain.

Keywords: E-commerce, E-readiness, Information Communication Technology, E-commerce readiness, global economy.

1 Introduction

With the advent of globalization, the implementation of Internet-based technologies has become common and a very important trend. ICTs play crucial role in achieving business targets as well as inspiring development to such an extent that most of the changes in our lives would have been impossible without them (Castells, 1999). Each and every country, depending on the penetration of ICT into its business and the different legal and policy environment factors affecting it, stands at its own unique position in the global world. Thus, it is essential to identify what position a nation has in the global digital economy and assess its readiness to adopt such innovations.

One such innovation is electronic commerce or e-commerce. It is a general concept covering any form of business transaction of information exchange executed using Information and Communication Technologies (Huosong et al., 2003). It includes electronic trading of goods and services, transaction among auctioneers who create

M.L. Nelson et al. (Eds.): Sustainable e-Business Management, LNBIP 58, pp. 76–86, 2010.

marketplaces for bidding and relates to a variety of business dealings conducted online. E-commerce systems generally can be classified by application types as electronic markets, electronic data interchange, and internet commerce (Meza, no year).

Ethiopia is one of the African countries at the horn that has a significant historical and geo-political status. Nevertheless, mainly due to its fast growing population and other natural calamities, its social and economic development indicators regrettably reveal that it is lagging behind the rest of the world. It is expected that the nation's available resources can be efficiently used for rapid development and economic growth using new technologies. So also, many leaders in governments, businesses and social organizations around the globe have considered how best to harness the power of ICT for development.

Thus this study sets out to assess what standing the country has in terms of its readiness to benefit from the provisions of e-commerce readiness in order to be able to compete in the global information economy. Knowing the readiness level will help the country to design strategies relevant to the implementation of e-commerce in order to be competitive in the fast changing global economic context.

2 Rationale of the Study

The benefits of the information technology revolution are still unevenly distributed between the developed and developing countries, and within societies themselves. While investment in ICT infrastructure in Africa has improved dramatically in recent years (Kabanda, 2008), there is a need to ensure that the huge potential of ICT and the promises of the information societies are geared towards poverty reduction and improving the quality of life for all. Particularly, in the contemporary information age, the continuing expansion of e-business and e-commerce provide opportunities for improved business processes.

Any government in power has the duty to make sure that the ICT revolution is not driven by technologies but by people's needs. Governments of developing economies need to rise up to the challenge of providing environments that can facilitate harnessing of ICT's potential for social and economic development as well as strengthening of good governance and citizens' participation. And to be able to do this, they need to make informed decisions as a result of research outcomes that IS specialists make. As the implementation of e-commerce requires certain input from the environment, knowing the current status of readiness at the macro-level would enable policy makers to facilitate such desirable conditions. The competitiveness of a country in the emerging global economy depends on its e-commerce development and it is a must for a nation to make the necessary preparations to successfully assimilate e-commerce, one such preparation being measuring e-commerce readiness (Bui, et al., 2003).

3 Objective of the Study

3.1 General Objective

The general objective of this research is to assess the level of e-commerce readiness in Ethiopia to identify gaps for its eventual implementation all over the country; and explore potentials of the existing key organizational capabilities for e-commerce system.

3.2 Specific Objectives

The specific objectives of this study are to:

- assess the national level readiness for e-commerce so that strategies can be set to improve positioning for the digital economy;
- explore the challenges and opportunities of e-commerce implementation in the country;
- set baseline data at the macro level for the adoption of e-commerce in Ethiopia;
- provide advice to the government on a set of actions for implementation of e-commerce to create the necessary changes that are relevant for the local business environment.

4 Literature Review

This section presents conceptual definitions of terms/phrases, and key terminologies used in the domain. It also reviews the various models available to measure e-commerce readiness and briefly discusses some of the relevant research works at national and international level.

4.1 E-Commerce, E-Readiness, and E-Commerce Readiness

E-commerce and e-readiness are phrases often discussed in association with e-commerce readiness. The following sub-section gives an explanation on the distinction among these basic concepts.

4.1.1 E-Commerce

Electronic commerce or e-commerce has been defined in several ways. Kalakota and Whinston (1997:7) broadly define e-commerce as "a modern business methodology that addresses the needs of organizations, merchants and consumers to cut costs while improving the quality of goods and services and increasing the speed of service delivery." They view e-commerce as a production process that converts digital inputs into value-added outputs through a set of intermediaries. The most comprehensive and widely used definition that has been found suitable for this study is the one provided by the Organization for Economic Cooperation and Development (OECD): e-commerce as "the electronic exchange of information that supports and governs commercial activities including organizational management, commercial management, commercial negotiations and contracts, legal and regulatory frameworks, financial settlement arrangements and taxation" (OECD 2001:21).

Some others have also defined e-commerce at its grass root level, describing it as an electronic method of doing business, typically over the Internet. It can be said that the definition of e-commerce is one that can be viewed from different angles (Kosiur, 1997). From a communications perspective, it is the delivery of information, products/services, or payments via telephone lines, computer networks, or any other electronic means. From a business process perspective, it is the function of technology toward the automation of business transactions and workflows. From a service perspective, e-commerce is a tool that addresses the desire of firms, consumers and management to cut service costs while improving the quality of goods and increasing the speed of service delivery. And from an online perspective, ecommerce provides the capability of buying and selling products and information on the Internet and other online services. World Bank (2009) uses a more specific definition of e-commerce by OECD as: "commercial transactions occurring over open networks, such as the Internet. Both business-to-business and business-to-consumer transactions are included." This paper uses this definition of e-commerce for simplicity and clarity.

There are some considerable advantages that the spread of electronic commerce introduces into market functions (Bui and Sankaran, 2003). Primarily providing producers with improved access to distant markets at the cost of reduced time taken to supply those markets is a major benefit. Producers and consumers can communicate directly, without the intervention of the traditional intermediaries such as importers, exporters, wholesalers and retailers. As a result of such a direct communication between producers and consumers, some of the frictions of the marketplace are reduced. This is a step further in economic activities to come closer to some of the ideals of perfect competition: low transaction costs and improved access to information for the consumer. However, e-commerce at the same time introduces with it new issues related to: speed, in terms of time to market, cross border jurisdiction, security and the creation of global markets. These themes are also related to concerns about nations' ability to regulate electronic commerce and governments' capability to maintain tax revenue, the growth of telecommunications infrastructure with sufficient speed to cope with the demands of e-commerce, protection of consumers' privacy, protection of intellectual property and the like.

4.1.2 E-Readiness

The information society has affected all aspects of social and economic life. Every economy, regardless of its level of development, has a readiness profile on the global stage, based on its national policies, level of technology integration, and regulatory practices. A framework study report on e-readiness by Bui and Sankaran (2003:6) gives six different definitions for e-readiness to show the various perspectives of the concept. The same study mainly expounds the concept as follows:

> "the aptitude of an economy to use Internet-based computers and information technologies to migrate traditional businesses into the new economy, an economy that is characterized by the ability to performbusiness transactions in real-time – any form, anywhere, anytime, and at any price."

This definition presupposes that important application of ICTs offer interconnectivity between governments, businesses and individual citizens. There are sets of fundamental political, social and legal provisions that any nation needs to incorporate into its system to successfully adopt technological innovations, and subsequently benefit from them to remain competitive in the global market. Thus, e-readiness covers a wider scope and can include readiness for all the electronic potentials (like e-education, e-government, e-commerce, e-health,…e-everything).

4.1.3 E-Commerce Readiness

The measure of the availability of necessary preconditions to adopt ecommerce can be referred to as e-commerce readiness. Oxley and Yeung (2001) and Molla and Licker (2005) discuss some fundamental technological, political, social and legal factors that allow or inhibit the development of e-commerce progress: the pace of technological change, acceptance by consumers and businesses, and the response of governments. Several studies in developing countries have also emphasized the influence of such contextual impediments as major determinants of e-commerce adoption. E-commerce readiness of a country is, therefore, an indicator of where that country stands in availing the requirements to successfully implement e-commerce. E-commerce readiness can be viewed as having a narrower scope than the generic e-readiness, focusing on measuring the requirements for conducting business transactions electronically through intranets and extranets or over the global internet. However, successful e-commerce can take place if and only if there are robust foundations of e-readiness (Choucri et al., 2003).

It is important that every country identifies, as much as possible, what is happening, as well as what is not, for the purposes of strategic planning for growth and development (ISCR, 2005). To this effect, various models of measurement for e-commerce readiness have been used by different nations and regions. One such frame that gives major measurable aspects of e-commerce is the one developed by the Asia Pacific Economic Cooperation (APEC) in 20021. According to this model, there are three main issues that can be assessed in relation to e-commerce:

- Readiness - in terms of potential usage and access and technology/socio-economic infrastructure;
- Intensity - in terms of transaction/business size and nature of transaction/business); and
- Impact - in terms of efficiency gains and employment/skill composition; work organization, new products/services, new business models, contribution to wealth creations and changes in product/value chains.

A similar study, by Esselaar and Miller (2001), focuses on three African countries - Rwanda, Namibia and South Africa. These countries have large and relatively impoverished citizens mainly located in rural areas, where the benefits of ICT have not been felt though there are major differences in the sizes of their overall economies. A comparative study of Tanzania and Ethiopia on ICT and e-commerce showed that Ethiopia appears to have more Internet entrepreneurs emerging although Tanzania had a better physical e-commerce infrastructure (Lake, 2000).

There are also studies related to ICTs in general and e-commerce in particular, in Ethiopia. A background study on ICT access in Ethiopia shows that the Internet service was introduced in 1996/97 with 1042 subscribers and has increased to 6487 in the first five years (Demeke and Birru 2002). Coverage of Internet services has expanded to 12 major towns but about 96% of the total subscribers are from the capital - Addis Ababa. It is also stated that the Internet bandwidth is very small i.e., the bandwidth from ISP to the Internet backbone is only 4Mb for uploading and 10Mb for downloading. The maximum bandwidth from user to ISP is 56Kb for dial-up access and 64Kb for leased lines. In line with this, the total number of local web-sites, out of which a significant number belong to private commercial firms, increased from 68 in

2000/01 to 88 in 2001/02 and it was projected to rise to 100 in 2002/03. Another baseline study has also been conducted in relation to e-commerce in Ethiopia, sponsored by Ethiopian ICT Development Agency - EICTDA (Demeke et al 2008). As the general objective of this comprehensive study was to propose a road-map for the development of e-commerce in Ethiopia, it did not particularly address the issue of readiness for e-commerce adoption.

The use of the internet for SMEs (Small and Medium-sized Enterprises) was also studied (Admassie and Taye 2007). It has been indicated that SMEs in Ethiopia have started showing interest in using Internet services amidst multitudes of challenges relating to products/ services not being suitable for sale via the Internet; customers not being ready to use Internet purchases; absence of provision for online payment system; lack of legal framework for electronic commerce; logistic problems with the delivery network; and the low-level ICT skills available. In general, the level of awareness and knowledge of the ICT technology, among SMEs, does not encourage them to anticipate the apparent possibility of utilizing e-trade as an alternative way of doing business globally. The above mentioned studies contend that, among the areas that challenge the development of e-trade/e-commerce in Ethiopia, the major ones are the inadequate telecom infrastructure available in the country, the constraining regulatory framework, lack of skilled human resource and key technologies.

The general assertion (Admassie and Taye, 2007, Demeke et al., 2008, Demeke and Birru, 2002, and Fekadu 2006) depicts that E-commerce is at its infant stage in Ethiopia and there are only few organizations that use ICTs in business transactions. These organizations use ICT for online advertisement, selling Ethiopian music, film and food mainly to the Ethiopian diaspora, and providing e-mall services including selling electronic products to local customers. The studies reiterate that lack of conducive environment for e-commerce activities in Ethiopia is characterized by the following major constraints:

a) Absence of e-banking system in Ethiopia which forces the companies that sell products and services outside the country to use the foreign account of a person they know living abroad;
b) Lack of appropriate legal framework for electronic commerce;
c) Monopoly of the telecommunication industry (the fact that the Ethiopian Telecommunication Corporation is the only provider) which results in lack of competitive ICT service provision;
d) Limited internet service the corporation provides which caters for an unreliable, continuously failing and expensive connection that hardly meets the demands of a shallow user base.

Although e-commerce in Ethiopia is at its early stage, the business environment is rapidly changing. Thus, from the foregoing review of literature, it can be observed that e-commerce readiness in Ethiopia is not yet measured despite the upcoming importance of doing so.

4.2 Models to Measure E-Commerce Readiness

Over the last few years, a number of e-readiness assessment methods and tools have been developed. Each tool gauges how ready a society or economy is to benefit from the information technology and electronic commerce. Among different readiness measurement models, some focus on measuring the general e-readiness (covering wider perspective than measuring ecommerce readiness). Some others do the same with narrower perspectives (limited to infrastructure and manpower readiness) while others take a wider perspective (with comprehensive ecommerce readiness indicators).

This section briefly describes the various measurement tools that are available and what they measure particularly, to foster informed decisions about approaches to e-readiness assessment, as national governments consider their information technology policies and undeletable development initiatives.

Kirkman et al (2002) used the Networked Readiness Index (NRI) which has two components and several micro-indexes measured through 65 variables. This model is upgraded and used by Dutta and Mia (2009) which ranked the NRI of 134 countries. Instead of the two components of NRI, Dutta and Mia used three components - Environment, Readiness, and Usage. Both of these models focus mainly on technological (infrastructural) requirements to adopt e-commerce; they do not include other enabling factors like the human, economic, and cultural elements.

The Brazilian e-commerce readiness and diffusion model is about the diffusion and impacts of e-commerce in Brazil (Tigre, 2004). It discusses a number of questions related to early predictions about the Internet and e-commerce development. This model mainly focuses on measuring the impacts of e-commerce. It focuses on identifying what stage Brazil has reached in adopting e-commerce which in fact results from fulfilling the necessary requirements for its adoption.

As per ISCR (2005), OECD countries developed 11 e-commerce indicators which generally fall under two categories: either relating to telecommunications infrastructure available in a country, or to skills and training of the population using the infrastructure (IBID). Thus, in relation to the objective that this paper tries to achieve, this model is not comprehensive enough to measure other e-commerce readiness factors than manpower and telecommunications (such as policy, economic, and cultural issues).

The Asia-Pacific Economic Cooperation (APEC) E-Readiness is a self-assessment tool for use by developing economies to assess their e-commerce readiness. Eight Broad indicators of e-readiness are developed into a series of questions that provide direction as to desirable policies that will promote e-commerce and remove barriers to electronic trade. Each of the 52 indicators was rated using a 5-scale effectiveness rating. Table 1 lists the eight major factors and their 52 indicators used by APEC for calculating e-readiness.

Thus, despite the availability of many existing models in the literature, some of which are very particular to the context they are developed in, the APEC model will be the most suitable to customize for this study considering its comprehensive nature. The comprehensiveness of the selected model will create an opportunity for assessing every element related to ecommerce. Besides, the APEC e-commerce Readiness Assessment Guide is chosen in this study due to the relative similarity in level of economic development between the APEC countries and Ethiopia.

Table 1. The 8 factors and their 52 measures for calculating e-readiness

Knowledgeable Citizen	Access to Skilled Workforce (Supply Skills)
Adult literacy Rate	Public Spending of Education as % of GDP
Secondary Enrollment	University Education Meets the Needs of Economy
Tertiary Enrollment	Well-educated People do not Emigrate Abroad
8th Grade Achievement in Science	Extent of Staff Training
MGMT Education Available in first-class Business Schools	Research Collaboration Companies/Universities Number of Technical Papers per Million People
Flexibility of People to Adapt to New Challenges	
Macro Economy	Digital Infrastructure
Trade as % of GDP	Telephone per 1000 people
Adequate regulations & Supervision of Financial Institutions	Internet Hosts per 10000 People International Telecom, Cost of Call to US
Protection of property Rights	Investment in Telecom as % of GDP
Tariff and Non-tariff Barriers	Computer Processing Power (worldwide MIPS)
Soundness of Banks	E-government
Local Competition	ICT Expenditure as % of GDP
Regulatory Framework	Freedom on the Internet
Government Effectiveness	
Political Stability	
Press Freedom	
Rule of Law	
Control of Corruption	
Industry Competitiveness	Culture
Technology Achievement Index	National Culture is Open to Foreign Influence
Gross Tertiary Science & Engineering Enrollment Ratio	English Language
Admin. Burden for Start-ups	
Patent Applications Granted by USPTO	Percentage of Urban Population
Private Sector Spending on R&D as % of GNI	Percentage of Population 65 Years or Older
High-tech Exports (% of Manufactured Exports)	
Ability, Willingness to Invest	Cost of Living and Pricing
Composite ICRG Risk Rating	International Cost of Living based on $100 US
Availability of Venture Capital	Inflation Rate-CPI in %
Entrepreneurship among Managers	GDP per Capita in US$
FDI as % of GDP	

5 Scope of the Study

E-commerce readiness can be done at different levels – macro, intermediate and micro; however, this study focuses on the e-readiness assessment at the macro level, given the presumed level of ICT penetration and use in the business sector in Ethiopia. Besides, the macro level, which deals with infrastructural and institutional support issues, including public awareness, would add value to the quality of the study.

6 Methodology

The study would employ a descriptive survey of e-commerce readiness at the macro level. Specifically, the study will be a facility-based cross-sectional survey which will make use of both quantitative and qualitative study methods. The study will be conducted at the capital city (Addis Ababa) since all of the federal bureaus of the various sector of the economy are located at the capital.

6.1 Variables/Indicators

As the APEC e-commerce Readiness Assessment guide is selected to be used in this study. The 52 variables to be measured are categorized under the 8 broad groups: Knowledge citizen; Macro-economy; Competitiveness; Ability and willingness to invest; Access to skilled workforce; Digital infrastructure; Cost of living and pricing; and Culture.

6.2 Target Data Sources

Relevant data to measure each of the variables listed above will be gathered from appropriate sources. The monopolistic nature of businesses in Ethiopia has lead to the concentration of data solely on specific government organizations. Thus, such organizations will be identified to collect data as there are no other organizations with relevant data to the study. Some of these organizations which are found to be the sole owners of information relevant to measure each of the variables are Ethiopian Telecommunication Corporation, National Bank of Ethiopia, Ministry of Education, selected Public and Private Higher Educational Institutions, Ethiopian ICT Development Agency, Ethiopian Chamber of Commerce, Ministry of Capacity Building, Ministry of Finance and Economic Development and Science and Technology Agency. The fact that data on a single variable can be obtained from two or more sources helps to cross check its verifiability.

6.3 Instrument

To get quantitative data, a 52-item questionnaire of APEC E-commerce readiness assessment tool will be adopted and distributed to about 50 appropriate officials. The findings from the questionnaire will be supported by data from relevant documents. Moreover, to complement the quantitative data gathered from the questionnaire, and to see the issues from the key decision-makers point of view, qualitative data will be generated through in-depth interview with key informants from the selected organizations.

6.4 Data Collection Procedures

To collect the quantitative data, the adapted questionnaire will be pre-tested for correctness and clarity. Frequent follow-up will be made to get the questionnaires returned. As to collecting the qualitative data is concerned, the interview guide will be checked for completeness and logical flow; the respondents will be briefed about the objective of the study and, as much as possible, the interview will be conducted based on the convenient time of respondents. When appropriate, related and useful documents will be assessed. The collected data will be referenced against measures in the models used for the study.

6.5 Data Entry and Analysis

The quantitative data from the questionnaire will be analyzed using descriptive statistics. Regarding data from the interview, first, the data will be organized by breaking down large bodies of text into smaller units, perhaps in the form of sentences, or individual words. Then, particular attention will be paid to the entire data set several times to get a sense of what it contains as a whole. In the process, few memos will be jotted down that suggest possible categories or interpretations. Following this, general categories or themes, and perhaps subcategories or sub-themes will be identified, and then classify each piece of data accordingly with the objective of getting a general sense of patterns – a sense of what the data mean. Finally, the data will be integrated and summarized for the readers.

7 Expected Benefits of the Study

The fact that there are different models, with some common variables, available for different countries shows that there is no one standard measure of e-commerce readiness. In fact, it would be ideal for countries to identify e-readiness factors that would best align with their strategies as there is no single magic formula of measuring it (Bui, et al., 2003). Thus, e-commerce readiness in Ethiopia can be measured by developing a new model as a result of customizing the existing models, or by preparing the one that seems most suitable for Ethiopian conditions. Hence, this baseline research is believed to gauge readiness and show directions of adoption of such innovations for a nation to be part of the global digital economy.

This Research can be used by government policy makers to identify gaps in technology concerning facilities and address the pressing need of facilitating online commerce. Practitioners, research institutions and academics working on e-commerce in particular and IS in general could also draw potentially valuable information and data from it in the effort they are continuously making to harness the use of ICT for economic advantage.

References

1. Admassie, A., Taye, W.: The Role of ICTs In Enhancing Trade and Economic Growth In Ethiopia, United Nations, Addis Ababa (2007)
2. Asia-Pacific Economic Cooperation - APEC, The APEC E-commerce Readiness Assessment Guide, APEC Readiness Initiative (2000)
3. Bui, T.X., Sebastian, I., Jones, W., Naklada, S.: E-commerce Readiness in East Asian APEC Economies. In: The Pacific Research Institute for Information Systems Management (PRIISM), Honolulu, Hawaii, USA (2002)
4. Bui, T.X., Sankaran, S., Sebastian, I.M.: A Framework for Measuring National E-readiness. International Journal of Electronic Business 1(1), 3–22 (2003)
5. Castells, M.: Information Technology, Globalization and Social Development, United Nations Research Institute for Social Development - UNRISD; Discussion Paper No. 114 (1999)
6. Choucri, N., Maugis, V., Madnick, S., Siegel, M.: Global E-readiness- for What? Paper 177, Report of the Group for Globalization of e-Business, Center for E-Business at MIT, Sloan School of Management (2003)
7. Demeke, M., et al.: Promoting Electronic Commerce for Development in Ethiopia: Issues, Challenges and Road Map; Ethipoian ICT Development Agency, Addis Ababa (2008)
8. Demeke, M., Biru, T.: ICT Penetration and Usage in Ethiopia. Baseline Study (2002)

9. Dutta, S., Mia, I.: The Global Information Technology Report 2008-2009: Mobility in a Networked World; World Economic Forum (2009)
10. Esselaar, P., Miller, M.: Towards Electronic Commerce in Africa: A Perspective from Three Country Studies. Southern African Journal of Information and Communication 2(1) (2001)
11. Fekadu, D.: Analysis of Determinants of Business Demand for Internet Access in Addis Ababa, MA Thesis (2006) (unpublished)
12. Huosong, X., Kuanqi, D., Shuqin, C.: Enterprise knowledge tree model and factors of KMS based on E-C. Journal of Knowledge Management 7(1), 96–106 (2003)
13. ITU, IT Success Stories: E-commerce. International Telecommunications Union (2007), http://www.itu.int/ITU-D/ict_stories/themes/e-commerce.html (accessed on June 15, 2009)
14. ISCR, Scoping Study: E-commerce Performance Measurement Research for New Zealand, Ministry of Economic Development, New Zealand (2005), http://www.med.govt.nz/templates/MultipageDocumentTOC9993.aspx (accessed on April 29, 2009)
15. ISCR, Scoping Study: E-commerce Performance Measurement Research for New Zealand: Appendix 2. The OECD Methodology, Ministry of Economic Development, New Zealand (2005), http://www.med.govt.nz/templates/MultipageDocumentPage10015.aspx (accessed on June 16, 2009)
16. Kabanda, G.: Collaborative Opportunities for ICTs Development in a Challenged African Environment. Journal of Technology Management & Innovation 3(3), 91–99 (2008)
17. Kalakota, R., Whinston, A.B.: In: Kirkman, G.S. (ed.) Electronic Commerce – A Manager's Guide, Addison-Wesley, Reading (1997)
18. Cornelius, P.K., Sachs, J.D., Schwab, K.: The Global Information Technology Report 2001-2002: Readiness for the Networked World. Oxford University Press for the World Economic Forum, Oxford (2002)
19. Kosiur, D.: Understanding Electronic Commerce, 1st edn. Microsoft Press, Redmond (1997)
20. Lake, S.: E-Commerce and LDCs: Challenges for Enterprises and Governments; UNCTAD Electronic Commerce Section, Nepal (2000)
21. Meza, M.: E – Commerce, http://www.geocities.com/englishforinternationaltrade/Lesson_5_e_commerce.pdf (accessed on May 31, 2009)
22. OECD Report: Measuring Electronic Measurement, ICCP, DCDE 185, OECD, Paris (2001)
23. Oxley, J., Yeung, B.: E-commerce Readiness: Institutional Environment and International Competitiveness. Journal of International Business Studies 32, 4 (2001)
24. Tigre, P.: Globalization of E-commerce. E-commerce Readiness and Diffusssion: The case of Brazil; Center for Research on Information Technology and Organizations, University of California (2004), http://www.crito.uci.edu (accessed on May 2, 2009)
25. United Nations Development Report. United Nations Conference Report on Trade and Development. UNCTAD. ICT Glossary Guide, World Bank, New York and Geneva, 26 (2001) (accessed on May 31, 2009)
26. http://web.worldbank.org/WBSITE/EXTERNAL/TOPICS/EXTINFORMATIONANDCOMMUNICATIONANDTECHNOLOGIES/0,,contentMDK:21035032~menuPK:2888320~pagePK:210058~piPK:210062~theSitePK:282823,00.html

Corporate Blogging Today – Usage and Characteristics

Franziska Brecht, Anastacia Cudreasova, and Jing Zhou

Humboldt-Universität zu Berlin
{Franziska.Brecht,Anastacia.Cudreasova,
Jing.Zhou}@wiwi.hu-berlin.de

Abstract. In the much-observed field of weblogs, corporate blogs are of particular relevance and interest. This study[1] empirically examines the corporate blog phenomenon by reviewing the blog status of 250 companies from the consumer goods industry. Their blogs – if any – were tested with the help of different variables, such as the location of the company, the blog's updating frequency or its interactivity. This allowed for testing certain hypotheses, in particular concerning the existence of corporate blogs in certain companies, industries and regions, or whether a blog's traffic rank depends upon these variables. This survey suggests that a blog's traffic rank is significantly influenced by the frequency of blog postings and its interactivity features. These factors seem to greatly depend upon the sales volume of a company. However, the data sample at hand suggests that there is not yet a widespread usage of corporate weblogs.

Keywords: Blog, weblog, corporate blog, communication tool, public relations, blogs and marketing, new media.

1 Introduction

Corporate blogging is a rather new phenomenon. Initially, weblogs or 'blogs' were written by individuals to document their lives' and to express opinions on various topics (Nardi, Schiano, Gumbrecht and Swartz, 2004). Since then the blogosphere has evolved. Companies discovered the new medium for internal communication, and also for communication with customers, which offers additional marketing channels. According to Fredrik (2004), a corporate blog is "a blog published by or with the support of an organization to reach that organization's goals." Blogs differ from conventional websites by i) their interactive elements such as votings, comments and questions (contact form), which allows customers to give feedback; ii) by being written in a conversational voice; and iii) by being created using instant publishing software, which does not require technical expertise (Weil, 2006). Moreover, blogs can achieve higher rankings in search engine results than static sites if frequently updated. This is due to the fact that they are heavily linked to one another and they contain individual posts that can each be indexed as separate files by search engines (Li, Stromberg, North and McHarg, 2007).

[1] This research was funded by the German Federal Ministry of Education and Research under grant number 01IA08001E as part of the Aletheia project (http://www.aletheia-projekt.de/). The responsibility for this publication lies with the authors.

M.L. Nelson et al. (Eds.): Sustainable e-Business Management, LNBIP 58, pp. 87–99, 2010.

Even though many companies do employ corporate blogs, the existing research focuses mainly on tools employed to create and maintain corporate blogs. This paper aims to understand the factors that play a role for the corporate blog adoption decision. To reach this goal, the paper utilizes an exploratory quantitative analysis. The underlying research questions are: Where are companies which blog located? From which industry sectors are they? How successful are companies that maintain blogs? How often do they update their blog? Is the update frequency related to the popularity of the blog? What kind of features do corporate blogs have? Do these features determine the popularity? For the purposes of the study we have examined all companies listed in “Global powers of the consumer products industry: The Top 250 (2009)”, which is published by Deloitte each year.

The remainder of the paper is structured as follows: Firstly, related work is outlined. Secondly, different criteria and variables are developed in order to classify corporate blogs. These are selected according to their applicability with regard to our data sample. Thereafter, the empirical findings are presented and subsequently serve as a basis to test the validity of certain hypotheses with regard to existence and traffic of corporate blogs. The study concludes with a summary of the findings, its limitations and relevance for future work.

2 Related Work

2.1 Classification of Corporate Blogs

Blogs are generally classified based on the accessability (Fredrik, 2004), on their content or on certain characteristics of the authors (Lee, Hwang and Lee, 2006).

The main distinction of blogs is whether they are internal and external. Employees can access internal blogs via the intranet. These blogs can improve communication and thus contribute to the identification and loyalty of the employees with their company. They can be grouped as knowledge blogs, collaboration blogs and culture blogs, depending on their content (Fredrik, 2004). External blogs can be accessed publicly and be subdivided into sales blogs, relationship blogs and branding blogs (ibid.). They can provide information about products and services, about the history or the culture of the company. The most predominant external corporate blog is the sales blog. It usually aims at (potential) customers to show them existing or upcoming products. Due to interactive features, customers' feedback can be integrated into such blogs, adding credibility. Customers generally trust customer reviews more than the product information given by producers or retailers (Komiak and Benbasat, 2004). Another aspect is the dissemination of selective information. A company's 'culture' and branding can serve as one example: Many companies have a long history, which can potentially increase customer's confidence in their products and conduct. This is underlined, for instance, by a well-known soft drink company that was established at the end of the 19th century, and that has its blog written by their own historian and archivist.[2]

Another possible classification of blogs depends upon certain characteristics of the authors, the purpose, and the content (Lee et al., 2006), e.g. employee blogs, group

[2] http://www.coca-colaconversations.com/

blogs, executive blogs, promotional blogs, or newsletter blogs. Authors of product blogs normally work in the marketing/PR or in the management department, in private SEO companies, as journalists or as employees.

The CEO blog can be named as another type of blog, the outstanding feature of which is that the author is the CEO of the company. Considering the role and responsibility of a CEO, Taylor (2005) mentions that CEOs should not spend time on blogging, but rather focus on responsibilities coming along with their leading position. However, Sessum (2005) argues that blogs written by CEOs have advantages such as an increased interest in the blogs, a personalized relationship of the reader to the company; also, it is thought to encourage employees to work on their careers.

2.2 Advantages

Most blogging companies believe the customer's insights gained with the help blogs is invaluable compared to the relatively low investments required: "You can set a blog up for $0. You can host one for $8-$30 a month and you can have them designed and optimized for a price-range from $500-$5000." (Durbin Media, 2006). Corporate blogs can help to construct and maintain a certain image of the company, as well as building long-term relationships with customers. Through the two-way communication it provides, customers can interactively personalize their relation with the company. The company can benefit from the feedback of the customers (Singh, Liza and Cullinane, 2008). Another important aspect is the 'empowerment' of the customers. By being organized in a blog-based community, customers can easily exchange information and if necessary pressure the company with the help of public opinion. They can build awareness and loyalty by engaging the customer to participate in the product development process (ibid.), e.g. by voting upon product features. Furthermore, corporate blogs can contain customer reviews and thus facilitate the buying decision process by providing additional information.

2.3 Disadvantages

Setting up a corporate blog can be facilitated by plug-and-play software. Specialized companies offer blog content and blog monitoring (Singh et al., 2008). However, customers will only visit corporate blogs regularly if they are "rewarded" with new, interesting content. This updating process can be a communication very time-consuming task, although this highly depends upon the update frequency. It requires researching relevant information, reading other blogs and updating the blog with new posts and uploads. Furthermore, comments and questions have to be answered.

A crucial issue with interactive tools is the loss of control. Any person can leave (possibly anonymously) negative comments or reveal confidential information. Depending on the company's policies and on the validity of the criticism, such entries are deleted or replied to.

Another important point why companies are reluctant to blog is the difficulty to measure the impact of blogs in terms of their influence upon concrete business goals. Therefore the additional risk and exposure linked with blogs can be difficult to justify. Possible solutions are to compare blog-reading customers vs. non-readers in customer satisfaction surveys, to monitor the volume of revenue originating from bloggers, and to measure the reduction of customer service inquiries. Likewise, companies can extend their ROI (return on investment) metrics by taking into account goodwill, loyalty, and brand equity (Li, 2004).

2.4 Delineation

There are other studies examining corporate blogs from different sectors and according to specific variables: Mattson and Barnes (2009) examined US-based companies across different sectors (Fortune 500 List 2008) in an attempt to quantify the adoption of corporate blogs by using descriptive statistics. Adding to this approach, Xifra and Huertas (2008) use a correlation analysis, but they limit their analysis to public relation blogs, and also include both personal blogs and corporate blogs.

Our study aims at giving a representative overview over corporate blogs specifically, focussing on blogs across different industry sectors and from different countries. Furthermore, this study combines the variables of previous studies in order to get an insight into the interrelations between the characteristics of corporate blogs, the success of the blog and certain characteristics of companies that blog.

3 Research Method

We focused our analysis on external blogs due to their public accessability. 250 companies from the worldwide consumer products industry (Deloitte, 2009) were analyzed according to different variables by using descriptive statistical data and variable correlation. This sample was chosen because the consumer industry comprises different industry sectors. Also, there is a presupposition that they are more likely to blog than e.g. companies producing mainly B2B products. Finally, this sample allows to analyze geographical aspects since those companies are located all over the world. The "Top 250" Deloitte list contains an adequate preselection of such companies. The data was collected at the end of 2009 through the Internet.

3.1 Selection and Definition of Variables

In the following, we will discuss possible variables regarding their suitability and availability for the analysis and their scales of measurement. The variables are divided into four dimensions according to the research questions: company characteristics, company success characteristics, blog characteristics and blog success characteristics. Figure 1 depicts possible relations between the four dimensions.

The most important variable is the blog existence. All companies that do not blog are separated from those who do in the first step:

i.) Blog existence. Dichotomous nominal variable, i.e. 1-"yes" and 0 – "no".

Company characteristics

ii.) Region. Ordinal scale, where 1 – 'North America', 2 – 'Asia/Pacific', 3 – 'Europe', 4 – 'Africa/Middle East', and 5 – 'Latin America'. This information is taken from the Deloitte report (2009).

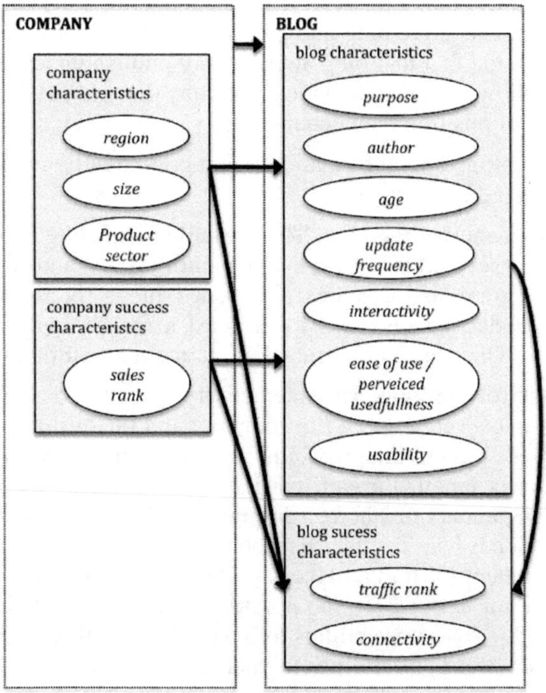

Fig. 1. Overview over dimensions and variables

iii.) Company size. This variable can be measured either according to the number of employees, or to the company turnover, or the balance sheet or market capitalization (Office for National Statistics, 2010; Little, 2010). For each industry segment, a different metric is significant, so there was no metric that was available for all blogging companies considered in this study. Hence, this variable is no longer considered hereafter.

Company success characteristics

iv.) Sales rank. This variable is linked to the company size by measuring the sales volume. It is measures by an ordinal scale and the information is provided in the classification of Deloitte (2009).

Blog characteristics

v.) Purpose of the blog. We attempted to classifiy the examined blogs according to Fredrik (2004) (i.e. sales blogs, relationship blogs or branding blogs), but many of them showed mixed characteristics. Therefore, the purpose was left out in our analysis. Xifra and Huertas (2008) employ the variable 'content', which would have left us with the same difficulties as with the variable ' purpose'.

vi.) Author of the blog. Lee et al. (2006) distinguish between employee blog, group blog, executive blog and promotional blog. This variable could not be used due to the fact that blog authors only publish under pseudonyms, which does not allow to conclude which company department they are working for, what kind of position they occupy, etc.

vii.) Age of the blog. This information is not consistently available and therefore not considered.

viii.) Update frequency of the blog. This variable is measured ordinally: 1 – 'every day', 2 – 'every week', 3 – 'every month', 4 – 'more than a month'. The fourth category also contains abandoned blogs, because these companies have not updated their posts for at least a month, and some of them even over years. This variable is crucial to maintain a faithful audience.

ix.) Interactivity of the blog. The interactivity of a blog describes the possibility of communication between the company and the customer. Interactivity can be achieved through the possibility to comment on postings, through a contact form via email, through participation in votings, downloading or uploading documents or photos, through enabling customers to send postings to their friends via Twitter, Facebook or email, or through subscribing to specific content (Xifra and Huertas, 2008). The variable 'interactivity' is divided into four groups: 0 –"no possibility to interact", 1 – "one possibility to interact", 2 – "two possibilities to interact", 3 – "three possibilities to interact" and 4 – "four possibilities to interact".

x.) Technology Acceptance Model (TAM) and usability. TAM variables (Davis 1989) such as perceived usefulness[3] (PU) and perceived ease-of-use[4] (PEOU) can only be measured by the evaluation of blog readers and are therefore not comprized by the scope of this study. However, some variables influence TAM variables: the update frequency problably influences the PU, and the interactivity of the blog probably influences the PEOU. The same reasoning applies to usability, which is is a necessary requisite to develop efficient interactivity (Hallahan, 2001) and is therefore partially measured by that variable.

Blog success characteristics

xi.) Traffic rank. This variable measures the popularity of a website. It was measured with an ordinal scale using a tool called Alexa traffic rank[5]. The rank is calculated by combining the average number of daily visitors and page views over the past 3 months.

xii.) Connectivity. Blogs are usually linked to other blogs and websites with related content. Those links lead to higher rankings in search engine results. This information cannot be measured accurately and is therefore not considered hereafter.

---

[3] This was defined by Davis as 'the degree to which a person believes that using a particular system would enhance his or her job performance'.

[4] This was defined by Davis as 'the degree to which a person believes that using a particular system would be free from effort'.

[5] http://www.alexa.com/

In summary, the following variables are included in the analysis: i) blog existence, ii) region, iv) sales rank viii) update frequency, ix) interactivity of blogs and xi) traffic rank.

4 Empirical Findings

4.1 Analysis of Variables

Existence of external corporate blogs regarding region and product sector

Of the 'Top 250' companies from the consumer products industry listed by Deloitte, 31 do external corporate blogging (i.e. 12%). The mayority of 88%, i.e. 219 companies do not have external blogs. This can be called surprising, as the consumer products industry expectedly should have the highest rate of corporate blogs.

Table 1. Blog existence with respect to the product sector

		Blog existence		Total
		yes	no	
Product sector	Electronic Products	22	11	33
	Fashion Goods	13	4	17
	Food, Drink & Tobacco	126	6	132
	Home Furnishings & Equipment	14	0	14
	Home Improvement Products	12	1	13
	Leisure Goods	3	4	7
	Personal & Household Products	20	5	25
	Tires	9	0	9
	Total	**219**	**31**	**250**

Out of the 31 companies that maintain a blog, 11 (36%) were from the electronic products industry, so it can be considered as the sector with the greatest presence in the blogosphere. Concerning the percentage within one sector, the leisure goods sector has the highest percentage of companies with a corporate blog (4 blogs, representing 57%). In the product sectors "home furnishing and equipment" and "tires", the companies examined have no corporate blogs at all (table 1).

The 250 companies surveyed are located in five regions (table 2). None of the relevant companies from Latin America and Africa/Middle East have any corporate blogs, however, this region is underrepresented and therefore this finding is not cogent. The highest number of corporate blogs was found in North America – 15 companies (17%). Asia/Pacific and Europe have very similar results - Asia/Pacific 9 companies (12%), Europe – 7 companies (10%).

Table 2. Blog existence with respect to the location of the company

		Blog existence		Total
		yes	no	
Region	North America	75	15	90
	Asia/Pacific	67	9	76
	Europe	64	7	71
	Africa/Middle East	5	0	5
	Latin America	8	0	8
	Total	**219**	**31**	**250**

Update frequency and interactivity of corporate blogs

As for update frequency, corporate blogs in this study showed various patterns. The blogs with the highest update frequency posted more than one entry a day, while the least frequently updated blog had last entry recorded in the year 2006. 32% (10 blogs) of the surveyed blogs had not been updated for more than a month. As irt can be assumed that these blogs that have been abandoned, this seems to be quite an outstanding finding (figure 2).

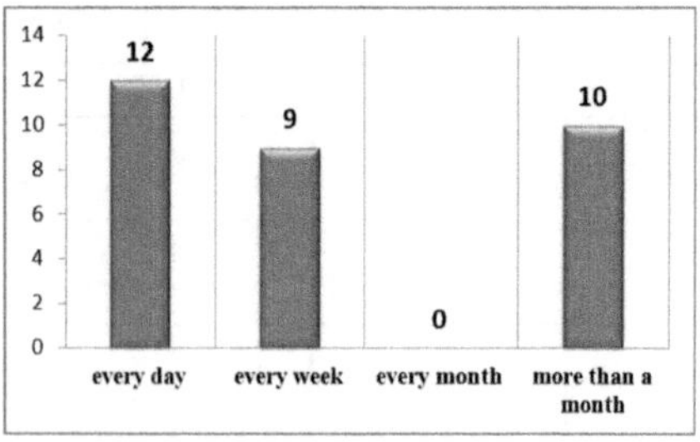

Fig. 2. Update frequency

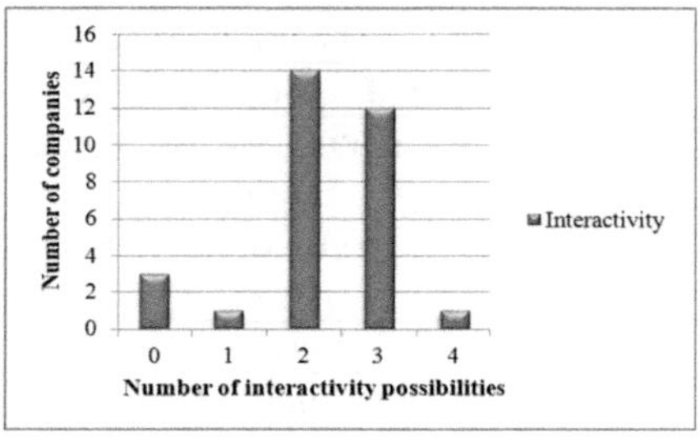

Fig. 3. Blog interactivity

Interactivity of the existing corporate blogs has a homogenous structure; most companies (84%) have two or three possibilities to interact (figure 3).

Sales rank apparently influences the adoption of blogging by our sample companies. As far as companies with a sales rank up to place 50 are concerned, 35% (11 companies) have a corporate blog. Of the group listed 51st-100th, 26% (8 companies) have a corporate blog. Among the group listed 101st-150th, 23% (7 companies) have a corporate blog. In contrast, the bottom 100 (those listed 151st-250th) account for 16% (5 companies) of the corporate blogs (figure 4).

4.2 Correlation Analysis

The data was analyzed using SPSS[6]. First, a Kolmogorov-Smirnov test showed that the data is not normally distributed. Therefore, we based our analysis on non-parametric correlation analysis tests such as Spearman's rho, Chi-square (χ^2) and

[6] Statistical Package for the Social Science.

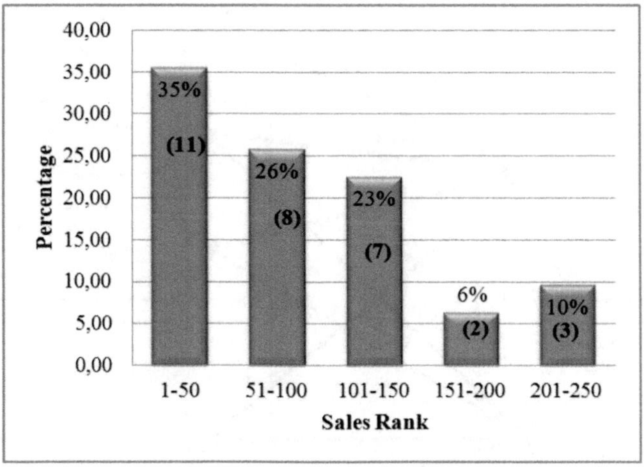

Fig. 4. Blog existence with respect to sales rank

Cramer V. Spearman's rho was used as a correlation coefficient between two ordinal variables. The crosstabs were used to get the chi-square and Cramer V test of association for the nominal and ordinal data (as suggested by Garson, 2004). A cross tabulation displays the joint distribution of two or more variables simultaneously, they can be used for any kind of measurement: nominal, ordinal, interval, or ratio. Cross tabs treat all data as if they were nominal. χ^2 tests the statistical significance of the cross tabulations. The Cramer V coefficient gives the strength of association of the cross tabulations (ibid.). It is a variant of the Phi coefficient that adjusts for the number of rows and columns. Values range from 0 (no association) to 1 (the theoretical maximum possible association).

The main four research questions that were solved through testing hypothesis theory using SPSS software were: i) Does the location of the company have an influence on blog existence and blog properties?; ii) Does a blog update frequency have influence on the blog's traffic rank?; iii) Does the blog's interactivity influence the blog's traffic rank?; and iv) Does the sales rank of the company influence blog existence and the blog properties?

Figure 5 depicts the variables and the hypotheses that are discussed subsequently.

H1. The location of the company has an influence on the blog existence and the blog properties.

This hypothesis stems from an article by Kolari, Finin, Lyons, Yesha, Yesha, Perelgut and Hawkins (2007) and claims an influence of geographical distribution on corporate blogging. However, it was unclear whether such influence was due to the common language that has bridged geographical distances. The following sub-hypotheses are conceivable:

H1.1. The location of the company has an influence on the blog existence.

H1.2. The location of the company has influence on the blog update frequency.

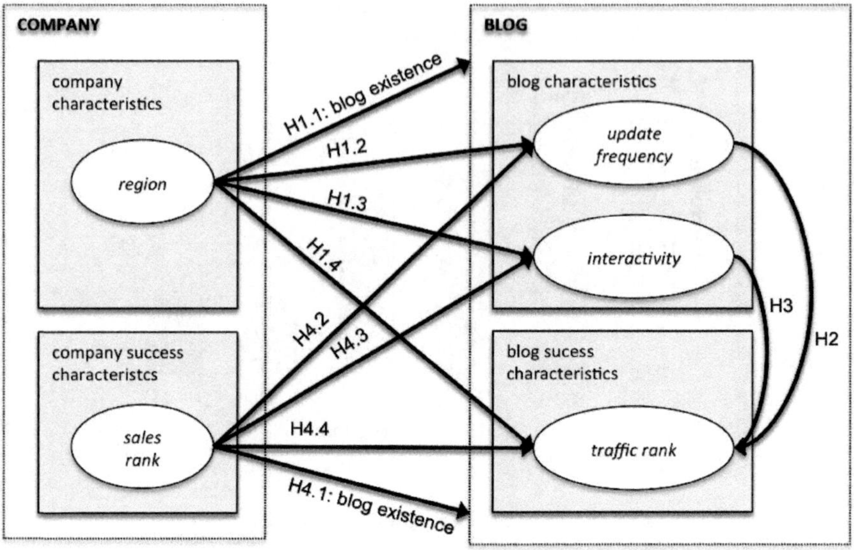

Fig. 5. Overview over the variables and the hypotheses

Table 3. Blog existence and region of the company

Symmetric measures: Blog existence				
Nominal by nominal	*Location of the company*		*Value*	*Appr.Sig.*
		Phi	*0,123*	*0,435*
		Cramer-V	*0,123*	*0,435*
Total			*31*	

Table 4. Blog update frequency and region of the company

Symmetric measures: Blog update frequency				
Nominal by nominal	*Location of the company*		*Value*	*Appr.Sig.*
		Phi	*0,410*	*0,266*
		Cramer-V	*0,290*	*0,266*
Total			*31*	

Table 5. Blog interactivity and region of the company

Symmetric measures: Blog interactivity				
Nominal by nominal	*Location of the company*		*Value*	*Appr.Sig.*
		Phi	*0,455*	*0,600*
		Cramer-V	*0,322*	*0,600*
Total			*31*	

Table 6. Blog traffic rank and region of the company

Symmetric measures: Blog traffic rank				
Nominal by nominal	*Location of the company*		*Value*	*Appr.Sig.*
		Phi	*1,414*	*0,335*
		Cramer-V	*1,000*	*0,335*
Total			*31*	

H1.3. The location of the company has an influence on the blog's interactivity.

H1.4. The location of the company has an influence on the blog's traffic rank.

With the available data it was possible to test these hypotheses, because the study took into account the location of the companies, and not the region's language. All four hypotheses could be rejected (see table 3-5 representing the crosstabs for the χ^2 and Cramer V test) i.e. the location of the company has no significant influence on the blog existence, nor on the update frequeny, nor on the blog's interactivity, nor on the blog's traffic rank in our sample.

H2: The blog update frequency influences the blog's traffic rank.

H3: The blog's interactivity influences the blog's traffic rank.

H2 is based on Du and Wagner (2006), who argue that blog success largely depends upon the value the blog provides to its readers. However, their study captures both static (popularity rank) and dynamic characteristics (popularity growth) of weblog success over a period of time. To test this hypothesis only the weblog popularity rank was used. H2 could not be rejected (table 7). The correlation between these two variables is very strong (0,6). This result indicates that increasing the blog update frequency increases the traffic rank of the blog.

To test H3, we used the blog's traffic rank, which is referred to as 'weblog popularity rank' by Du and Wagner (2006). This hypothesis was rejected (table 8). The correlation between the blog's interactivity and the blog's traffic rank is negative (–0,4), which can be explained by the ascending order of the blog's traffic rank.

Table 7. Blog traffic rank and update frequency

Correlations: Blog traffic rank			
Spearman-Rho	*Blog update frequency*	*Correlation coefficient*	*0,597*
		Sig. (2-tailed)	*0,000*
Total		*31*	

Table 8. Blog traffic rank and blog interactivity

Correlations: Blog traffic rank			
Spearman-Rho	*Blog interactivity*	*Correlation coefficient*	*-0,392*
		Sig. (2-tailed)	*0,029*
Total		*31*	

H4: The sales rank of the company has an influence on blog existence and the blog properties.

By using the example of blogs from the Fortune 500 companies, Mattson and Barnes (2009) show that the rank influences the adoption of blogs. However, the sample used in their study comprises only US-based companies, whereas our blog sample contains companies from all over the world. Furthermore, we want to examine these relations by the following hypothesis in greater detail:

H4.1. The sales rank of the company has an influence on the blog existence.

H4.2. The sales rank of the company has an influence on the blog update frequency.

H4.3. The sales rank of the company has an influence on the blog's interactivity.

H4.4. The sales rank of the company has influence on the blog's traffic rank.

H4.1 and H4.4 were rejected (see tables 9 and 12). However, we could state a strong correlation between the sales rank and the blog update frequency (H4.2) and the blog's traffic rank (H4.3) (see tables 10 and 11). The correlation coefficient for H.4.2 is negative (-0,468), which can again be explained by the ascending order of the sales' rank.

5 Conclusion

The analysis of the blogging status of 250 companies from all over the world that produce consumer goods showed that only very few run corporate blogs. Half of the companies from our sample that maintain blogs are located in the USA. Moreover, one third of the companies which have blogs produce electronic products. This may be explained by the fact that customers that buy electronic products are more open to technology in general, and to the Internet in particular.

Table 9. Blog existence and sales rank

Symmetric measures: Blog existence				
Nominal by nominal	*Sales rank*		*Value*	*Appr.Sig.*
		Phi	*1,000*	*0,470*
		Cramer-V	*1,000*	*0,470*
Total		*250*		

Table 10. Blog update frequency and sales rank

Correlations: Blog update frequency			
Spearman-Rho	*Sales rank*	*Correlation coefficient*	*0,401*
		Sig. (2-tailed)	*0,025*
Total		*31*	

Table 11. Blog interactivity and sales rank conclusion

Correlations:Blog interactivity			
Spearman-Rho	*Sales rank*	*Correlation coefficient*	*-0,468*
		Sig. (2-tailed)	*0,008*
Total		*31*	

Table 12. Blog traffic rank and sales rank

Correlations: Blog traffic rank			
Spearman-Rho	*Sales rank*	*Correlation coefficient*	*0,238*
		Sig. (2-tailed)	*0,197*
Total		*31*	

This paper suggests that the update frequency influences the number of visitors of the blog. All hypotheses concerning the location of a company could be rejected, i.e. according to our findings it has no significant influence on the blog existence, update frequency, interactivity, nor on traffic rank. However, a significantly high influence was detected between the blog's traffic rank and the blog update frequency, respectively its interactivity. By increasing the blog's interactivity and update frequency, one should be able to increase satisfaction of the target group and thus considerably increase the traffic rank of the blog. The last group of hypotheses which connect the sales rank of a company with the blog's existence, respectively its update frequency, interactivity and traffic rank, revealed that only the influence of the sales rank on the blog's update frequency and on the blog's interactivity is stastically significant. This means that the higher the sales volume, the higher is the frequency of updates in a company blog, and the more likely it is that one would find a diversity of interactive features in the respective blogs.

6 Limitations and Future Research

The results presented above could be biased by the small sample size. Although our initial data basis comprised 250 companies, this was soon reduced by the fact that out of these only 31 did maintain corporate blogs. Many of the variables that could have been relevant had to be neglected because of a lack of data. Therefore, future studies should examine the corporate blog status of a broader number of companies, possibly chosen from more specific regions or industries.

Regardless of the limitation mentioned before, our study supports certain hypotheses and set a trend that others must be rejected. These results can and should be tested in subsequent studies which use similar statistical tests and methods.

Acknowledgements

We thank Oliver Guenther, Matthias Kuehn and Christoph Goebel for their ideas and support.

References

1. Davis, F.D.: Perceived usefulness, perceived ease of use, and user acceptance of information technology. MIS Quarterly 13(3), 319–340 (1989)
2. Du, H.S., Wagner, C.: Weblog success: Exploring the role or technology. International Journal of Human-Computer Studies 64, 789–798 (2006)
3. White Paper: Corporate Primer On Business Blogging, Durbin Media Group (2010), http://durbinmedia.com
4. 2010 Enterprise size, Office for National Statistics, http://www.ons.gov.uk/about-statistics/user-guidance/lm-guide/concepts/employers/enterprise/index.html (accessed January 01, 2010)
5. Fredrik, W.: Your Guide to Corporate Blogging (2010), http://www.corporateblogging.info/ (accessed January 15, 2010)
6. Garson, G.D.: Nominal Association: Phi, Contingency Coefficient, Tschuprow's T, Cramer's V, Lambda, Uncertainty Coefficient (2008), http://faculty.chass.ncsu.edu/garson/PA765/assocnominal.htm (accessed January 02, 2010)
7. Hallahan, K.: Improving public relations web sites through usability research. Public Relations Review 27, 223–239 (2001)
8. Lee, S., Hwang, T., and Lee, H.H. (2006) Corporate blogging strategies of the *Fortune* 500 companies, Management Decision, 316-334.
9. Li, C., Stromberg, C., North, J., McHarg, T.: The ROI Blogging, Forrester Research (2007), http://www.forrester.com/rb/Research/roi_of_blogging/q/id/41064/t/2 (accessed January 05, 2010)
10. Little, K.: Size Matters in Investing (2010), http://stocks.about.com/od/tradingbasics/a/Sizemat013105.htm (accessed January 15, 2010)
11. Mattson, E., Barnes, N.G.: Corporate Blogging: Fortune 500 indicates trends in blog usage and adoption (2009), http://www.masternewmedia.org/corporate-blogging-fortune-500-indicates-trends-in-blog-usage-and-adoption/ (accessed January 02, 2010)
12. Nardi, B.A., Schiano, D.J., Gumbrecht, M., Swartz, L.: Why We Blog. Communications of the ACM 47(12), 41–46 (2004)
13. Kolari, P., Finin, T., Lyons, K., Yesha, Y., Yesha, Y., Perelgut, S., Hawkins, J.: On the Structure, Properties and Utility of Internal Corporate Blogs. In: ICWSM 2007, Boulder, Colorado, USA (2007)
14. Komiak, S.X., Benbasat, I.: Understanding Customer Trust in Agent-Mediated Electronic Commerce, Web-Mediated Electronic Commerce, and Traditional Commerce. Information Technology and Management 5, 181–207 (2004)
15. Sessum, J. D.: Adding Your Voice to the Conversation: Why CEOs Should Blog (2005), http://www.globalprblogweek.com/2005/09/19/sessum-why-ceos-should-blog/2005 (accessed January 05, 2010)
16. Singh, T., Liza, V.J., Cullinane, C.: Blogging: A new play in your marketing game plan. Business Horizons 51, 281–292 (2008)
17. Taylor, D.: Why CEOs Shouldn't Blog (2005), http://www.globalprblogweek.com/2005/09/19/taylor-why-ceos-should-not-blog/ (accessed January 05, 2010)
18. Weil, D.: The Corporate Blogging Book. Penguin Group (2006)
19. Xifra, J., Huertas, A.: Blogging PR: An exploratory analysis of public realtions weblogs. Public Relations Review 34, 269–275 (2008)

Agent-Based Simulation for Evaluation of a Mobile Emergency Management System

Heiko Roßnagel[1], Jan Zibuschka[1], and Olaf Junker[2]

[1] Fraunhofer IAO
{heiko.rossnagel,jan.zibuschka}@iao.fraunhofer.de
[2] Airport Research Center
olaf.junker@arc-aachen.de

Abstract. Large public events such as sporting events, concerts, fairs and street festivals are quite common in metropolitan areas. Because of the high frequency of such events and the increasing number of involved parties, the stakeholders responsible for the organization and execution have to cope with increasing complexity and shortening time frames for planning and preparation. Especially in public transportation, unplanned incidents that occur during these events can have devastating effects because of the high concentration of passengers. Emergency management systems that utilize mobile communication infrastructures can provide prompt information delivery to save human lives. In this contribution we propose a system design for mobile emergency management. We also present an evaluating approach for this system design using a multi-agent based simulation, based on empirical data for a particular large event as well as for normal rush hour traffic. We also consider characteristics of the mobile communication infrastructure.

Keywords: Public events, Agent-based simulation, Mobile Services, Emergency Management.

1 Introduction

Large public events such as sporting events, concerts, fairs and street festivals are quite common in metropolitan areas. During these events, the mass of visitors alone can put quite a strain on public transport. Because of the high frequency of such events and the increasing number of involved parties, those being responsible for the organization and execution have to cope with increasing complexity and shortening time frames for planning and preparation. This can lead to several transport and security challenges.

Because of the high concentration of passengers, unplanned incidents that occur during these public events can have devastating effects and may lead to crises and disasters. Furthermore, large events are an attractive target for terrorists, because of the high number of potential victims, and high level of media exposure. In order to mitigate disaster effects and to accelerate the healing process, it is essential to undertake steps to increase the level of disaster preparedness, including infrastructure investments for warning systems and training activities (Johnston et al. 2007).

M.L. Nelson et al. (Eds.): Sustainable e-Business Management, LNBIP 58, pp. 100–114, 2010.

Emergency management systems (EMS) provide the capability to address this dilemma and to enable disaster forces to manage disasters, including detection and analysis of incidents (Carver and Turoff 2007). Persons in charge should be supported to prepare evacuations, control and support disaster forces and to locate victims (Carver and Turoff 2007). Since mobile communication infrastructures offer standardized wireless communication services in almost all countries (GSMworld 2010) and allow a fast diffusion of information, they provide a promising technological basis for saving human lives in emergencies. If a disaster event occurs, they enable emergency managers to distribute warnings to the effected areas by cell broadcast to ensure timely warnings of potential victims (Fritsch and Scherner 2005).

In the German research project VeRSiert (Projekt VeRSiert 2008) such an infrastructure has been proposed for coordinating major events in Cologne (a German city). Following the classical design science approach, the utility, quality, and efficacy of a design artifact must be rigorously demonstrated via well executed evaluation methods (Hevner et al. 2004). In this research in progress paper we will present our approach to evaluate the proposed artifact.

This paper is structured as follows. We first present the methodological framework of our work in section 2. In section 3, we present requirements for emergency management systems from the literature and briefly discuss how current systems rate against these requirements. A system design based on (Scherner et al. 2009), that addresses these requirements, is presented in section 4 and in section 5 we outline our approach to evaluate this artifact. Section 6 gives an outlook on the next steps of our research, before we conclude our findings.

2 Methodology

We address the introduced problem with a conceptual system design providing a technological basis for emergency management. This system design represents an IT artifact instantiation that aims at contributing to the problem's solution, i.e. at (1) minimizing the impact of the emergencies and at (2) offering novel services to customers. As system architectures, system designs or prototypical software applications, IT artifact instantiations demonstrate the feasibility of an approach developed. Due to its utility-centric focus, design science research contributions present novel IT artifacts and suitable evaluation approaches that address the artifact's appropriateness to contribute to the problems' solution (Nunamaker et al. 1991). These two facets of rigorous design science-oriented research contribute to the foundations and the methodologies pool of Information Systems research, i.e. they contribute to its knowledge base (Hevner et al. 2004). In the following, we present a design of an emergency management system, which utilizes communication facilities of mobile communication networks. Our system design provides facilities for integrating EMS functionalities and commercial value-adding services on the basis of a common platform. Evaluation is provided by an agent based simulation of passenger egress from Cologne central train station that is based on empirical real life data of passenger movements. Simulation for the evaluation of designed artifacts is discussed in some detail in (Kriz and Hense 2006) (Hevner et al. 2004). We follow the classic approach of design science-oriented research (March and Smith 1995) as we first present a developed IT artifact and we second evaluate the artifact's benefits for potential users. Therefore, and e.g. in contrast to behavioral science oriented research, the goal of this contribution is utility, namely the benefits our system design can provide (Simon 1969).

3 Related Work

(Scherner et al. 2009) derived the following high-level requirements from the literature that need to be addressed by an emergency management system. They comprise (1) system effectiveness (Johnston et al. 2007), (2) reliability (Zeckhauser 1996), (3) cost efficiency (Zeckhauser 1996), (4) smooth service integration (Ritchie 2004), (5) multilateral user interaction (Turoff et al. 2004a), (6) availability (Faulkner 2001) and (7) security (Valtonen et al. 2004).

They also argued that one of the most crucial requirements for preparedness is that ordinary people are used to the system in order to react on warning signals without any delay (Gruntfest and Huber 1989). Meeting this requirement is extremely difficult if the system is solely used for warnings. The success of emergency management systems clearly depends on well-trained users being familiar with the service functionalities provided (Turoff et al. 2004b). For an infrequently used emergency management system, limited practical experience of users can be expected (Manoj and Hubenko Baker 2007). However, on a technological level, many services used for emergency management systems do not differ from services used in day by day use cases. For example, the upload of a picture could be used to inform emergency managers, but also for online community services. The challenge is that both functionalities have to be integrated in a coherent design, which allows both perspectives and supports the user to become familiar with the functionalities (Scherner et al. 2009).

Existing emergency management systems like the GDACS (European Communities 2008) and the SMS-alert initiative in the Netherlands (which is based on the Short Message Service (SMS)) concentrate on disseminating already existing information to a broad audience in case of emergencies, rather than providing multilateral interactions with decision makers. A backchannel for providing reliable information, provided by people in the affected area, could significantly improve the quality of decisions that have to be made by authorities (Sutton et al. 2008). Due to applying point-to-point technologies for notifying potential victims, both initiatives require that the recipient has registered in advance which violates the requirement of effectiveness and reliability.

The simulation component used in this work is similar to (Pan et al. 2007) (Pidd et al. 1996) (Pelechano et al. 2007) (Pan et al. 2006) extended by parameters representing notification via mobile phone (see the Evaluation Approach section for more details), such as agents changing their plan based on a received notification, agents passing received notifications along to neighboring agents, and limitations of the underlying mobile infrastructure. The simulation component itself has already been evaluated using automatic monitoring of actual pedestrian movements (Junker et al. 2010).

4 A Mobile Emergency Management System

4.1 Proposed System Design

The proposed system design is an extension of (Scherner et al. 2009). To adapt the system design to the event management domain, we have defined roles of the public sector and the event management industry. Figure 1 illustrates how the different parties interact within our system design and which services are provided.

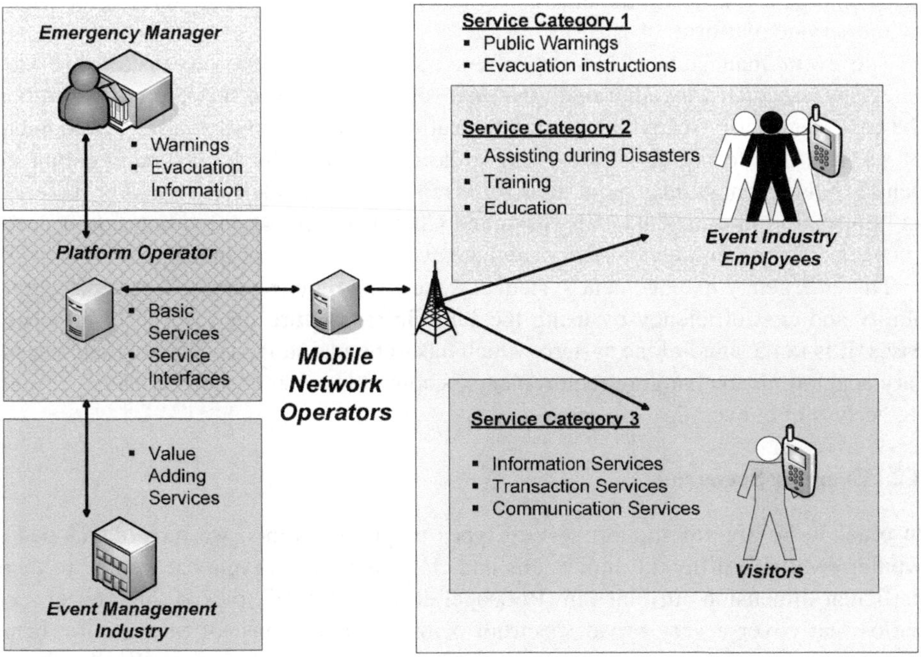

Fig. 1. Proposed System Design

The central component in our design is the service platform, which is maintained by the platform operator. The platform communicates with mobile network operators and provides basic services for service providers from the event management industry and the emergency manager via standardized service interfaces. A full list of the implemented basic services is given in the Artifact Implementation section.

The platform operator can be a public or private entity. Its main task is to operate the information system infrastructure and to provide basic services via service interfaces to the involved parties. Several different entities could take on this role. The platform could for example be operated by the city council. The event experience could be improved by new value adding services offered using this platform and by establishing a powerful EMS, signaling preparedness to potential visitors. Also, companies with a strong commitment to the destinations community, such as public transport providers, could take on the role of platform providers. The role of platform operator could also be fulfilled by commercial service providers, who charge for the basic services that are offered over the service platform.

The emergency manager provides all emergency management related services to the public and ensures efficient notifications, which is henceforth classified as service category 1. Furthermore, this role makes services available to the event management sector and its employees (service category 2) in order to help them to prepare for emergencies and to offer guidance in emergency situations. For the implementation of these emergency services, the emergency manager utilizes the basic services provided by the service platform.

The event management industry offers commercial services to visitors (service category 3), which we elaborate in the next subsection. These services are built upon the basic services provided by the service platform, which allows a rapid development of services due to the already existing building blocks. The service aggregation on behalf of the event management industry is realized by the platform operator who acts as information intermediary (Bhargava and Choudhary 2004), providing n to m links between different entities of visitors and the event management industry.

The emergency management system can meet the requirements effectiveness, reliability and cost efficiency by using the same infrastructure for several different use cases. It is not a stand-alone system, which has to be maintained separately and necessary adaptations to changing requirements become more likely. Stakeholders get used to the system in everyday use cases.

4.2 Example Scenarios

In order to be able to support several types of public events, we have developed a typology with 16 different dimensions and classified public events according to their particular dimension attributes in (Roßnagel et al. 2008). We picked three event scenarios that cover a very broad spectrum of those dimensions for presentation here. Those events are a soccer match, the "Kölner Lichter" and German Kirchentag, a religious grassroots meeting.

Soccer Match Scenario

Soccer matches are events that occur on a weekly basis. They are sporting events that take place in a stadium. They have a rather mild effect on public transport, because they occur very often and authorities and public transport providers have a lot of experience handling the traffic consequences. The event lasts for a couple of hours and attracts less than 100.000 visitors. Most of these visitors are from the local area and some of them may be violent hooligans.

"Kölner Lichter" Scenario

"Kölner Lichter" is an annual event that takes place at the Rhine River in Cologne. Several music bands perform on stage and the music is broadcasted along the riverside. There is no fee for attending the event and it takes place in an open environment. The event ends at midnight with spectacular fireworks that last about half an hour.

Usually this event attracts between 500.000 and 1,000,000 visitors. Due to the short timeframe of the main event the peak of visitors associated with it, this event has a huge effect on public transport. However, since this is an annual event, authorities and transport providers can prepare themselves based on prior experiences.

Kirchentag Scenario

Kirchentag ("church day") is a grassroots religious event that takes place annually but changes venues every year. So from the perspective of the city that hosts the Kirchentag, it is a one-time event. It attracts over a million visitors, including a lot of foreigners. Event organizers have a lot of experience, but local authorities and transport providers are usually confronted with this event for the first time. The Kirchentag itself takes place in a non-restricted environment and comprises several sub-events that take place at different locations (e.g. stages) all over the city.

Identified Value-adding Services

Based on interviews with stakeholders involved in those scenarios, we identified key services for implementation. The ability to spontaneously communicate with other visitors, using chat or twitter services, is an attractive mobile service in the context of large scale events. Also, the ability to document the event using pictures and videos and to publish them on the internet is of interest to users. Another promising service category are services that support group management, because a lot of the visitors travel to events in groups, and members might be spread out over the event area and might lose sight of each other. In addition, location-based services such as routing to points of interests, e.g. sights, pharmacies or bars with after event specials, could provide added value. A broader discussion of suitable services for those scenarios can be found in (Roßnagel et al. 2008).

4.3 Artifact Implementation

The service platform provides a centralized access point to the mobile communication infrastructure, which can be utilized for emergency management and commercial mobile value-adding service as described in the previous section. It offers modular basic services that were identified based on the value-adding event management and emergency services. These basic services include:

- chat platform
- micro-blogging platform
- localization of users
- multicast and broadcast messages
- mobile ticketing
- mobile payment

As the same underlying technologies can be used for both value-added and emergency management services economies of scale significantly reduce the associated costs. In addition, by offering a service platform implementing those building blocks, a quick development of value-adding mobile services can be achieved.

We have implemented a system prototype, based on customized Open Source components for the server side, and using Google's Android[1] platform for implementation of the client application.

On the server side, we use StatusNet's Laconica micro-blogging service[2] (providing support for persistent, asynchronous, bidirectional communication between stakeholders). To also offer a synchronous, non-persistent communication channel allowing for group communications, we use the OpenFire[3] server implementing the eXtensible Messaging and Presence Protocol (XMPP). Both forms of communication are useful in both disaster response and commercial settings.

On the client, components like routing, chat client, micro-blogging connector and friend finder have been implemented using the Android API, in part based on additional online services like Google Maps[4] and components of the mobile phone, e.g. the Global Positioning System (GPS). Further basic services can be implemented as modular components. A rebranding of the client application was integrated, to allow for additional distribution channels, and enabling the system to reap the benefits associated with strong brand names in the context of new product deployment (Tauber 1981).

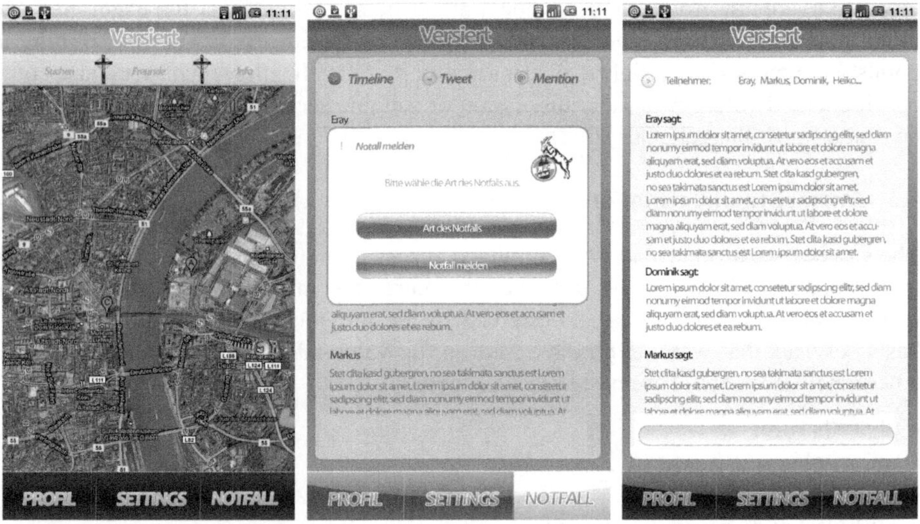

Fig. 2. Prototype screenshots

[1] http://www.android.com/
[2] http://status.net/
[3] http://www.igniterealtime.org/projects/openfire/
[4] http://maps.google.com/

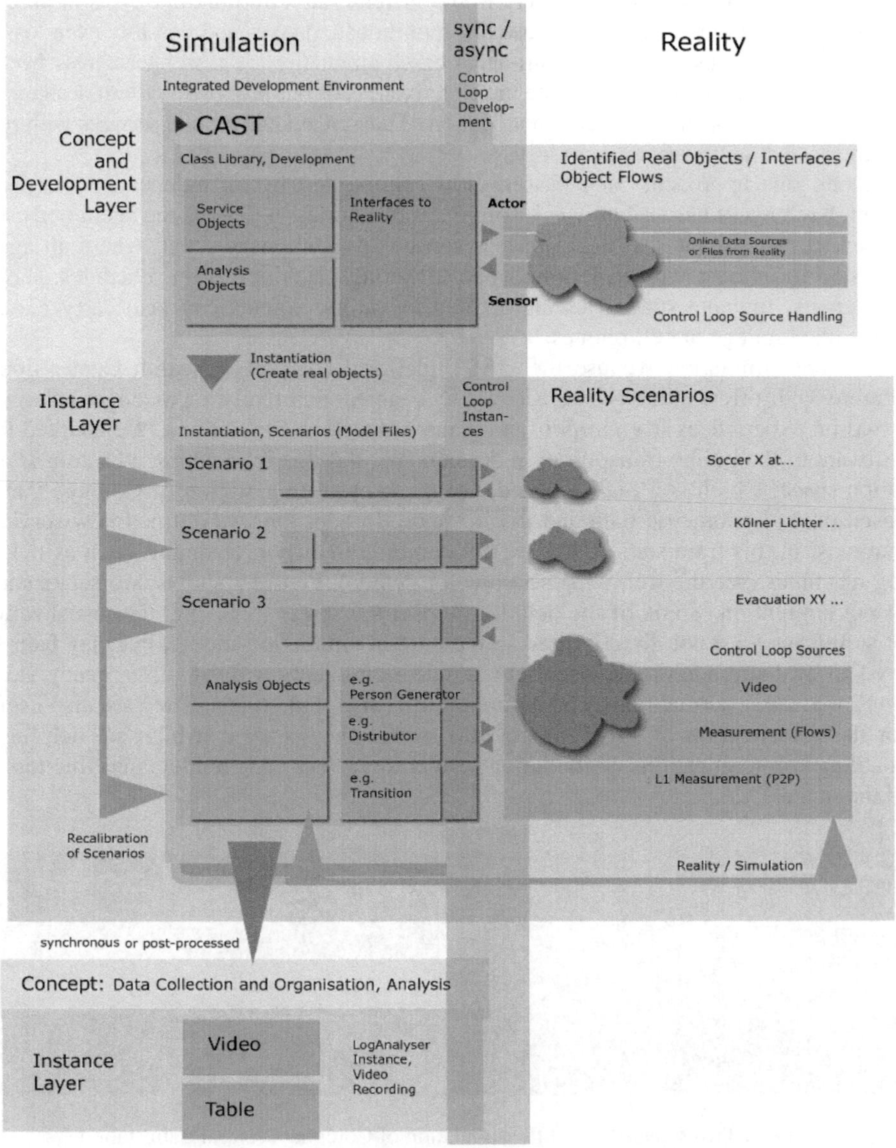

Fig. 3. CAST Platform and Integration with Scenarios

5 Evaluation of System Effectiveness Using Simulation of Passenger Egress

5.1 Evaluation Approach

Obviously, the set-up of a real scenario including real cell phone users, general infrastructure including actor communication, regional distinctions and peer group specialties as well as real emergencies and disasters would increase the effort and the costs of an efficient evaluation immensely, and cause disproportionate danger and possibly even loss of life. Because of this, we use a multi-agent based simulation of passenger egress from a simulation space in order to evaluate the effectiveness of our proposed system design. We compare results for runs including notification of passengers via mobile services with runs where no such notification takes place.

Using this approach, each passenger is represented by an independent software agent. Each agent has a plan which comprises of a series of actions the agent performs or services the agent is using. Services can be any stationary point, where an agent can stop to interact with it. Examples are ticketing machines, train schedules, shops, restaurants, luggage spaces, escalators and elevators. Agents can also carry certain items like luggage or cell phones.

For our simulation we use the CAST platform (Airport Research Center 2009) (Figure 3). It offers a three-dimensional environment and realistic passenger behavior, based on experiences from airport and plane evacuation simulations. We adapted this software to the public transportation domain. We did this by creating a custom simulation space, which is a realistic model of the central train station of Cologne that is based on real geometric data and true to scale. In addition, we defined new services that exist in this train station and are not common in airport terminals such as ticketing machines (see the following sections for details). Figure 4 shows two screenshots of our simulation. Some of the details given in the screenshots, e.g. the visualization of storefronts, are not directly used in the current simulation model, but may later be used to evaluate additional visual communication channels during emergency situations, e.g. using virtual reality as described in (Tang et al. 2009). They are also useful for the visualization of simulation results within the scenario, which are helpful in enabling communication of simulation results to various stakeholders and fine tuning of the model.

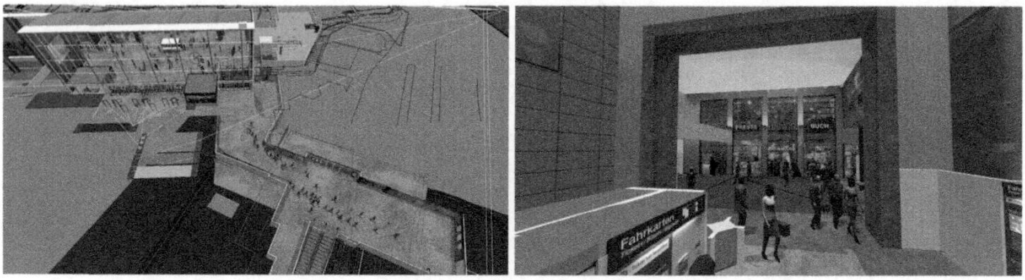

Fig. 4. Two screenshots of the simulation of Cologne's central train station

5.2 Empirical Basis for Simulation

The quality of simulation results depends on the level of detail of the simulation model sufficiently reflecting reality. Information about the topology of the simulation space, location and quantity of passengers, individual agent behavior as well as the capacity of mobile communication cells have to be taken into account in order to get realistic results. Furthermore, statistic information about the distribution of passenger properties such as gender, cell phone usage and state of mind (drunk, aggressive, fearful, uncomfortable, communicative, oblivious) can be important parameters. Once that data has been collected, a variation of parameters inside the model in addition to a high number of simulation runs is used to understand the dependencies between agent properties, their behavior and applied disaster warning strategies.

To achieve a high quality of our simulation runs we gathered the necessary data in the context of the scenarios described above. We based our simulation model on real geometric data of Cologne's central train station. We identified and photographed all service points, exits and platform access, and included representations in our simulation. We also counted the number of passengers entering and leaving the station at all exits during a defined time frame of two hours using 10 minute intervals of measurement. We performed this passenger count for a particular large event ("Kölner Lichter 2009") as well as for normal rush hour traffic. In order to acquire information about the particular plans of passengers, we used the method of single person pursuit. The researchers picked random passengers to follow and to record their activities during their stay in the central train station. Based on these activity reports, the plans of the simulation agents were developed. The simulation of passenger movements was evaluated by comparing it to data acquired via real-time video analysis at the station (Junker et al. 2010).

We also obtained information about location, capacity and range of the mobile communication cells in the central station from the network providers, and interviewed experts to determine holistic assessments of the most relevant factors to limit the complexity of the model, i. e. we do not want to simulate the propagation of radio waves to determine the spectral efficiency that can be expected for the base stations. Our interviews showed that simplifying assumptions can be made without impacting the overall quality of the simulation results.

5.3 Calibration of Simulation Model to Scenario

Several adjustments were made to the simulation of the underlying mobile infrastructure and agent behavior. In order to enable a certain mobile phone provider to send evacuation messages to a dedicated cell, the component Mobile Cell has been developed. On request, this simulation object sends messages to agents if they are located in the range of the cell. The agent can adjust its current path and planned route dependent on the message that has been sent.

To quantify the effectiveness of our artifact we identified several potential key performance indicators (KPI) (measurable performance indicators that can be obtained during a simulation run in a predefined scenario). For the initial runs, we chose as single KPI the time that was used for evacuating the train station after a bomb alert. To prove the reproducibility and to ensure reliable results, multiple simulation runs of the same scenario were performed.

In order to test the efficiency of a dedicated broadcast message to the persons inside a room, a simulation model with bidirectional person flow from exit A to exit B was created (Figure 5). The functional components flow generator, distributor, and property interpreter are used to configure the passenger flow.

The green area which covers the whole room represents the mobile cell which will send a dedicated evacuation recommendation during the simulation run to all persons inside the influence area of the cell. Depending on the message received, agents' plans will be changed.

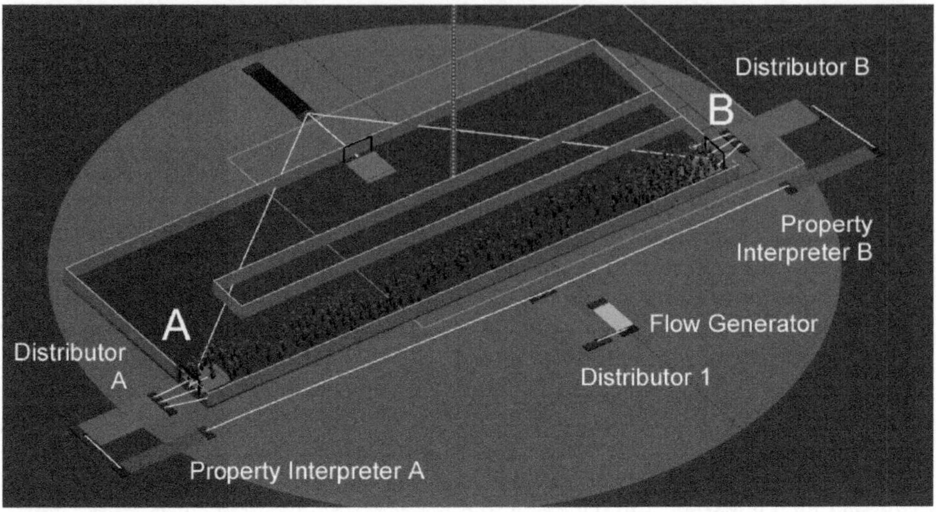

Fig. 5. Model of bidirectional passenger flow using CAST platform

5.4 Initial Simulation Results

Two different scenarios have been built to prove that a dedicated evacuation message leads to a faster evacuation.

Case 1 – without additional exit (Figure 6): The first model setup shows what happens if the passengers are not aware of the additional exit in the rear area of the building – the persons decide for the closest exit A or B, thus generating congestion at both exits. This is in line with the topological structure of Cologne station, which has a hard to find back exit that is widely ignored by passengers.

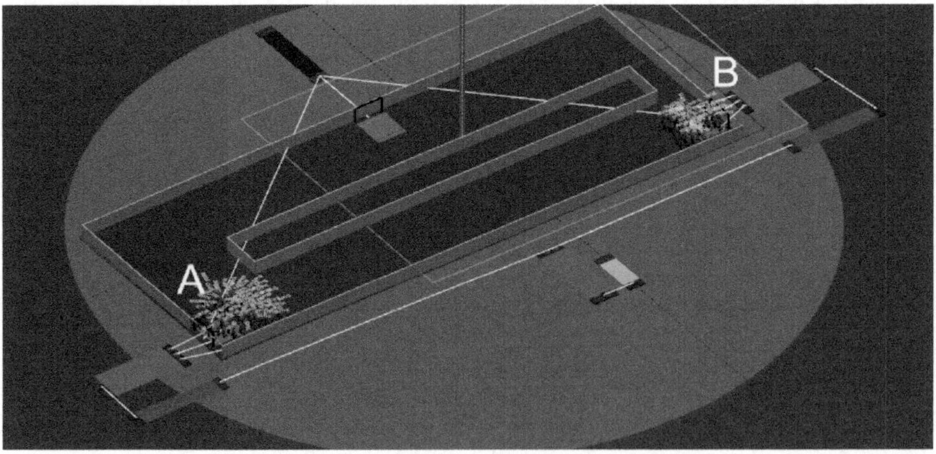

Fig. 6. Case 1 - Without additional exit

Case 2 – using an additional exit (Figure 7): In the second case, egress is faster – this is because an additional exit will be used by the passengers once they have been informed about it by a text message. Holistically speaking, passengers are much more evenly distributed across available space and emergency exits due to the mobile notification.

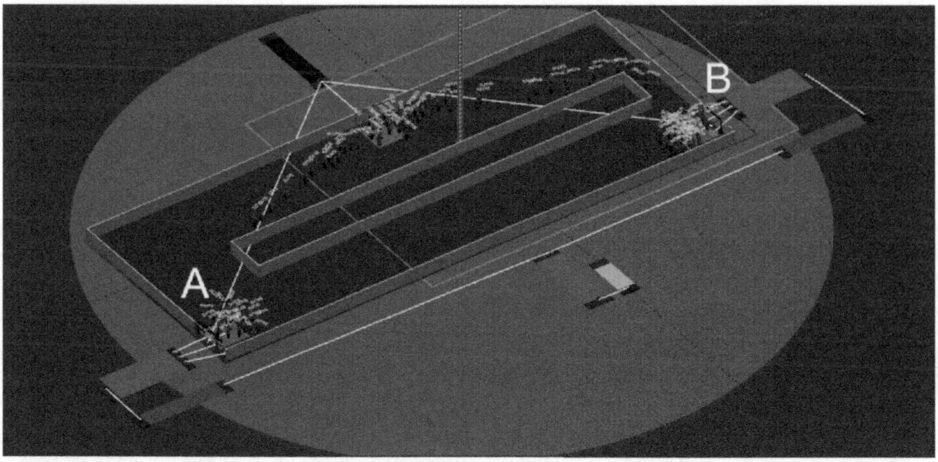

Fig. 7. Case 2 - Using additional exit

The reaction of the passengers as well as the functionality of the mobile components can easily be configured and evaluated in CAST once the appropriate components have been developed. However, even the initial results show a clear advantage enabled by mobile alerting measures in the given scenario (Figure 8).

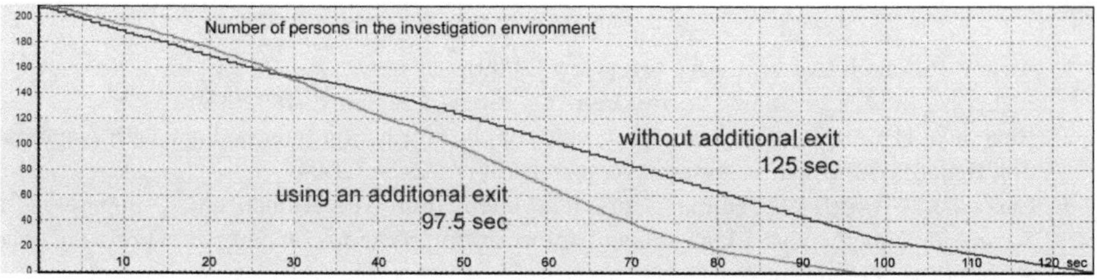

Fig. 8. Effectiveness of evacuation in simulated scenarios

6 Next Steps

In order to bridge the gap between reality and the simulation model iteratively, we plan to use both videos illustrating simulation results based on our model of passenger movements and the prototype demonstrator based on the underlying design artifact to enable stakeholder feedback. By continuous refinement of the existing object models and the calibration of simulation parameters against the real behavior of the agents, the model will converge to reflect a representation of the mobile emergency management scenario that is shared by all stakeholders. Additionally, the functionality of the artifact can also be fine tuned in additional iterative cycles as mandated by our approach (Hevner et al. 2004).

The demonstrated model represents a very simple case. In future models, more detailed mobile cell and phone configuration shall be used. For instance, it will be interesting to see how the passenger agent behavior and the overall evacuation time and model behavior changes dependent on different parameter settings. Such parameters could be message delays, reduced signal reception, dedicated communication between mobile phone providers etc. Further KPIs, e.g. avoided injuries due to congestion situations, can also be considered.

7 Conclusion

During large public events, the mass of visitors alone can put quite a strain on the public transport system. Unplanned incidents that occur during these events can have devastating effects and can lead to crises and disasters. Emergency management systems based on mobile communications could be used to mitigate the effects of such incidents. We adapted the system design proposed by (Scherner et al. 2009) for a mobile emergency system for tourist destinations to the event management domain. In order to evaluate the effectiveness of this system design we performed a multi-agent based simulation. This approach promises to be quick, powerful, flexible and cost-efficient. Also, it allows the creation of scenarios which can not be created in reality, because this would require the endangerment of passengers on a large scale. In order to achieve a realistic representation of the passenger movements we gathered a large amount of empirical data.

References

1. Airport Research Center, CAST Overview (2009), `http://www.airport-consultants.com` (accessed 13-09-2009)
2. Bhargava, H.K., Choudhary, V.: Economics of an Information Intermediary with Aggregation Benefits. Information Systems Research 15(1), 22–36 (2004)
3. Carver, L., Turoff, M.: Human Computer Interaction: The Human and Computer as a Team in Emergency Management Information Systems. Communications of the ACM 50(3), 33–38 (2007)
4. European Communities, Global Disaster Alert and Coordination System (GDACS) Homepage (2008), `http://www.gdacs.org/` (21-11-2008)
5. Faulkner, B.: Towards a Framework for Tourism Disaster Management. Tourism Management 22, 135–147 (2001)
6. Fritsch, L., Scherner, T.: A Multilaterally Secure, Privacy-Friendly Location-based Service for Disaster Management and Civil Protection. In: Proceedings of the AICED/ICN 2005, pp. 1130–1137. Springer, Heidelberg (2005)
7. Gruntfest, E., Huber, C.: Status report on flood warning systems in the United States. Environmental Management 13(3), 279–286 (1989)

8. GSMworld, GSM Operators, Coverage Maps and Roaming Information (2010), `http://www.gsmworld.com/roaming/gsminfo/index.shtml` (accessed 07-02-2010)
9. Hevner, A.R., March, S.T., Park, J., Ram, S.: Design Science in Information Systems Research. MIS Quaterly 28(1), 75–105 (2004)
10. Johnston, D., Becker, J., Gregg, C., Houghton, B., Paton, D., Leonard, G., Garside, R.: Developing warning and disaster response capacity in the tourism sector in coastal Washington. Disaster Prevention and Management 16(2), 210–216 (2007)
11. Junker, O., Strauss, V., Majer, R., Link, N.: Real-time video analysis of pedestrians to support agent simulation of people behavior. In: Fifth International Conference on Pedestrian and Evacuation Dynamics (PED 2010), Gaithersburg, MD, USA, March 8-10 (2010)
12. Kriz, W.C., Hense, J.U.: Theory-oriented evaluation for the design of and research in gaming and simulation. Simulation & Gaming 37(2), 268–283 (2006)
13. Manoj, B.S., Hubenko Baker, A.: Communication Challenges in Emergency Response. Communications of the ACM 50(3), 51–53 (2007)
14. March, S.T., Smith, G.F.: Design and Natural Science Research on Information Technology. Decision Support Systems 15(4), 251–266 (1995)
15. Nunamaker, F.J., Chen, M., Purdin, T.D.M.: Systems development in information systems research. Journal of Management Information Systems 7(3), 89–106 (1991)
16. Pan, X., Han, C.S., Dauber, K., Law, K.H.: Human and social behavior in computational modeling and analysis of egress. Automation in Construction, 448–461 (2006)
17. Pan, X., Han, C.S., Dauber, K., Law, K.H.: A multi-agent based framework for the simulation of human and social behaviors during emergency evacuations. AI & Society 22(2), 113–132 (2007)
18. Pelechano, N., Allbeck, J.M., Badler, N.I.: Controlling individual agents in high-density crowd simulation. In: Proceedings of the 2007 ACM SIGGRAPH/Eurographics symposium on Computer animation, San Diego, CA, USA, pp. 99–108 (2007)
19. Pidd, M., de Silva, F.N., Eglese, R.W.: A simulation model for emergency evacuation. European Journal of Operational Research 90(3), 413–419 (1996)
20. Project VeRSiert, Versiert Homepage (2008), `http://www.versiert.info/` (accessed 01-03-2010)
21. Ritchie, B.W.: Chaos, Crises and Disasters: A Strategic Approach to Crisis Management in the Tourism Industry. Tourism Management 25, 669–683 (2004)
22. Roßnagel, H., Engelbach, W., Frings, S., Weisbecker, A.: Mobile Dienste zur Erhöhung der Sicherheit bei Großveranstaltungen. In: Spath, D., Höß, O., Weisbecker, A. (eds.) Stuttgarter Softwaretechnik Forum 2008: Science meets Business, pp. 91–102. Fraunhofer IRB Verlag, Stuttgart (2008) (28-11-2008)
23. Scherner, T., Muntermann, J., Roßnagel, H.: Integrating Value Added Services into an Emergency Management System for Tourist Destinations. In: Proceedings of the European Conference on Information Systems (ECIS 2009), Verona (2009)
24. Simon, H.A.: The Sciences of the Artificial. The MIT Press, Cambridge (1969)
25. Sutton, J., Palen, L., Shklovski, I.: Backchannels on the Front Lines: Emergent Uses of Social Media in the 2007 Southern California Wildfires. In: Fiedrich, F., Van de Walle, B. (eds.) Proceedings of the 5th International ISCRAM Conference, Washington D.C, USA (May 2008)
26. Tang, C., Wu, W., Lin, C.: Using virtual reality to determine how emergency signs facilitate way-finding. Applied Ergonomics 40(4), 722–730 (2009)
27. Tauber, E.M.: Brand franchise extension: New product benefits from existing Brand Names. Business Horizons 24(2), 36–41 (1981)

28. Turoff, M., Chumer, M., Hiltz, R., Klashner, R., Alles, M., Vasarhelyi, M., Kogan, A.: Assuring Homeland Security: Continuous Monitoring, Control & Assurance of Emergency Preparedness. Journal of Information Technology Theory and Application (JITTA) 6(3), 1–24 (2004b)
29. Turoff, M., Chumer, M., Van de Walle, B., Yao, X.: The Design of a Dynamic Emergency Response Management Information Systems (DERMIS). Journal of Information Technology Theory and Application (JITTA) 5(4), 1–36 (2004a)
30. Valtonen, E., Addams-Moring, R., Virtanen, T., Jrvinen, A., Moring, M.: Emergency Announcements to Mobile User Devices in Geographically Defined Areas. In: Proceedings of Information Systems for Crisis Response and Management (ISCRAM), Brussels, Belgium, May 3-4, pp. 151–156 (2004)
31. Zeckhauser, R.: The Economics of Catastrophes. Journal of Risk and Uncertainty 12, 113–140 (1996)

Using Ontologies in an E-Commerce Environment: Help or Hype?

Franziska Brecht and Kerstin Schäfer

Humboldt-Universität zu Berlin
{Franziska.Brecht,Schaefke}@wiwi.hu-berlin.de

Abstract. Even though online shopping is becoming increasingly popular, many consumers are still reluctant to buy online, especially when it comes to apparel. One approach to improve adaption is to base e-commerce search engines on ontologies to allow a more intuitive search process. This paper[1] presents the results of an analysis how a sample of online shoppers perceived various ontology-based features in an online shop. The data was gathered in two focus groups with panelists coming from different socio-demographic backgrounds (middle-aged women, students in their twenties). Most of the middle-aged women panelists actively shopped for apparel by means of catalogues. However, across the focus groups, most panelists are very reluctant buying apparel online. Our study suggests that age has a higher influence on the information search behaviour of consumers in online shops than gender. The study concludes with suggestions for adapting ontology-based systems to these findings.

Keywords: consumer decision process, e-commerce, ontology-based search, ontology engineering, low-fidelity prototyping.

1 Introduction

Even with more than 10 years of experience in e-commerce, online shops are still not able to address all consumer needs, especially during the information search online. Shopping online entails many advantages for the consumer, e.g. cost and time savings. Disadvantages originate, among other factors, from the replacement of the sales assistant who could give recommendations by an information system (IS) (Bakos, 1997). In online shopping, products cannot be tested, touched, lifted or tried on, and important product information for taking a buying decision may be missing. Further problems originate from the consumer's interaction with the online shop, such as unclear query formulation or a lack of relevance of search results. Finally, organizational disadvantages such as the availability of products, possible delays in shipping and additional costs (shipping and handling) can reduce customer satisfaction.

However, online shops try to confront these challenges. One approach aims at bridging the offline-online gap by employing interactive consumer decision aids. For

[1] This research was funded by the German Federal Ministry of Education and Research under grant number 01IA08001E as part of the Aletheia project (http://www.aletheia-projekt.de/). The responsibility for this publication lies with the authors.

M.L. Nelson et al. (Eds.): Sustainable e-Business Management, LNBIP 58, pp. 115–126, 2010.

example, Amazon is known for its successful implementation of item and user-based collaborative filtering recommender systems, addressing consumers' needs for recommendation and sales conversation (Konstan, Miller, Maltz, Herlocker, Gordon and Riedl, 1997; Sawar, Karypis, Konstan and Reidl, 2001; Wang, de Vries and Reinders, 2006).

Another possible approach is to employ ontologies in e-commerce search engines. An ontology is an explicit representation of a domain of discource (a conceptualization) usually composed of a set of concepts and relationships (Gruber, 1993). The conception of ontologies is not new, there is a myriad of technical studies discussing interoperability, mapping and matching of ontologies. However, beyond academia they are rarely employed: only few authors analysed technology acceptance (Davis, 1989) of ontologies from a user perspective, in particular regarding the employment of ontologies in the context of e-commerce (Fensel, McGuiness, Schulten, Ng, Lim and Yan, 2001).

This study i) provides an inventory of current problems in online shopping; ii) analyses the technology acceptance of certain ontology-based features employed in an online shop; and iii) deduces requirements for engineering ontology-based systems based on the results of i) and ii). Parts i) and ii) are an explorative analysis based on focus groups. The analysis in part ii) was based on low-fidelity prototype testing.

The paper is structured as follows: After describing the theoretical background, ontology-based features are presented that serve as a basis for the low-fidelity prototype being used in the focus groups. Subsequently, the research methods and the results are depicted. Finally, implications and conclusions are presented.

2 Related Work

Our study touches upon several research areas: consumer research, human-computer-interaction, information retrieval, and technology acceptance.

In online decision processes, the extent of a consumer's information search depends upon certain antecedents. These particularly influence aspects of user-system-interaction and the evaluation of the usefulness and effectiveness of an IS for satisfying consumer information needs. Product-related antecedents such as involvement (Mittal, 1989; Mittal and Lee, 1989) and prior product knowledge (Brucks, 1985; Flynn and Goldsmith, 1999) are especially important. The extent of an information search correlates positively with situational involvement or enduring involvement in the information search process (Beatty and Smith, 1987). It correlates negatively with the amount of prior product knowledge, however (Jepsen, 2007). Finally, consumers with imprecise information needs usually employ exploratory search tactics, and strategies that induce an evolvement of the information need during information search, achieved by learning processes during search (Bates, 1979, 1989; White, Muresan and Marchionini, 2008). Consumer research also deals with the issue of risk. According to this, the main task of information search is the reduction of perceived product and transactional risks. The perceived risk relates to the concreteness of an information need, which in turn depends mainly on the amount of prior product knowledge (Swaminathan, 2003).

Consumer satisfaction will increase consumer loyalty and revenue. It can be measured by perceived ease of use and perceived usefulness (Davis, 1989; Venkatesh, Morris, Davis and Davis, 2003) as well as the resulting overall information and system satisfaction (Delone and McLean, 2003, 2004; Wang, 2008). Consumer satisfaction can be increased by a higher relevance of the search results and creating new features (Hill, Roche and Allen, 2007; Lee and Joshi, 2006; Shankar, Smith and Rangaswamy).

Three general approaches for influencing information search in online buying decision processes can be distinguished. First, human-computer-interaction approaches emphasize the importance of task-orientated user search interfaces (Marchionini, 2006; White et al., 2008). Second, system-based approaches aim at improving information retrieval processes by query expansion and query specifications (Kumar and Lang, 2007; Shen, Pan, Sun, Pan, Wu, Yin and Yang, 2006). In an e-commerce context, the evaluation of IS effectiveness should include user-centric relevance (Baeza-Yates and Ribeiro-Neto, 1999) such as the concept of situational relevance, which describes the relevance of a search result at a certain point in the search process (Borlund, 2003; Schamber, Eisenberg and Nilan, 1990). The third approach employs recommendation agents in order to deal with issues regarding product evaluation and selection (Ansari, Essegaier and Kohli, 2000; Bodapati, 2008; Bruyn, Lietchy, Huizingh and Lilien, 2008; Häubl and Trifts, 2000; Murray and Häubl, 2008; Schafer, Konstan and Riedl, 2001; Senecal and Nantel, 2004; Swaminathan, 2003).

However, a holistic approach that integrates and extends the approaches mentioned above seems most suitable to tackle conceivable barriers in information search. Semantic technologies may contribute to such solutions. As few studies have systematically addressed possible B2C applications of ontologies (Meij, Mika and Zaragoza, 2009), and as they predominantly focus on technical aspects, this study analyses consumer-related aspects.

3 Ontologies in E-Commerce

Ontologies consist of concepts, relations of those concepts, attributes, rules and instances (see above). In today's shopping context, the latter will normally be the products. Ontologies allow i) to define rules for soft product attributes and soft product categories; and ii) to extend the search space by including concepts that are similar to the search term, as opposed to a mere search for synonyms.

Thereby, ontologies create a model of reality, which is based on rather subjective stipulations. Thus, the influence of ontologies on functionality and information retrieval will always depend upon the overall setting, such as the type of online store (brand store, general retailer, specialized retailer), the type of products offered, the degree of specialisation (heterogeneity of products), and also upon the degree of heterogenity of customers regarding age, gender, income, education and IT experience. Using navigation, however, will not necessarily solve this due to the fact that soft product categories or navigational categories and indexes are also not commonly agreed upon.

4 Research Method

4.1 Data Collection

The relevant data for this study was collected with the help of two independent focus groups of eight panelists each. A focus group is an acknowledged method of exploratory research used to understand consumers' motivation and experiences, and to derive hypotheses that can be tested in further analyses (Churchill and Iacobucci, 2002). The number of focus groups was limited due to resource restrictions, but as there was a sufficient saturation of the data material during the second focus group, we do not consider this a disadvantage. The panelists were recruited through convenience sampling, as they were either students of Humboldt University or related to the private and professional network of the researchers. To counteract a possible bias, they represent different customer segments. As the study aims at understanding the influence of demographic aspects of current and future behaviour in online shops, we invited a student sample and a middle-age women sample. The students (majors: business, mathematics and web design) had greater experience with the Internet than the other sample. The middle-age woman sample consisted of panelists between 35 and 60 years of age. Participation only was possible if the candidate affirmed some experience with online shopping.

The discussion in the focus groups was guided with the help of two sets of structured open questions. It took place within 90 minutes at the end of 2009 at Humboldt University and was recorded and transcribed. In the first part, each group discussed general experiences in online information search and the type of products they buy online. In the second part, panelists evaluated ontology-based features by means of low-fidelity prototypes (graphical mockups). Although such prototypes do not provide any functionality, they can considerably support the evaluation of design alternatives early in the product development cycle (Rudd et al., 1996). To maximize the representativity of the discussion, we chose the two prevailing user interfaces used in online shops, i.e. the 'direct search' and 'navigation' and combined them with two main product categories, i.e. digital cameras and apparel. The direct search enables the customer to type in a query term, whereas the navigation offers a choice of product categories (i.e. digital cameras or apparel) and navigational categories (i.e. digital camera for beginners). The two scenarios for digital cameras are graphically depicted in figure 1 and 2.

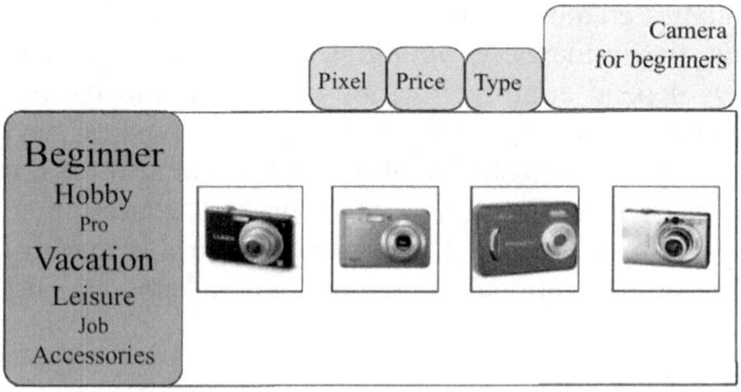

Fig. 1. Mockup "direct search and tag cloud"

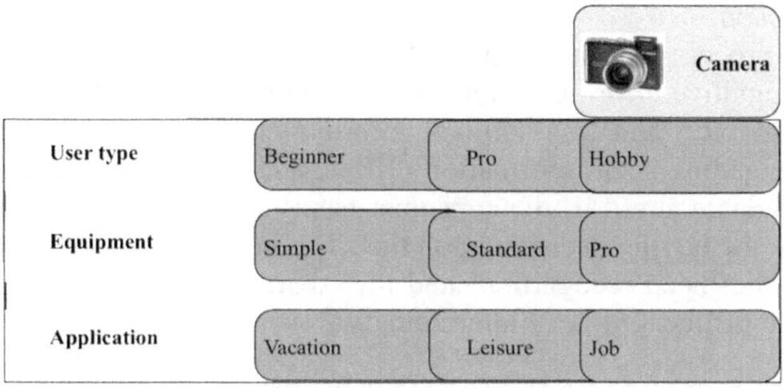

Fig. 2. Mockup "categories for navigation"

The scenario that combined "navigation" with "apparel" offered navigational categories according to style (modern, elegant, etc.), occasion (casual, office, etc.) and season. The scenario for the direct search was combined with a tag cloud (a graphical depiction of words related to the search term) displayed on the left side of the user interface. For the direct search, panelists were confronted with soft search terms such as "summerly dress".

4.2 Data Analysis

In order to analyse the focus groups transcriptions we have used an interpretive approach (Miles and Huberman, 1994) based on grounded theory (Glaser and Strauss, 1967). Interpretivism stresses that theory does not emerge from data, but data are constructed from observations (Strauss and Corbin, 1998). Due to the subjectivity of the emergent theory, we do not claim objectivity, but instead we argue that the emergent theory is one possible explanations of reality, which can be more or less relevant, credible and acceptable. In the first stage, we identified concepts and discovered their properties, similarly to what Strauss and Corbin (1998) and Miles and Huberman (1994) refer to as open coding. Then we grouped these concepts into categories according to their properties and dimensions, also referred to as selective coding (ibid.). Finally, we validated our results by taking over theoretical concepts from consumer research such as antecedents (demographics, Internet experience, search routines, etc.).

5 Empirical Findings

The concepts and categories resulting from our qualitative analysis are introduced in this section. The implications derived from these findings are presented in the section thereafter. In general, we perceived reluctance in both groups to buy goods online that habitually are only being bought after trying them on physically. Surprisingly, panelists from the first group, the middle-age woman sample, who are frequently buying apparel via catalogues refuse to buy online even though there is much more product information available, e.g. pictures with side and back views of the model wearing the item of interest.

Channel selection

The decision process is influenced by the following aspects: i) the consumer has to balance the cognitive effort, time and costs for retrieving product information (price, features, color, etc.) and transactional information (such as the time of delivery) online against getting such information offline, and sometimes the required information is not available at all; ii) the consumer has to compare the information retrieved and must base the buying decision upon this. The initial phases of the consumer decision process, the 'need recognition' and the 'search for information' (Blythe, 2006) can be realized offline, online or alternatingly.

Use of search interface and motivation for shopping

The panelists' amount of product knowledge acquired prior to an online information search mainly influences the use of search interfaces: panelists with high prior product knowledge prefer direct search interfaces. Panelists with low prior product knowledge usually combine this with the navigation search. However, the choice of a search interface seems also to be related to the shopping motivation. We could classify three motivations for online shopping: i) boredom / inspiration: the panelist wants to pass time or get inspired to purchase products (however, the latter result was strictly limited to female panelists); ii) the panelist is searching for a product in a specific product category, e.g. a pair of jeans; and iii) the panelist is looking for a specific product, i.e. a particular brand and model. Whereas panelists in category i) use the navigation, panelists in category iii) use the direct search and panelists in category ii) alternate.

Using the direct search interface, some panelists experienced problems formulating a query resulting in a resonable amount of search results. Most panelists feared choosing too narrow query terms, thereby excluding relevant search results. Panelists complained that they never know whether a product is linked to more than one product category or not.

Product information and relevance of search results

Panelists often mentioned the importance of an "appropriate" number of search results meaning that they felt overwhelmed when getting too many and frustrated when getting too few search results. This phenomena seems to present a psychological barrier to consumer satisfaction. Panelists do not feel satisfied when they only get few results even if they are highly relevant to their search. The relevance of the search results depends not only on the number of search results, but also on the perceived quality of the product information provided. In general, we discovered a gap between the retailers' product description and the panelists' information need. Panelists stated that they often search for experienced-based knowledge, which cannot be provided by the retailer but only by consumers having consumed the product. Furthermore, the credibility of customer reviews and ratings is perceived to be much higher by the panelists than the information provided by the retailer. Providing adquate product information considerably reduces the functional, social and financial risk from the panelist's point of view.

Evaluation of ontology-based features

The definition of soft criteria in ontologies influences the choice of the categories for the navigation, as well as the search terms for the direct search. Panelists were generally very interested and open to the new features; however, most of them asked about the functionalities of the features presented to them. This implies that the chosen functionalities were not as intuitive as we assumed.

Panelists felt that the ontology would be useful for interpreting their query terms when using the direct search. However, most panelists stated that independent from the product category they would refrain from using soft criteria. The reason is that they fear to exclude relevant search results because of a possible incongruence of their own search terms and the ontology. Some panelists predicted that consumers would adapt to using soft product criteria. The navigational interface was perceived more useful and transparent since the structure of the ontology can partially be seen through the choice of the categories.

However, the panelists' evaluation of the usefulness of the categories depended upon the product category and user-related characteristics. For example, we could state a clear age divide concerning the usefulness of the given apparel categories. While older panelists found all categories useful, the student panelists stated that they would only use the categories for seasonal apparel, and some panelists for style. The student sample collectively agreed that they would not use the navigational category "occasion" (casual, office, festive). Further discussion revealed that fashion is becoming less constrained with regard to occasion, e.g. short pants or skirts are worn in winter combined with leggings. Panelists stated that they were not aware of how the given categories were generated, respectively of how the soft product criteria were defined.

This was different with regard to digital cameras. As before, the older panelists were very satisfied with the categories suggested. The student panelists were also keen to use the proposed categories but claimed information of how these are defined.

A surprising result was the altered shopping behaviour of the panelists when buying for someone else, e.g. when a gift is bought. All panelists agreed that they would rely much more on the navigation categories in such cases.

Another surprising result was the rejection of the tag cloud by all panelists according to usability criteria such as ease of use and perceived usefulness: it was being evaluated as "very confusing" and "not intuitive". Even the student sample - where all panelists were accustomed with tag clouds in blogs - could not explain how the tag cloud functions, nor its purpose. Across the focus groups and their opinions, we did not note disagreements between the genders.

5 Managerial Implications for Deploying and Modeling Ontology-Based Systems in Online Shops

The interpretation of our data revealed the following problems: i) *featuritis or creeping featurism*: releasing new software always bears the risk of overloading the user with features. However, if insufficient features are used to structure the displayed information, the consumer could suffer from ii) *information overload*: there are many different online shops and there is a large amount of product information available. However, one of the main problems in online shopping is a lack of specific product information presented online, such as experienced-based information The challenge for online shops is therefore to provide the right features and the right information; iii) *paternalism*: by employing soft product attributes (e.g. "summerly" dress) or navigational categories (e.g. digital cameras for beginners), consumers might get confused if they do not agree with the definition of the attribute or navigational category. This phenomenon is also related to iv) *trust*: consumers may lose confidence if they do not agree with or do not understand the choice of categories made. In the following, we suggest solutions to reduce the challenges mentioned above.

Engineering an ontology-based system

How can an ontology be modeled to meet the expectations of a majority of the relevant consumers? The formulation of rules is highly subjective and therefore particularly critical. Such rules, for example, define which products are suggested for product bundling, or they assign soft product attributes to certain product characteristics (e.g. "handy" to describe digital cameras weighing less than 200 grams).

Contrary to common practice in companies, we therefore suggest that at least two employees should contribute to the modelisation of ontologies. Especially when defining relations between concepts and rules, ontology modelers should additionally base their work on empirical findings. These can be generated by i) conducting focus groups or interviews with consumers. Also, ii) consumers could be incited to tag products when visiting the online shop, or iii) machine learning can be applied to adapt ontologies to consumer queries, and iv) existing logfiles can be analysed through web analytics.

Using soft categories for navigation bears certain risks: on the one hand, when incorporating soft categories next to hard categories, consumers might feel overwhelmed by the number of categories (cf. i) *featuritis* above). One solution could be to display only soft categories and offer the possibility to filter the search results according to hard product criteria at the same time. On the other hand, consumers might feel patronized when they disagree with the definition of a certain navigational category. This could be addressed by displaying the definitions used. In doing so, the searching process becomes more transparent and consumers can avoid the unwanted exclusion of relevant search results.

The impact of the ontology in a direct search is less obvious, because a search conducted with hard product attributes will lead to similar results regardless of the ontology. However, when introducing a new search engine, consumers should be adverted to its possibilities. This could be achieved by inserting a default query into the search slot (e.g. "I am looking for an elegant summer dress").

Ontologies can support recommendation functions such as "products matching the product you selected" (bundling), or "find similar products". Ontologies can support the establishment of newsletters and help to integrate Web2.0 sources containing consumer reviews. As our panelists attested high credibility to such reviews, it seems advisable to integrate internal or external consumer reviews. However, for many products the writing of consumer reviews is not common, e.g. for fashion. This may be due to the ephemerality and the opacity of the apparel market.

User specific aspects

As human-computer-interaction research has shown, system development has to address different needs of different user types (Fischer, 2001). Accordingly, demographic characteristics of the consumer such as age, which often strongly correlates with technology affinity and Internet shopping experience can be considered. However, situational characteristics (such as the shopping motivation, the prior product knowledge and involvement) are not as relevant, because they may change frequently or abruptly.

6 Limitations

Deploying ontologies in search engines is only one approach to reduce problems in online shopping. All of the discussed functionalities could also be achieved with other solutions, e.g. statistical analysis, or relational databases. Moreover, the search function is only one of multiple factors influencing online shopping experiences, e.g. availability of products or costs for shipping and handling.

As to this study, methodological limitations arise concerning the representativeness of focus groups and due to low-fidelity prototyping. Panelists often mispredict their behaviour when asked about their future feelings in hypothetical situations as shown in a study by Loewenstein and Schkade (1997).

7 Conclusion

This study develops requirements for ontology-based system engineering by combining empirical findings about current usage of e-commerce with consumers' opinions about ontology-based features. Such features have not yet found widespread acceptance in e-commerce, mainly due to a lack of research and experience in this field.

An analysis of the focus group discussions showed that both the student panelists and the middle-age panelists classified as useful the navigational categories presented to them in a search for digital cameras. Only the middle-age panelists found the navigational categories for apparel useful, whereas the student panelists explained that due to the dissolution of fashion conventions they would feel patronized by engineers who define such navigational categories. However, all panelists would use soft product categories when buying presents.

The analysis also emphasized the importance of the information displayed in a search process for the consecutive phases of the buying decision process, because purchase and after-purchase aspects - such as transaction and delivery - already determine the purchase decision.

The following implications can be derived from this analysis: Not only one but preferably all phases of the buying decision process should be considered in ontology-based system engineering; ontologies should be modeled based on empirical findings concerning consumer opinion; definitions of soft product categories should be provided; and experience-based product information should be included by integrating internal or external consumer reviews.

Our findings presented above are based on low-fidelity-protyping realized with the help of a small sample size. These results should be validated by quantitative high-fidelity prototyping. If such future studies take all the above implications and limitations into account, it is possible to further refine the guidelines for ontology engineering and to offer additional advice concerning the selection and configuration of ontology-based features in online shops.

References

1. Ansari, A., Essegaier, S., Kohli, R.: Internet recommendation systems. Journal of Marketing Research XXXVII, 363–375 (2000)
2. Bakos, R., Ribeiro-Neto, B.: Modern Information Retrieval. ACM Press, New York (1999)
3. Bakos, J.Y.: Reducing buyer search costs: implications for electronic marketplaces. Management Science 43(12), 1676–1692 (1997)
4. Bates, M.J.: Information search tactics. Journal of the American Society for Information Science and Technology, 205–214 (1979)
5. Bates, M.J.: The design of browsing and berrypicking techniques for the online search interface. Online Information Review 13(5), 407–424 (1989)
6. Beatty, S.E., Smith, S.M.: External search effort: an investigation across several product categories. The Journal of Consumer Research 14(1), 83–95 (1987)
7. Blythe, J.: Principles and practices of marketing. Thomson, London (2006)
8. Bodapati, A.V.: Recommendation systems with purchase data. Journal of Marketing Research XLV, 77–93 (2008)
9. Borlund, P.: The concept of relevance in IR. Journal of the American Society for Information Science and Technology 54(10), 913–925 (2003)
10. Brucks, M.: The effects of product class knowledge on information search behavior. The Journal of Consumer Research 12(1), 1–16 (1985)
11. Bruyn, A.D., Liechty, J.C., Huizingh, E., Lilien, G.L.: Offering online recommendations with minimum customer input through conjoint-based decision aids. Marketing Science 27(3), 443–460 (2008)
12. Churchill, G.A., Iacobucci, D.: Marketing research: methodological foundations. 8th, South-Western College Pub., Australia (2002)
13. Davis, F.D.: Perceived usefulness, perceived ease of use, and user acceptance of information technology. MIS Quarterly 13(3), 319–340 (1989)
14. Delone, W.H., McLean, E.R.: The DeLone and McLean model of information systems success: a ten-year update. Journal of Management for Information Systems 19(4), 9–30 (2003)
15. Delone, W.H., McLean, E.R.: Measuring e-commerce success: applying the DeLone and McLean information systems success model. International Journal of Electronic Commerce 9(1), 31–47 (2004)
16. Fensel, D., McGuiness, D.L., Schulten, E., Ng, W.K., Lim, E.P., Yan, G.: Ontologies and electronic commerce. IEEE Intelligent Systems 16(1), 8–14 (2001)
17. Fischer, G.: User modeling in human-computer interaction. User Modeling and User Adapted Interaction 11(1-2), 65–86 (2001)
18. Flynn, L.R., Goldsmith, R.E.: A short, reliable measure of subjective knowledge. Journal of Business Research 46, 57–66 (1999)
19. Glaser, B.G., Strauss, A.L.: The Discovery of Grounded Theory – Strategies for Qualitative Research. Aldine de Gryuter, NY (1967)
20. Gruber, T.: A translation approach to portable ontology specifications. Knowledge Acquisition 5(1), 199–200 (1993)
21. Häubl, G., Trifts, V.: Consumer decision making in online shopping environments: the effects of interactive decision aids. Marketing Science 10(1), 4–21 (2000)
22. Hill, N., Roche, G., Allen, R.: Customer satisfaction: the customer experience through the customer's eyes, Cogent, London (2007)
23. Jepsen, A.L.: Factors affecting consumer's use of the Internet for information search. Journal of Interactive Marketing 21(3), 21–34 (2007)

24. Konstan, J.A., Miller, B.N., Maltz, D., Herlocker, J.L., Gordon, L.R., Riedl, J.: Grouplens: applying collaborative filtering to usenet news. Communications of the ACM 40, 77–87 (1997)
25. Kumar, N., Lang, K.R.: Do search terms matter for online consumers? The interplay between search engine query specification and topical organization. Decision Support Systems 44(1), 159–174 (2007)
26. Lee, K., Joshi, K.: Development of an integrated model of customer satisfaction with online shopping. In: Proceedings of the sixth Special Interest Group of the ACM on Management Information Systems, Claremont, USA, April 13–15, pp. 53–56 (2006)
27. Loewenstein, G., Schkade, D.: Wouldn't it be nice? Predicting furure feelings. In: Kahneman, D., Diener, E., Schwarz, N. (eds.) Well-being: the foundations of hedonic psychology, pp. 85–105. Sage, NY (1999)
28. Marchionini, G.: Exploratory search: from finding to understanding. Communications of the ACM 49(4), 41–46 (2006)
29. Meij, E., Mika, P., Zaragoza, H.: Investigating the demand side of semantic search through query log analysis. In: Proceedings of the Semantic Search 2009 Workshop located at the 18th International World Wide Web Conference WWW 2009, Madrid, Spain, April 21 (2009)
30. Miles, M.B., Huberman, A.M.: Qualitative Data Analysis. SAGE Publications, London (1994)
31. Mittal, B.: Measuring purchase-decision involvement. Psychology and Marketing 6(2), 147–162 (1989)
32. Mittal, B., Lee, M.S.: A causal model of consumer involvement. Journal of Economic Psychology 10, 363–389 (1989)
33. Murray, K.B., Häubl, G.: Interactive consumer decision aids. In: Wierenga, B. (ed.) Handbook of Marketing Decision Models, pp. 55–84. Springer Science & Business Media, NY (2008)
34. Rudd, J., Stern, K., Isensee, S.: Low vs. high-fidelity prototyping debate. interactions 3(1), 76–85 (1996)
35. Sawar, B., Karypis, G., Konstan, J., Reidl, J.: Item-based collaborative filtering recommendation algorithms. In: Proceedings of the 10th International Conference on World Wide Web, Hong Kong, pp. 285–295 (2001)
36. Schafer, J.B., Konstan, J.A., Riedl, J.: E-commerce recommendation applications. Data Mining and Knowledge Discovery 5, 115–153 (2001)
37. Schamber, L., Eisenberg, M.B., Nilan, M.S.: A re-examination of relevance: toward a dynamic, situational definition. Information Processing and Management 26(6), 755–776 (1990)
38. Senecal, S., Nantel, J.: The influence of online product recommendations on consumers' online choices. Journal of Retailing 80(2), 159–169 (2004)
39. Shankar, V., Smith, A.K., Rangaswamy, A.: Customer satisfaction and loyalty in online and offline environments. International Journal of Research in Marketing 20, 153–175 (2003)
40. Shen, D., Pan, R., Sun, J.T., Pan, E.J., Wu, K., Yin, J., Yang, Q.: Query enrichment for web-query classification. ACM Transactions on Information Systems 24(3), 320–352 (2006)
41. Strauss, A., Corbin, J.: Basics of Qualitative Research. SAGE Publications, London (1998)
42. Swaminathan, V.: The impact of recommendation agents on consumer evaluation and choice: the moderating role of category risk, product complexity, and consumer knowledge. Journal of Consumer Psychology 13(1-2), 93–101 (2003)

43. Venkatesh, V., Morris, M.G., Davis, G.B., Davis, F.D.: User acceptance of information technology: toward a unified view. MIS Quarterly 27(3), 425–478 (2003)
44. Wang, J., de Vries, A.P., Reinders, M.J.T.: Unifying user-based and item-based collaborative filtering. In: Proceedings of the 29th annual international ACM SIGIR conference on Research and development in information retrieval, Seattle, Washington, pp. 501–508 (2006)
45. Wang, Y.S.: Assessing e-commerce systems success: a respecification and validation of the DeLone and McLean model of IS success. Information Systems Journal 18(5), 529–557 (2008)
46. White, R.W., Muresan, G., Marchionini, G.: Evaluating exploratory search systems. Information Processing and Management 44(2), 433–436 (2008)

B2B Electronic Marketplaces in Supply Chain Management: Analyzing Recent Research Activities

Christoph Pflügler and Klaus Turowski

Inter-organizational Systems Group
University of Augsburg
{christoph.pfluegler,klaus.turowski}@wiwi.uni-augsburg.de

Abstract. Since their rise during the 1990s, business-to-business (B2B) electronic marketplaces have been subject to numerous scientific articles. Especially during the dot-com era, these research efforts have been accompanied by several start-ups such as *CommerceOne*, with mixed market success. For researchers looking for promising areas of IS research, these facts raise the question whether B2B electronic marketplaces still constitute a viable option which is worth focusing on. The work at hand strives to answer that question by conducting a literature analysis covering the period from 2005 to 2009. We examined 11 major IS-journals as well as three major IS conferences in search of articles dealing with or relating to B2B electronic marketplaces. The analysis of the data gathered throughout that process provides an overview of the B2B electronic marketplace research of the past five years from multiple perspectives. Our analysis indentifies several research opportunities for researchers, e.g., by indentifying research methods that have not been applied to examine certain topics, or by identifying geographical regions that have been underresearched regarding the application of B2B electronic marketplaces. Further, our work will help practitioners seeking reliable information regarding B2B electronic marketplaces to indentify publication outlets relevant for this field of research.

Keywords: B2B electronic marketplaces, electronic markets, e-procurement, negotiation, auctions, agents, adoption, reputation, trust, flexibility, semantic web, literature analysis.

1 Introduction

After an initial set of publications during the late 1980s (e.g., Malone, Yates and Benjamin (1987), Malone, Yates and Benjamin (1989)), B2B electronic marketplaces attracted a large amount of interest in the IS research community during the 1990s. This development was also reflected by numerous start-ups related to the topic during the dot-com era. However, these commercial initiatives, e.g. *CommerceOne*, a producer of marketplace software, succeeded only partially in the market. Although *CommerceOne* participated, e.g., in the implementation of the well-known B2B marketplace *Covisint,* it was acquired by *PerfectCommerce* in 2006. In turn, *Covisint*'s sourcing and services business was sold to *FreeMarkets*, which subsequently was

M.L. Nelson et al. (Eds.): Sustainable e-Business Management, LNBIP 58, pp. 127–144, 2010.

acquired by *Ariba* (Forbes, 2004). *Covisint*'s more promising data messaging business was sold to *Compuware* (Forbes, 2004). In general, a key feature of commercial B2B electronic marketplaces has been the high failure rate (Klueber, Leser and Kaltenmorgen, 2001).

The area of B2B electronic marketplaces is under research for quite a long time now and its commercial exploitation is not always a success story. However, despite the high failure rate, B2B electronic marketplaces have become an indispensable component of various supply chains, especially in the car, metal and chemical industry (Computerworld, 2004; Economist, 2004). From a scientific point of view, this raises the question whether B2B electronic marketplaces still constitute a viable area of research, worth focusing on for researchers. The work at hand strives to answer that question by conducting a literature analysis covering the period from 2005 to 2009. We examined 11 major IS-journals as well as three major IS conferences in search of articles dealing with or relating to B2B electronic marketplaces.

After this introduction, section "B2B Electronic Marketplaces" depicts current definitions of the term B2B electronic marketplace and presents a classification scheme based on our literature review. The literature selection process is detailed in section "Research Methodology". Section "Analyzing Recent Research Activities" reveals the results of our multi-perspective literature analysis, section "Limitations" outlines its limitations. Future research endeavors in the field of B2B electronic marketplaces are briefly described in section "Conclusion and Future Work".

2 B2B Electronic Marketplaces

There are various terms used almost synonymously for a B2B electronic marketplace: electronic market, EMP, e-hub, B2B exchange, or (B2B) e-market are some of them. Although the definitions for each term may slightly differ, the core concept is mostly the same. A selection of definitions based on our literature analysis is depicted in table 1.

Numerous classifications of B2B electronic marketplaces have been proposed (Grieger, 2003). Our approach is to depict how the articles analyzed throughout our study classify B2B electronic marketplaces. An overview of the resulting classification scheme is provided in table 2.

First of all, it is worth mentioning that only two of the 77 analyzed articles conduct a classification. Son and Benbasat (2007) as well as Dominguez (2009) distinguish *vertical* and *horizontal* B2B electronic marketplaces. Horizontal marketplaces serve more than one industry (e.g., Worldbid.com, Global Trade Village), whereas vertical ones are industry specific (e.g., Covisint, ChemConnect). Further, Son and Benbasat (2007) distinguish *private* and *non-private* marketplaces. Private marketplaces are owned and operated by a single firm (e.g., SupplyPower by General Motors) (Howard, Vidgen and Powell, 2006). Non-private marketplaces such as Alibaba, ChemConnect or WorldWide Retail Exchange are owned and operated by either an independent third-party intermediary (also referred to as *public marketplace*) or by a consortium of competing firms (*consortium- based marketplace*) (Son and Benbasat, 2007). Dominguez (2009) further distinguishes B2B electronic marketplaces by the *type of good* they exchange (MRO goods or goods directly linked to the manufacturing process), as well as by their *value proposition*. Regarding the value proposition, she differentiates between *transactional* electronic marketplaces aiming at executing exchanges, and *collaborative* electronic marketplaces which encourage collaboration of the market participants.

Table 1. Selected definitions for B2B electronic marketplaces

Author(s)	B2B electronic marketplace definition
Ash (2005)	"…define a B2B e-marketplace (or e-Marketplace) as a virtual marketspace where multiple buyers and sellers can interact with information and transactions supported by additional value-add facilities."
Soh et al. (2006)	"Electronic marketplaces (EMPs) are independently owned, IT-enabled intermediaries that connect many buying organizations with many selling organizations."
Rossignoli et al. (2006)	"…consider e-marketplaces as an ICT based organizational form that mixes markets coordination mechanisms (prices) and network coordination mechanisms (trust and common values)."
Guo and Xu (2006)	"Internet-based B2B e-marketplaces are a kind of inter-organizational information system in the online-environment, in which multiple buyers and sellers come together to gather information and exchange goods or services. They serve as electronic intermediaries to facilitate the exchange of information about products and/or support business transactions between participating buyers and sellers"
Finnegan and O'Reilly (2008)	"…an organisational intermediary that electronically provides value added communication, brokerage and integration services to buyers and sellers of direct and/or indirect products and/or services in specific horizontal or vertical markets by supporting basic market functions, meeting management needs for information and process support, and/or operating the required IS/IT infrastructure."
Dolpanya et al. (2009)	"…can be considered as an inter-organisational information system with which participating buyers and sellers utilize electronic markets for a dynamic price-making mechanism (such as electronic auctions), as well as for the exchange of information related to price, product specification, and terms of trade."
Dominguez (2009)	"…EMPs can be seen as intermediaries between buyers and suppliers devoted to answering purchasing and supply chain needs. They can also be defined as inter-organizational information systems (IOIS) that interact to create, store, transform, and communicate data between buyers and suppliers"

Table 2. Classification scheme for B2B electronic marketplaces based on our literature analysis

Attribute	Possible Values		
Ownership	*Private*	*Consortium-based*	*Public*
Industry Focus	*Vertical*	*Horizontal*	
Goods Traded	*MRO goods*	*Primary Materials*	
Value Proposition	*Collaborative*	*Transactional*	

3 Research Methodology

In our work, we adopted the framework for literature search proposed by vom Brocke, Simons, Niehavens, Riemer, Plattfaut and Cleven (2009). This research methodology consists of five phases which are depicted in figure 1. Each phase is explained in full detail in the following paragraphs.

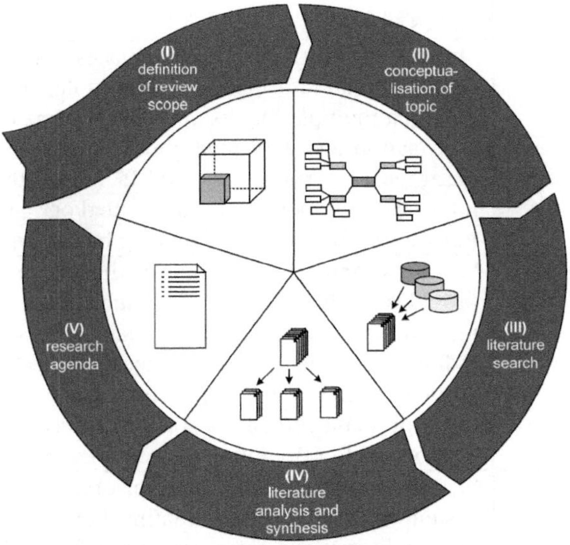

Fig. 1. The research methodology (vom Broke et al., 2009)

Pfeffers and Ya (2003) identified 326 journals that publish IS research, the Index of Information Systems Journals[1] lists 649 IS journals today. Thus, a comprehensive literature analysis is illusive. To indentify a set of high-quality journals, rankings are frequently used (e.g., Ho, Jin and Dwivedi (2009), vom Brocke et al. (2009)). To achieve a reasonable degree of internationality, we employ both the German Academic Association for Business Research's JOURQUAL2[2] and the official AIS

[1] http://lamp.infosys.deakin.edu.au/journals/
[2] http://vhbonline.org/en/service/vhb-jourqual/jq2/

ranking[3]. In the first step, we selected the 15 highest ranking journals of the JOURQUAL2 *IS and Information Management* and *Electronic Commerce* rankings. Then we intersected this set of journals with all AIS-listed journals that have 20 average rank points or less. The resulting set of journals includes *ISR, MISQ, SIAM Journal on Computing, JMIS, ISJ, JAIS, INFORMS Journal on Computing, IEEE Transactions on Engineering Management, ACMTDS, IJEC* and *DATABASE.* We also evaluated an intersection with AIS-listed journals that have 15 average rank points or less, however, the resulting set of journals was considered too small. As the AIS does not include conferences into its ranking, we directly included the three highest ranking conferences of the JOURQUAL2 *IS and Information Management* and *Electronic Commerce* rankings, which are the *ICIS*, *ECIS* and the *ER* conference.

After selecting relevant journals and conferences, we conceptualized the topic B2B electronic marketplaces by means of a respective seminar consisting of two graduate business students and four graduate computer science students. The seminar was held by one of the authors of the work at hand. The objective of that seminar was the formulation of a textbooks dealing with B2B electronic marketplaces in the context of electronic commerce.

The actual literature search was conducted in the next phase. Thereby, the archives of each journal and conference selected in phase I were searched manually, issue by issue, year by year. During this initial search, we decided upon relevance by title and abstract. As title and abstract do not always allow for an inference on the actual content of an article (Palvia and Pinjani, 2007), we included every article potentially covering our topic, resulting in a very broad literature index covering most aspects of electronic commerce and inter-organizational systems. We reduced that rather broad index for the first time by eliminating all articles with explicit B2C or C2C focus that was detectable by considering the abstract only. After this initial reduction step, we tried to get a full-text version of each remaining article by using various internet sources or soliciting the respective authors for a copy. After having received full-text versions of most of the articles (see table 3 for the articles not available full-text und thus not considered any longer in the analysis), we removed the remaining ones that focus B2C or C2C exchanges. An article was considered B2C or C2C related, if respective datasets were analyzed (e.g., EBay or Amazon datasets), or if the articles frequently referred to consumers. All remaining papers were included into the final literature index, if they explicitly referred to electronic marketplaces, resulting in a final set of 77 papers.

The final selection of articles was analyzed in phase IV. Therefore, we first of all collected author names, organization of each author, location of each organization, research method applied, and year of publication of each article. To identify the research method of each analyzed article, we incorporated the classification scheme of Palvia and Pinjani (2007). In the next step, we iteratively clustered the locations of the organizations as well as the topics the analyzed articles are centered around. The resulting data model is depicted in figure 2.

Throughout the entire literature search process, we developed a specific research agenda which we describe in section "Conclusion and Future Work".

[3] http://ais.affiniscape.com/displaycommon.cfm?an=1&subarticlenbr=432

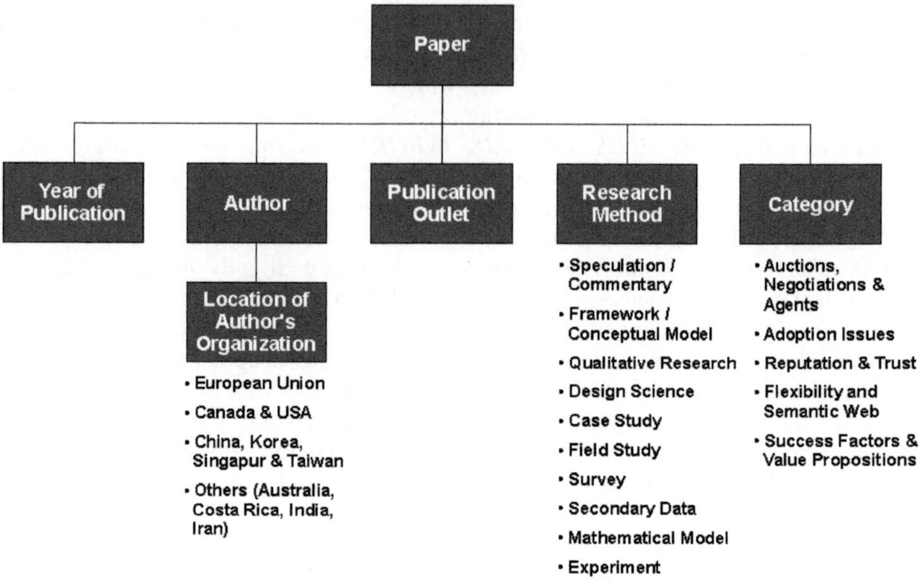

Fig. 2. Data model for the literature analysis

4 Analyzing Recent Research Activities

Two journals and one conference of the 11 journals and 3 conferences selected for our literature analysis did not publish articles on B2B electronic marketplaces. These are the *SIAM Journal on Computing*, the *ACMTDS* and the *ER conference*. The distribution of the 77 articles considered for our analysis on the remaining publication outlets is shown in figure 3. Most of the articles were published in the *JMIS*, followed by the

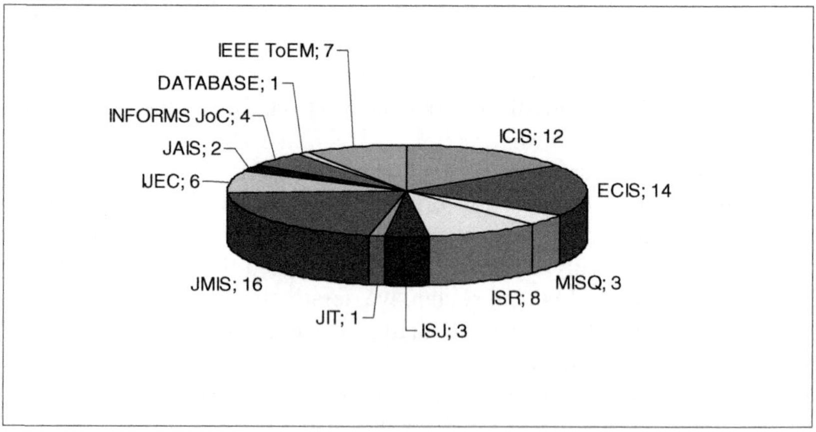

Fig. 3. Distribution of the analyzed articles on publication outlets

ECIS and the *ICIS*. Considering journals only, the top three publication outlets are the *JMIS*, the *ISR* and the *IEEE Transactions on Engineering Management* with 16, 8 and seven published articles, respectively. From our point of view, the low number of publications on B2B electronic marketplaces in the *IJEC* was surprising as the journal's name let us suggest a higher amount of respective articles in it. However, the IJEC seems to have its focus on B2C exchanges. Another interesting point is the research method dominating in each outlet: Especially the ECIS did provide a lot of case or field studies, whereas in the journals mathematical models or experiments are dominating.

The rest of this section provides a multi-perspective analysis of the research activities regarding B2B electronic marketplaces in the period from 2005 to 2009. We add explanatory notes for and try to derive possible research opportunities from each perspective.

4.1 Year of Publication vs. Type of Publication Outlet

One of the objectives of our literature analysis is to reveal the chronological development of the number of publications on B2B electronic marketplaces in supply chain management. First of all, we discovered that the overall amount of articles on the topic remained constant from 2005 to 2007, and is increasing since 2007. The amount of conference publications constantly increased since 2007, whereas the amount of journal publications remained relatively constant. As conference publications often report on ongoing research projects which frequently result in journal publications, we estimate an increasing amount of journal publications on B2B electronic marketplace-related topics in the course of the next years. Figure 4 depicts the chronological distribution of the analyzed articles.

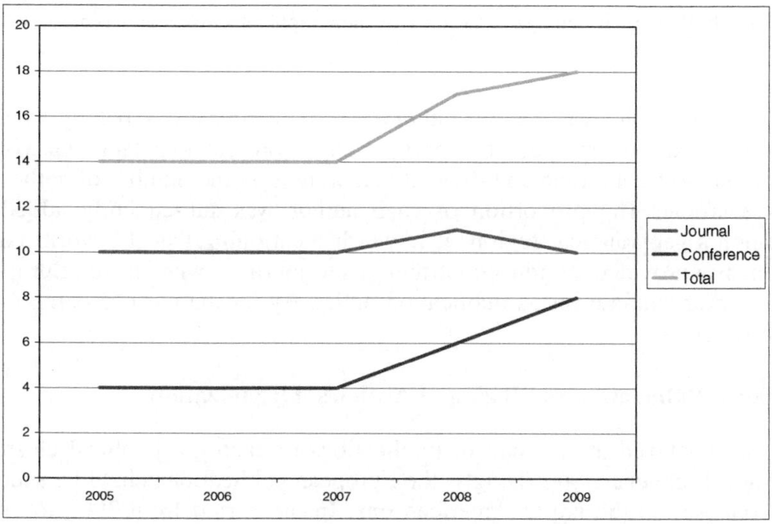

Fig. 4. Chronological distribution of the analyzed articles

4.2 Region of Authors' Organization vs. Type of Publication Outlet

In order to get an impression of the research effort regarding B2B electronic marketplaces in different regions of the world, we iteratively clustered the geographical location of each author into the four clusters *European Union, Canada & USA, China, Korea, Singapur & Taiwan,* and *Others (Australia, Costa Rica, India, Iran).* We further distinguished the type of publication outlet (i.e., conference or journal). The results are shown in figure 5.

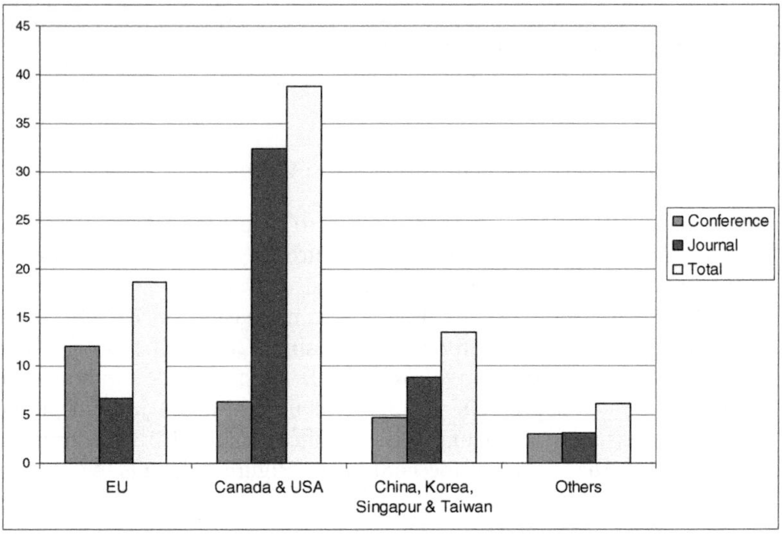

Fig. 5. Distribution of the analyzed articles by geographical cluster and type of publication outlet

Several articles are written by authors whose organizations belong to different geographical clusters; in order to appropriately represent this fact, we assigned a weight of one to each article and divided that weight by the number of authors of the respective article. The proportion of each author was subsequently added to her organization's geographical region. It is worth mentioning that the North American IS-community provided the most contributions to journals, whereas the European one seems to prefer conferences as publication outlet. By far the most research was done in North America.

4.3 Year of Publication vs. Region of Authors' Organization

Further, we analyzed the amount of publications of each geographical cluster in its chronological sequence. Surprisingly, the European publication behaviour seems to be directly opposed to the North American one. In the period from 2005 to 2006, the dramatic decrease in publications on B2B electronic marketplaces from North America was cushioned by publications from Europe and Asia. Please see figure 6 for an overview of this perspective.

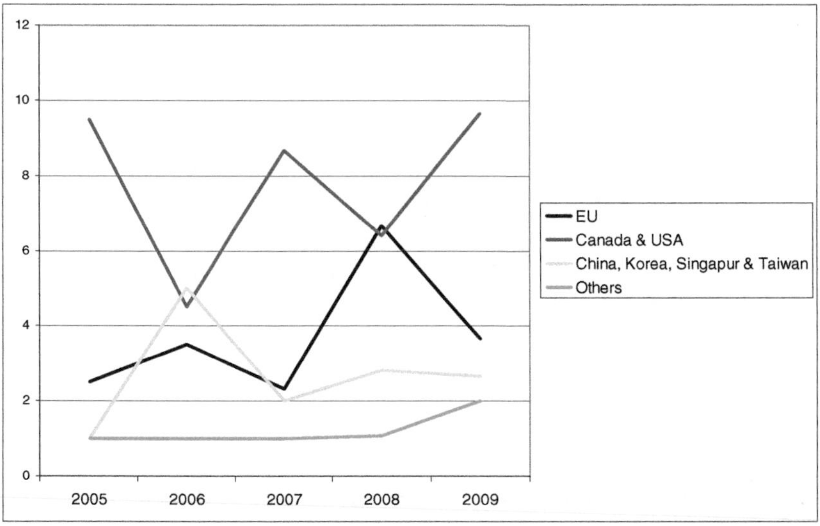

Fig. 6. Amount of publications per geographical region in chronological sequence

From our point of view, the huge gap between the number of publications from Europe and North America in the year 2009 is of particular interest, as it may allow for an inference on potential regional research opportunities in the field of B2B electronic marketplaces in Europe.

4.4 Focus of Analyzed Articles

As already described in section "Research Methodology", we iteratively clustered the topics the analyzed articles are centered around. The analysis of the resulting data reveals that most of the research on B2B electronic marketplaces concentrates on the clusters *Success Factors and Value Propositions*, as well as *Auctions, Negotiations and Agents*. As shown in figure 7, these topics are examined in more than half of the analyzed articles.

4.5 Focus of Article vs. Region of Authors' Organization

To identify possible research opportunities within the geographical clusters, we analyzed the focus of the articles in conjunction with the geographical clusters. The results are depicted in figure 8. The relative small percentage of research on *Adoption Issues* in Europe may indicate further research opportunities in this field and geographical region. *Trust and Reputation* seem to play a more important role in research on B2B electronic marketplaces in Europe than in the rest of the world. The more technology-oriented cluster *Flexibility and Semantic Web* is subject to intense research in Asia. This may indicate technology-oriented research opportunities in this field in the western world.

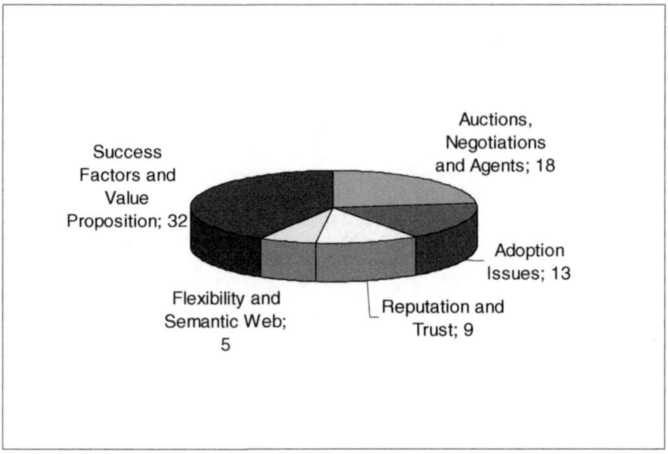

Fig. 7. Distribution of analyzed articles on research topics

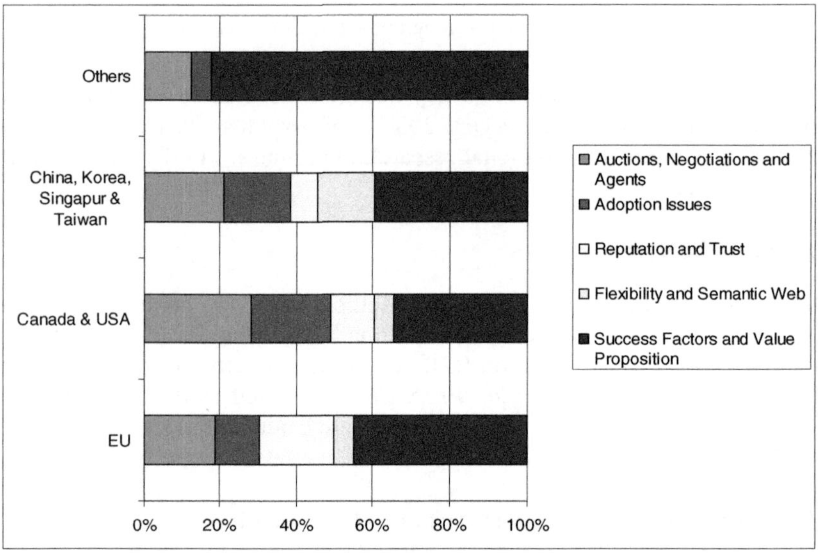

Fig. 8. Focus of the articles in conjunction with the geographical clusters

4.6 Focus of Article vs. Year of Publication

As depicted in figure 8, there is a strong increase of publications on *Success Factors and Value Propositions*, as well as *Auctions, Negotiations and Agents* in the period from 2007 to 2009, whereas there is not a single publication on *Reputation and Trust* or *Flexibility and Semantic Web* in 2009. The overall increase of publications related to B2B electronic marketplaces in the period from 2007 to 2009 can thus be attributed to the increase in publications dealing with *Success Factors and Value Propositions*, as well as *Auctions, Negotiations and Agents* in B2B electronic marketplaces.

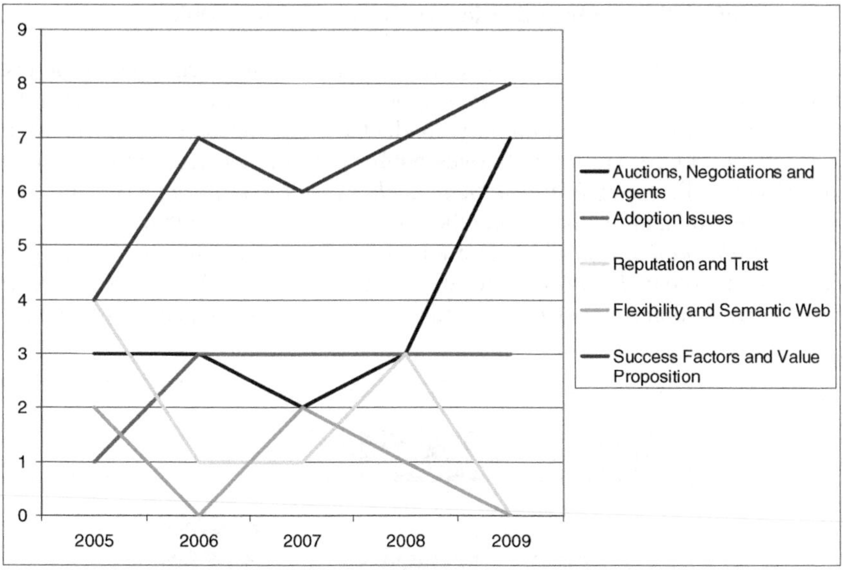

Fig. 9. Focus of the articles in chronological sequence

4.7 Research Methodologies

The dominating research methodology in B2B electronic marketplace research is the *Experiment*, followed by *Survey*, *Secondary Data, Field Study* and *Case Study*. An overview of all research methodologies applied in the analyzed articles is provided in figure 10.

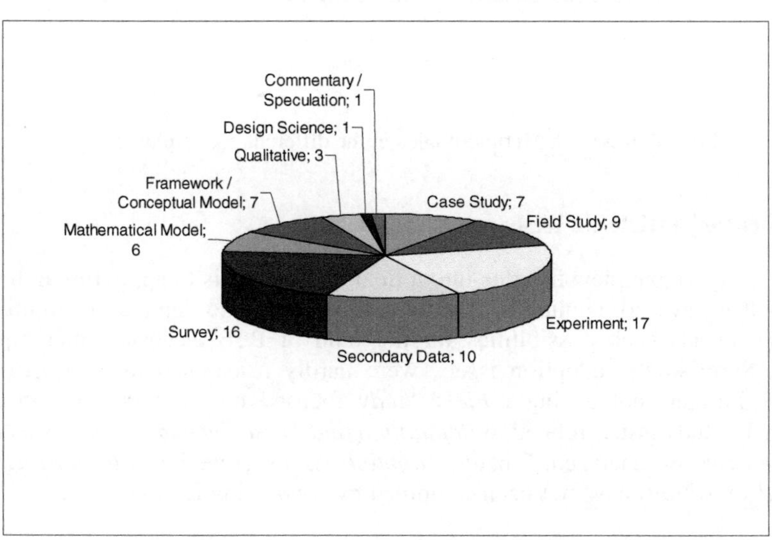

Fig. 10. Overview of applied research methodologies

4.8 Region of Authors' Organization vs. Research Methodology

This perspective on the B2B electronic marketplace research activities of the last five years reveals a very small number of *Case* or *Field Studies* in North America. In contrary, Europe's IS research community conducted only few *Surveys*. North American IS researchers, in turn, are the only ones publishing *Mathematical Models*. However, it must be noted that many *Mathematical Models* result in *Experiments*. Thus, it might be a possible explanation that researchers of the other geographical clusters do not publish a *Mathematical Model* without a corresponding *Experiment*. We assigned the research methodology *Experiment* to articles that contain a *Mathematical Model* as well as a corresponding *Experiment*. Figure 11 depicts this perspective in detail.

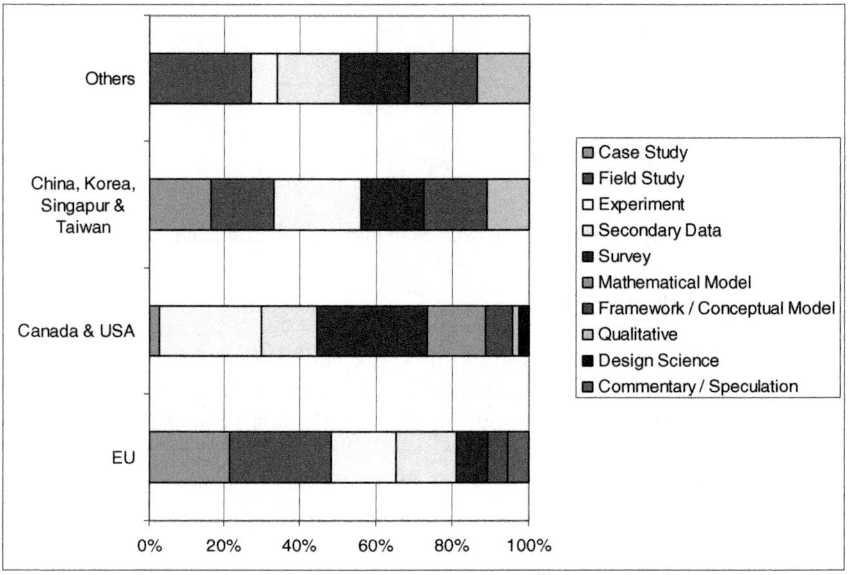

Fig. 10. Research Methodologies in the different geographical regions

4.9 Focus of Article vs. Research Methodology

A possibility to gain new insights into a field of research is to apply research methodologies that have not applied to that field before. As also depicted in figure 11, our analysis reveals such possibilities for the field of B2B electronic marketplace research. Surprisingly, adoption issues were hardly researched using *Case* or *Field Studies*. Further, not a single *Field Study* focused on *Auctions, Negotiations or Agents*. To study issues related to *Reputation and Trust*, *Secondary Data* was not used in the articles we analyzed. Finally, *Adoption Issues* as well as *Success Factors and Value Propositions* have not been examined by conducting *Experiments*.

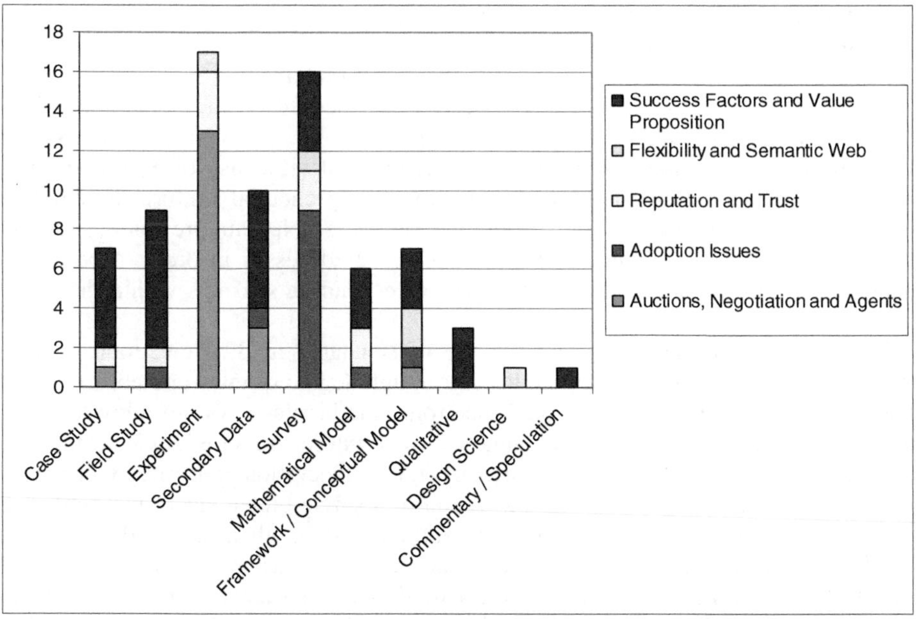

Fig. 11. Focus of article vs. research methodology

5 Limitations

The short time period covered by our literature analysis and the number of examined publication outlets are two major limitations of the work at hand. The resulting small number of analyzed articles implies a limited validity of our findings and conclusions. Further, we took the German JOURQUAL2 ranking and intersected it with the AIS ranking. As the German JOURQUAL2 is highly business-oriented, technical issues are disregarded to a certain extent. Thus, we may have created a bias regarding the topics the analyzed articles are centered around. Finally, the AIS ranking contains by far more US-originated journals than journals originated from other countries, which may create a bias regarding our analysis of research efforts on B2B electronic marketplaces in different geographical regions of the world.

6 Conclusion and Future Work

Although B2B electronic marketplaces have been subject to extensive research for more than two decades now, the increase of publications on the topic throughout the last three years led us to the conclusion that there is still a demand for further research. Moreover, several case or field studies report on successful B2B electronic marketplaces, which may indicate a successful incorporation of experience gathered by the analysis of past failures and successes. Summarizing our results, we believe that B2B electronic marketplaces still are a viable area of research which we consider worth focusing on.

A synthesis of literature is expected to result into a research agenda comprised of promising questions for future research. We briefly describe the research agenda we developed during our literature analysis in the next paragraphs.

Most B2B electronic marketplace research has focused on the value and role of B2B electronic marketplaces in industrial marketing. We are convinced that examining B2B electronic marketplaces from another point of view may offer new insights. For example, conducting a field study covering entrepreneurial ventures may help to answer the question "Do B2B electronic marketplaces help entrepreneurs to identify markets niches?". A challenge that will need to be addressed in order to be able to answer that question is the identification of corresponding start-ups within the different industries.

Further, we consider studies on the use of standards in B2B electronic marketplaces as interesting. As standards allow for a high degree of inter-operability, a high degree of standardization within B2B electronic marketplaces would allow business processes that cross marketplace boundaries. Such interoperable B2B electronic marketplaces could open opportunities for marketplace federation concepts by private or public organizations, thus fostering the vision of a single global electronic market. In order to measure the degree of standardization, first of all a standard framework for B2B electronic marketplaces needs to be developed, using a design science approach. On the basis of this framework, a field study or survey comprised of major B2B electronic marketplaces of each industry could be conducted in order to measure the actual degree of standardization.

References

1. Ash, C.G.: Managing E-Business Change within a Global E-Marketplace: A Buyer's Perspective. In: Bartmann, D., Rajola, F., Kallinikos, J., Avison, D., Winter, R., Ein-Dor, P., Becker, J., Bodendorf, F., Weinhardt, C. (eds.) Proceedings of the Thirteenth European Conference on Information Systems, Regensburg, Germany, May 26-28, pp. 1139–1150 (2005), http://is2.lse.ac.uk/asp/aspecis/
2. vom Brocke, M., Simons, A., Niehavens, B., Riemer, K., Plattfaut., R., Cleven, A.: Reconstructing the Giant: On the Importance of Rigour in Documenting the Literature Search Process. In: Newell, S., Whitley, E., Pouloudi, N., Wareham, J., Mathiassen, L. (eds.) Proceedings of the Seventeenth European Conference on Information Systems, Verona, Italy, June 8-10, pp. 2206–2217 (2009), http://is2.lse.ac.uk/asp/aspecis/
3. Computerworld, B2B Exchange Survivors, Computerworld (February 2, 2004)
4. Dolpanya, K., Land, L., Dick, G.: Understanding suppliers' participation in business-to-government (B2G) electronic auction markets in the thai context. In: Newell, S., Whitley, E., Pouloudi, N., Wareham, J., Mathiassen, L. (eds.) Proceedings of the Seventeenth European Conference on Information Systems, Verona, Italy, June 8-10, pp. 871–882 (2009), http://is2.lse.ac.uk/asp/aspecis/
5. Dominguez, C.: Competitive Advantages of Electronic Marketplaces in the Retail Automotive and Maintainance, Repair and Order (MRO) Industries. In: Newell, S., Whitley, E., Pouloudi, N., Wareham, J., Mathiassen, L. (eds.) Proceedings of the Seventeenth European Conference on Information Systems, Verona, Italy, June 8-10, pp. 2399–2419 (2009), http://is2.lse.ac.uk/asp/aspecis/
6. Economist, A market too far, Economist (May 15, 2004)

7. Forbes, Automotive (2004), http://www.forbes.com/bow/b2b/industry.jhtml?id=3 (Accessed February 17, 2010)
8. Grieger, M.: Electronic marketplaces: A literature review and a call for supply chain management research. European Journal of Operational Research 144(2), 280–294 (2003)
9. Guo, R., Xu, Y.: The adoption of internet-based business-to-business e-marketplaces among small and medium-sized enterprises in their international marketing practices. In: Ljungberg, J., Andersson, M. (eds.) Proceedings of the Fourteenth European Conference on Information Systems, Göteborg, Sweden, June 12-14, pp. 494–505 (2006), http://is2.lse.ac.uk/asp/aspecis/
10. Ho, D.T.Y., Jin, Y., Dwivedi, R.: Business Process Management: A Research Overview and Analysis. In: Proceedings of the Fifteenth Americas Conference on Information Systems. AIS Electronic Library, San Francisco, CA, USA, August 6-9, paper. 785 (2009)
11. Howard, M., Vidgen, R., Powell, P.: Automotive e-hubs: Exploring motivations and barriers to collaboration and interaction. Journal of Strategic Information Systems 15(1), 51–75 (2006)
12. Klueber, R., Leser, F., Kaltenmorgen, N.: Concept and Procedure for evaluating E-Markets. In: Strong, D., Straub, D., DeGross, J. (eds.) Proceedings of the Seventh Americas Conference on Information Systems, Boston, MA, USA, August 3-5, paper. 135. AIS Electronic Library (2001)
13. Malone, T.W., Yates, J., Benjamin, R.I.: The logic of electronic markets. Harvard Business Review 67(3), 166–172 (1989)
14. Malone, T.W., Yates, J., Benjamin, R.I.: Electronic markets and electronic hierarchies. Communications of the ACM 30(6), 484–497 (1987)
15. O'Reilly, P., Finnegan, P.: Exploring Electronic Marketplace Performance: The 3 Pillars. In: Proceedings of the Twenty Ninth International Conference on Information System, Paris, France, December 14-17, paper. 9. AIS Electronic Library (2008)
16. Palvia, P., Pinjani, P.: A profile of information systems research published in Information & Management. Information & Management 44(1), 1–11 (2007)
17. Peffers, K., Ya, T.: Identifying and evaluating the universe of outlets for information systems research: Ranking the journals. Journal of Information Technology Theory and Application 5(1), 63–84 (2003)
18. Rossignoli, C., Cordella, A., Mola, L.: E-marketplace and transaction cost theory: a possible set of new ideas. In: Ljungberg, J., Andersson, M. (eds.) Proceedings of the Fourteenth European Conference on Information Systems, Göteborg, Sweden, June 12-14, pp. 2039–2053 (2006), http://is2.lse.ac.uk/asp/aspecis/
19. Soh, C., Markus, M.L., Goh, K.H.: Electronic Marketplaces and Price Transparency: Strategy, Information Technology, and Success. MIS Quarterly 30(3), 705–723 (2006)
20. Son, J.Y., Benbasat, I.: Organizational Buyers' Adoption and Use of B2B Electronic Marketplaces: Efficiency-and Legitimacy-Oriented Perspectives. Journal of Management Information Systems 24(1), 55–99 (2007)

Appendix

Table 3. Overview of Articles (only articles available full-text where included in the analysis)

Year	Author(s)	Outlet	full-text
2009	Hsiao, Ou, Chen	ICIS	x
	Overby, Forman	ICIS	x
	Raventos, Zolezzi	ICIS	x
	Tan, Pan, Lu, Huang	ICIS	x
	Yang, Singhal, Xu	ICIS	x
	Gsell, Gomber	ECIS	x
	Dominguez	ECIS	x
	Dolpanya, Land, Dick	ECIS	x
	Bapna, Chang, Goes, Gupta	MISQ	x
	Adomavicius, Gupta, Zhdanov	ISR	x
	Ray, Wu, Konana	ISR	x
	Bichler, Shabalin, Pikovsky	ISR	x
	Rai, Brown, Xinlin	JMIS	x
	Xia, Xia	JMIS	x
	Bapna, Goes, Gupta	JMIS	x
	Karimi, Somers, Bhattacherjee	IJEC	x
	Johnson, Piccolotto, Filippini	IEEE ToEM	x
	Pardoe, Stone, Saar-Tsechansky, Keskin, Tomak	INFORMS JoC	x
2008	Guvence-Rodoper, Benbasat, Cenfetelli	ICIS	x
	O'Reilly, Finnegan	ICIS	x
	Adomavicius, Gupta, Sanyal	ICIS	x
	Benbasat, Dellarocas, Krishnan, Pavlou	ICIS	
	O'Reilly, Finnegan	ECIS	x
	Mola, Rossignoli, Carugati	ECIS	x
	Adam, Hagenau, Neumann, Weinhardt	ECIS	x
	Martinsons	ISJ	x
	Chang, Wang, Chiu	ISJ	x
	Dedrick, Xu, Zhu	JMIS	x
	Bolton, Loebbecke, Ockenfels	JMIS	x
	Bakos, Katsamakas	JMIS	x
	Lau, Wong, Li, Ma	JMIS	x
	Montazemi, Siam, Esfahanipour	JMIS	x
	Charki, Josserand	JMIS	x
	Iyer, D` Aubeterre, Singh	JAIS	x

Table 3. (*Continued*)

	Soares-Aguiar, Palma-dos-Reis	IEEE ToEM	x
	Bapna, Goes, Gupta, Karuga	INFORMS JoC	x
2007	Adomavicius, Sanyal, Gupta, Curley	ICIS	x
	Zhu, Zhou	ICIS	x
	Christ, Schroth, Janner	ECIS	x
	O`Reilly, Finnegan	ECIS	x
	Mishra, Konana, Barua	ISR	x
	Malhotra, Gosain, Sawy	ISR	
	Kim, Ahn	JIT	x
	Son, Benbasat	JMIS	x
	Grover, Saeed	JMIS	x
	Chi, Holsapple, Srinivasan	IJEC	x
	Standing, Lin	IJEC	x
	Lee, Chun, Shim, Lee	IJEC	x
	Ravichandran, Pant, Chatterjee	IEEE ToEM	x
	Wu, Zsidisin, Ross	IEEE ToEM	x
	Chari, Agrawal	INFORMS JoC	x
2006	Radkevitch, van Heck, Koppius	ICIS	x
	Rossignoli, Cordella, Mola	ECIS	x
	Guo, Xu	ECIS	x
	Nagle, Finnegan, Hayes	ECIS	x
	Soh, Markus, Goh	MISQ	x
	Nissen, Sengupta	MISQ	x
	Oh, Lucas	MISQ	
	Dellarocas	ISR	x
	Lee, Kwon	JMIS	x
	Kim, Umanath, Kim	JMIS	x
	Patnayakuni, Rai, Seth	JMIS	
	Jones, Easley, Koehler	JMIS	
	Huang, Lin, Yuan	IJEC	x
	Granados, Gupta, Kauffman	JAIS	x
	Khalifa, Davison	IEEE ToEM	x
	Teo, Ranganathan, Dhaliwal	IEEE ToEM	x
	Standing, Love, Stockdale, Gengatharen	IEEE ToEM	x
2005	Montano, Porter, Malaga, Ord	ICIS	x
	Fairchild, Finnegan, O'Reilly, Ribbers	ECIS	x
	Chiu, Poon, Lam, Tse, Sui, Poon	ECIS	x
	Ash	ECIS	x

Table 3. (*Continued*)

	Adomavicius, Gupta	ISR	x
	Dellarocas	ISR	x
	Bandyopadhyay, Barron, Chaturvedi	ISR	x
	Bunduchi	ISJ	x
	Galbreth, March, Scudder, Shor	JMIS	x
	Son, Narasimhan, Riggins	JMIS	x
	Gosain, Malhotra, ElSawy	JMIS	x
	Molla, Licker	IJEC	x
	Al-Naeem, Rabhi, Benatallah, Ray	IJEC	
	Fearon, Philip	JIT	
	Jones, Koehler	INFORMS JoC	x
	Travica	DATABASE	x

Proximal Business Intelligence on the Semantic Web

David Bell and Thinh Nguyen

Department of Information Systems and Computing (DISC),
Brunel University, UK
{David.bell,thinh.nguyen}@brunel.ac.uk

Abstract. Ubiquitous information systems (UBIS) extend current Information System thinking to explicitly differentiate technology between devices and software components with relation to people and process. Adapting business data and management information to support specific user actions in context is an on-going topic of research. Approaches typically focus on providing mechanisms to improve specific information access and transcoding but not on how the information can be accessed in a mobile, dynamic and ad-hoc manner. Although web ontology has been used to facilitate the loading of data warehouses, less research has been carried out on ontology based mobile reporting. This paper explores how business data can be modeled and accessed using the web ontology language and then re-used to provide the invisibility of pervasive access; uncovering more effective architectural models for adaptive information system strategies of this type. This exploratory work is guided in part by a vision of business intelligence that is highly distributed, mobile and fluid, adapting to sensory understanding of the underlying environment in which it operates. A proof-of-concept mobile and ambient data access architecture is developed in order to further test the viability of such an approach. The paper concludes with an ontology engineering framework for systems of this type – named UBIS-ONTO.

Keywords (Required): Pervasive Informatics, Business Intelligence, Semantic Web.

1 Introduction

The Ubiquitous computing (Ubicomp) goal of an enhanced computer that makes use of the many devices embedded within the physical environment - effectively invisible to the user - impacts all areas of computing, including hardware components, network protocols, interaction substrates (e.g. software for screens and haptic entry), applications, privacy, and computational methods (Weiser 1993). Since this vision, the Web has provided a platform for applications to outgrow the local machine (Penyala and Shim 2009) and provide a rich source of ubiquitous content (often invisible to the mobile user). Invisibility within the physical environment is a central theme in Ubicomp. John Seely Brown at PARC calls it the periphery (Weiser 1991). In order to decouple the information that we associate with our current applications and move it into the periphery, a means to transform the content and support the user in their current place is required. A number of opportunities and challenges need to be met if business systems (and business data) are to be made available in such environments.

M.L. Nelson et al. (Eds.): Sustainable e-Business Management, LNBIP 58, pp. 145–159, 2010.

A large numbers of devices (from mobile phones to ambient screens), variation in how information should be adapted and the large number of source systems combine to make architecting such system challenging. The cost of display technology is dropping and traditional posters and billboards are being replaced with digital displays (Schmidt 2009). Accessing enterprise data warehouses or enterprise system database back-ends has had little coverage in a pervasive computing context.

In contrast, “wireless sensor networks based on mobile devices will drive a wide range of new urban scale and eventually global-scale applications” (Cambell et al., 2008 pp. 12-21). Raman and Chebrolu (2008) identify a number of issues with regard to sensor network success though; arguing the superficial level at which problems are investigated is a limiting factor. Only by widening (and connecting) research at all levels from hardware design to information system strategy can substantial progress be made. Chen, Finin & Joshi (2003) identified weakness of traditional UBIS as: (1) limited support for knowledge sharing and context reasoning, (2) limited agreement between programs that wish to share data, (3) Software is typically modified in response to the dynamic nature of contextual information and the environments.

This paper presents an exploration into how commercial business data warehousing solutions can benefit from both sensor and semantic web technologies in order that business data can be both mobile and adaptive. The paper is structured as follows and opens with background material on commercial data warehouse approaches using SAP and introduces proximity sensors. A number of semantic web tools are then presented; followed by a description of a research plan that brings together business reporting, ontology and sensors. This is followed by more detailed description of the artifacts that resulted from the research – comprising two ontology, a Web service based architecture and performance measures – before the work is summarized.

2 Background

2.1 Business Data Meets Ubiquitous Architecture

Data warehousing allows organizations to organize and store a large amount of business data in a format that can be easily analyzed (Bose & Mahapatra, 2001); while data mining techniques use methods of artificial intelligence to facilitate the discovery of data patterns – relationships between underlying data. These components, coupled with visualization of information, user alerting events, are the basis of a new category of Business Intelligence (BI) tools. This research project utilizes the SAP Business Warehouse (BW) as a business data source and attempts to provide a novel data presentation approach based on proximity (to people, places and devices). In a contemporary business setting, business transactions result in a large amount of electronic data stored within information systems. Heterogeneous data (e.g. text, number, format, video, audio, etc.) created by various application systems needs to be extracted, transformed, loaded and consolidated into a form that can be analyzed. These functions – extraction, transformation, loading, consolidation - are applied by many warehouse technologies in order that data can be analyzed and stored using forms (Bose & Mahapatra, 2001). Constant flow of electronic transaction data can make the analytical process difficult (one reason for such external snapshots of transactional and other data). Data warehouses are designed

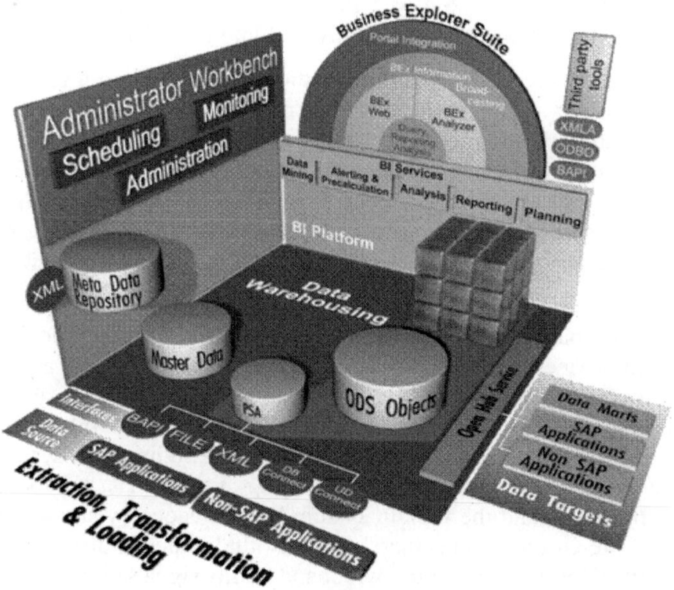

Fig. 1. SAP Business Warehousing (http://www.sap.com)

to provide query processing of integrated data views. Large amounts of data are brought together in data warehouses (from different sources) providing multi- dimensional views of the data.

Using SAP's toolset, end-users are able to create queries and aggregate related data in order to produce appropriate business reports. The Business Explorer's interface (based on an Excel add-on) allows SAP end users to create and save such reports. The popular SAP infrastructure (typical of many data warehousing systems) provides a number of data loading and reporting options – all reliant on successful data cleansing and importation. Exploring the decoupling of both information storage and presentation is at the heart of this paper – moving away from the centralized approaches and using context to filter data for presentation (to support decision making). A need for more timely data access using pervasive business intelligence has gained some recent interest (Watson and Wixom 2007).

In order to determine appropriate devices (mobile, ambient or other) for rendering business information, proximity measurement and response is required. Importantly, proximity not only determines the rendering device in view but is able to direct inferences on what specific business data is appropriate.

2.2 Scale of Proximity – Starting with RFID Technologies

An RFID tag is built with an antenna, a small silicon chip including a radio receiver, a radio modulator, control logic, memory and power system (Simson & Beth, 2006). The silicon chip is fundamentally an IC-based tag chip consisting of an integrated circuit (IC) with memory, essentially a microprocessor. There are various kinds of tags on the market. However, tags may be divided into three basic categories:

- Passive tags: powered by incoming radio frequency from a reader and with a range of a few centimetres to 9 meters. Active tags: powered by on-board battery and with a range of 30. "High end onboard capabilities can integrate analogue and digital interfaces to the outside world" (Stanford, 2003, p. 11).
- Semi-active tags (semi-passive tags): powered by on-board battery but using incoming radio signals for power. Reliability is improved (over passive tags) but still has the passive tags short reading range (Simson & Beth, 2006).

Variation in tag functionality provides some interesting possibilities for associating data of interest with particular scales of proximity. This is also applicable to a range of location based devices – Bluetooth, Wifi, GPS and others. Simon and Bath (2006) categorize such positioning systems as either: (1) Coarse-Grained systems such as Global positioning system (GPS), Assisted GPS, Wi-Fi, Bluetooth technology, and few other types of radio frequency infrastructures including RFID tag and RFID reader, Mobile phones (e.g. Cambridge Positioning systems has accuracy of location tracking up to 20 meters and the Rosum system has the accuracy about 3 meters to 25 meters) and (2) Fine-Grain systems that use ultrasound to detect distance from a tag to a dedicated point. Ubisense use ultra wideband radio signals for real time location system tracking system that can detect a target (tag) in a 15 centimeter range (Simson & Beth , 2006).

In order to make use of proximity measures in data provisioning, the source data must first be modeled in such a way that it can then be selected for subsequent presentation on the mobile or ambient devices present. Tools of the semantic web provide one approach to this problem - ontology and ontology query languages in particular – allowing relationships between business data, device capabilities and proximity to be modeled.

2.3 Semantic Web Tools

An ontology is "an explicit specification of a conceptualization" (Gruber 1995, pp. 1) and provide a formal description of concepts and their relationships within a domain. This result is a shared understanding and/or shared vocabulary for a domain of interest. The W3C Web Ontology (OWL) is itself based on XML using the RDF/XML specification. OWL provide more expressive power, extensibility, modifiability and interoperability (Mizoguchi, 2004). Constraints can be placed on property values, instances of classes and on classes themselves. For example, cardinality constraints, equivalence and reverse property functions. To support the semantic web in a distributed environment, OWL increases functionality for interoperability and scalability, allowing mapping (via Web URIs) between existing ontologies, importing existing ontology for reuse and interoperability (Chen, Finin & Joshi, 2003). Two projects are relevant to this research - CoBrA and SOUPA.

The CoBrA (Context Broker Architecture) system (Chen, Finin & Joshi, 2003) is a context-broker that detects context-aware devices or contexts in intelligent spaces. The system is able retrieve context-information from devices or environments. CoBrA-ONT is an ontology written in OWL and provides knowledge on contexts, agents and external sources. For example, a context broker in XCo detects a person's unique RFID number when entering Office Y. Policies on context privacy are included, which determine which contexts/data should be displayed at which locations. Ridhawi et al. (2008) created context policy ontology being used in the authors' own context-aware system.

Architectural bottlenecks limit each context broker to a specific geographical environment such as meeting rooms, laboratories, etc. In practice, Broker agents in CoBrA are "responsible for maintaining and aggregating a shared model for context information. The broker agent facilitates the distributed reasoning capabilities for service agents that make use of CoBrA by including a knowledge model and therefore removes the need to deal with the reasoning part for each service and application." (Ridhawi et al., 2008, p.559). SOUPA extends COBRA-ONT and reuses a number of existing ontologies: (1) FOAF for people, (2) DALM for Time, (3) OpenCyc and RCC for location, (4) COBRA-ONT for contexts, (5) MoGATU BDI for modeling the belief, desire, and intention of human users and software agents and (6) Rei Policy Ontology for access control rules Others have used ontology with data warehousing (Baumbach et al. 2006; Salguero et al. 2008), typically as a means to integrate data when uploading.

3 Research Approach

One question in ubiquitous business intelligence is how proximal and business data can be synthesized more effectively in a mobile setting – bringing together hardware devices and software/application data services. The research described in this paper initiates this process by exploring the use of semantic web middleware (the OWL language and SPARQL query engine), applications (SAP's Warehouse) and proximity knowledge. The research follows a design research approach, which is a search process to discover an effective solution to a problem (Hevner et al. 2004 p.88). The research process can be seen in Figure 2.

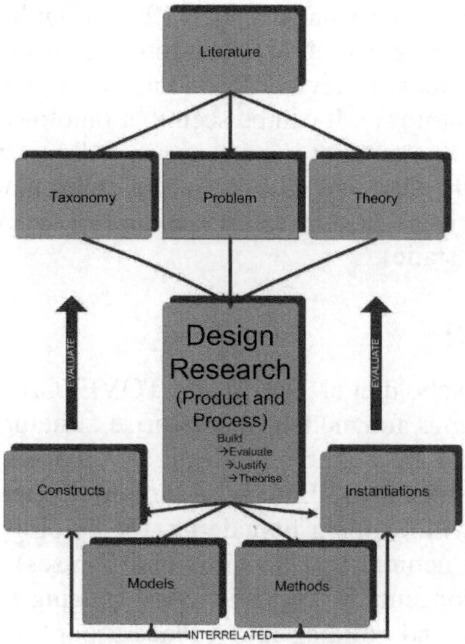

Fig. 2. Design research framework (terminology from March and Smith 1995)

The design research process presented in this paper, and depicted in the diagram above, is methodologically based on and adapted from the approach described by Nunamaker et al. (1991) and the guidelines presented by Hevner et al. (2004). The following sections address this problem of scalable business intelligence, confirming relevance of the problem being investigated, both in the architecture, ontology and software artifacts. The resulting artifacts are now presented. The starting point for the research is a number of reports that form part of the SAP training material on sales figures and the like. The data in these reports is used to develop a number of ontology and an associated querying mechanism.

4 Research Artefacts

4.1 Proximity Based BI Architecture

Figure 3 depicts our finalized UBIS reporting environment. The system comprises a domain ontology (deployed on the web server) that contains both business and proximity vocabulary. This ontology is then used to generate a number of BiGraphs (Business Intelligence graphs) – business instance data in the form of N3 triples (http://www.w3.org/2001/sw/RDFCore/ntriples/). Triples describe specific elements of business reporting data and relate the data to proximity objects. For example, describing a piece of data that is of interest to Salesman A when within proximity of Office B or City C. A tag in reading range will be read by an RFID reader passing the RFID tag's unique identification number to a host computer (a service named ProxiBI). A simple SPARQL processor on the host computer then chooses an appropriate SPARQL query in order to retrieve business data and render this on an LCD TV within view. A number of these processors are readily available on the Web already. In order to undertake the transcoding, the host computer uses references from a domain ontology document – BusinessStaticNTT.owl published on a web server - in order to understand reporting data in N3. The retrieved data can then be displayed on ambient screen or on a mobile device depending on user preference for this locale (again modeled in the ontology). It can be seen that ontology is at the heart of the system and its creation is of paramount importance in order to support the description of: 1) physical objects (both static and mobile) in the environment, 2) business data that is important to specific users or user categories and 3) the presentation form on specific devices (mobile or static).

4.2 Ontology Topology

Enterprise Ontology (Uschold et al., 1998) and TOVE (Gruninger and Fox, 1995) are well-known methodologies for modeling enterprise structures. Although their ontology specification outputs are quite similar, the development processes are different. There are a number of steps in the Enterprise Ontology approach defined by Uschold et al. (1998), starting with scoping boundaries for ontology. Brainstorming follows (typically from an unstructured list of words and phrases). Categorization is next – elaborating identified concepts to find relations - placing them into groups or work areas (i.e. parking space and building into a Place group). Elaborating on concepts in each group and arranging them in priority order is then possible (helping to discard or

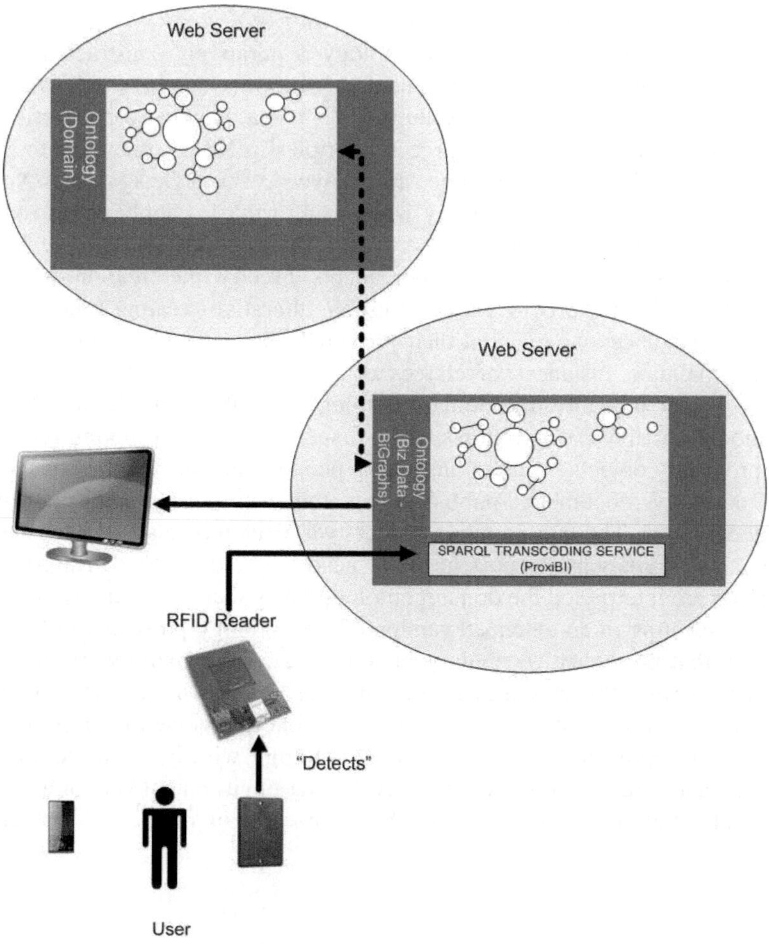

Fig. 3. High Level Architecture

move irrelevant ones to other groups). Each group is then analyzed, defining a term for each concept in a group with concepts being renamed in order that they can be understood more easily by users who will use them as context information for the domain. For example, AtomicPlaceNotInBuilding terms are created to group ParkingSpace and Garden. Building and zone are assigned to the newly created term called CompoundPlace. Terms are then refined in the group by deleting existing ones or adding new terms if necessary - adding definition to each term. The definition is not analogous to the definition of a word in the dictionary but must describe its own meaning and relations with other terms (Uschold et al., 1998). To capture/define precise term definitions, Uschold et al. (1998) identified building blocks such as Entity – class or instance of class - , Relationship – predicate - , and State of Affair. The purpose is to identify types of terms and assign them accordingly. This process was used as an input method for this research.

The Protege-OWL editor supports working with RDF and OWL and was used at the outset of this project. The domain ontology is iteratively constructed using Protégé. In contrast, the graphical environment is somewhat cumbersome when dealing with business instance data. Turtle/Notation 3 (N3) – a quick way of describing RDF triples – is used for this part of the process. Triples in N3 are then able to reference the domain ontology. Berners-Lee (http://www.w3.org/DesignIssues/Notation3) mentions the advantages of readability when using triples – applying also to derivative works such as Turtle (http://www.w3.org/TeamSubmission/turtle/). Instead of creating instances of classes in OWL documents directly, the creation of Notation 3 (N3) files (i.e. SAP.n3) provides a more usable alterative creating statements representing these instances – e.g. about their proximal relevance. Users are able to easily create and maintain instances of classes using vocabulary described in the OWL document. Understandably, the domain ontology in OWL must be developed first. The methodology above was followed with a specific focus on linking reporting objects to proximity objects – places, distances, people etc. The result of this work is a domain ontology document, published on the web server and named BusinessStaticNTT.owl. The interpretation process was driven by a set of business reports – systematically analyzing report headers, headings and data. Unsurprisingly, as more reports are interpreted the domain ontology takes shape. Seven test reports were interpreted resulting in an extended version of the ontology presented in Figure 4. It can be seen that proximity vocabulary such as place and proximity are included (including subclasses with respect to an example business environment). Although the domain ontology was created, this process would likely involve the re-use of existing ontology where applicable. Creating a new ontology with both business and proximity vocabulary enables a more controlled testing environment (i.e. in a production environment, future reviews would then harmonize the ontology with golden source ontology).

Fig. 4. Domain Ontology Example (after 1st Report Interpretation Pass)

The next step in the process is the production of a BiGraph – RDF ontology in N3 that contains report instance data. The example below (Figure 5) presents a small part of the N3 store created using the OWL domain ontology syntax and terms. Creating N3 files was an easier process with a vocabulary already defined and although undertaken manually can easily be automated from source documents. The storage of business data in N3 also opens a number of opportunities for distributing data over the network with placement directed by the query service, source system or available host. While building the N3 document (and relating business data to object proximity) it became apparent that rules can be formulated and placed within the domain ontology. Future work on automating this process is envisaged. Examples of such rules were groupings of specific data elements and patterns of use related to specific locations.

```
@prefix sapd:    <http://......./BusinessStaticNTT.owl#> .
@prefix ns:      <http://example.org/ns#> .
@prefix :        <http://example.org/services/> .

:Report1
  sapd:Document     "SaleOrgFulfilmentRate_FrankfurtOrg" ;
  sapd:Place        "St.John building" ;
  sapd:Proximity    sapd:YellowZone ;
  sapd:Interest     sapd:SalesRoles
  sapd:BusData1     1234
  sapd:BusData2     "abcd"
......
```

Fig. 5. Sample N3 document created - referencing OWL domain ontology (sapd)

The N3 document contains the following:

1. @prefix : is used to declare namespaces (URIs).
2. sapd : is attribute name – prefix namespace – referring to the namespace for the domain ontology - BusinessStaticNTT.owl.
3. The "#" at the end of the namespace is a symbol to link namespace and entity in the document. If it is not included in the namespace, it should be included inside document. For example, in this case, sapd:Document should be rewritten as sapd:#Document.
4. sapd:Document refers to " http://...../BusinessStaticNTT.owl#Document".

In summary, the N3 file can be seen as simple triple stores. Most semantic query languages are compatible and support N3, and are able to process (i.e. retrieve, remove, edit, etc.) data in triple store appropriately. The ARQ query engine for Jena written in Java is used to experiment with the ontology (as the Jena SPARQL libraries are embedded within a web based data access service - Proxibi). It allows users to create standard SPARQL which facilitates query processing of RDF triples. Basically, SPARQL defines pattern matching statements for interrogation of N3 and OWL documents and retrieves appropriate data. The purpose of this proof of concept is to test the efficiency of using ontology in a simple UBIS for intelligent data provisioning.

```
PREFIX sapd: <http://........./BusinessStaticNTT.owl#>
SELECT ?Document ?calendarYearMonth ?openOrderQuantity ?incomingOrderQuantity
?fulfilmentRateQuantityOnPercentage
FROM <SAP.n3>
WHERE
{
        ?loc  sapd:Document       ?Document .
        ?loc  sapd:Organization   ?Organisation .
        ?loc  sapd:Organization   "Frankfurt" .
        ?loc  sapd:Document   "SaleOrgFulfilmentRate_FrankfurtOrg".
        ?loc  sapd:calendarYearMonth       ?calendarYearMonth .
        ?loc  sapd:openOrderQuantity       ?openOrderQuantity .
        ?loc  sapd:incomingOrderQuantity  ?incomingOrderQuantity .
        ?loc  sapd:fulfilmentRateQuantityOnPercentage?  fulfilmentRateQuantityOnPercentage.
   }
```

Fig. 6. Test SPARQL query

Document	calendarYearMonth	openOrderQuantity	incomingOrderQuantity	fulfilmentRateQuantityOnPercentage
"SaleOrgFulfilmentRate_FrankfurtOrg"	"01.2003 to 12.2003"	"637.500 MIX"	"17.110.000 MIX"	"96% MIX"

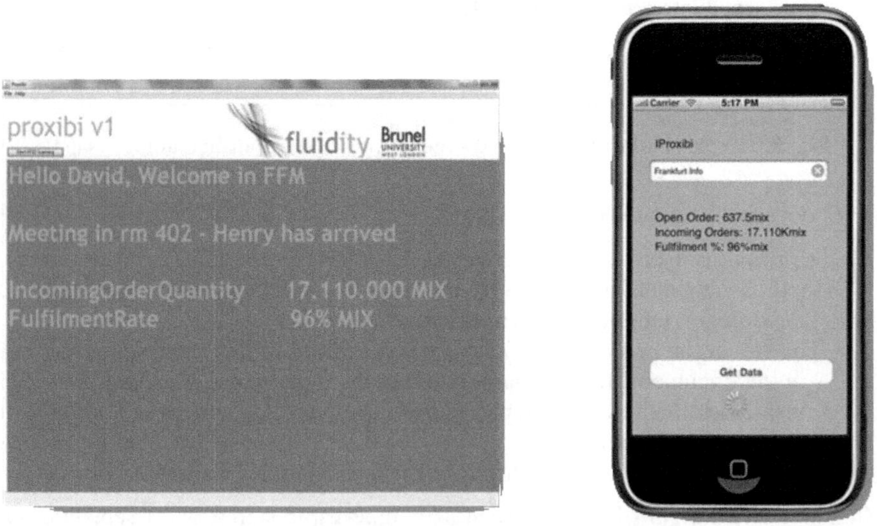

Fig. 7. Test output from the SPARQL query and service (test environment, ambient and mobile)

Therefore, the motivating use cases are made up for testing only and the proposed scenarios are used to demonstrate how part of the developed system will operate rather than focusing too much on developing the whole application system.

Three scenarios were used for experimentation in this project:

- Scenario 1: A user enters a building ("St Johns") reception and some available reporting (BiGraphs) should be displayed (i.e. reports of interest to the user).
- Scenario 2: Two users (a Salesman and Client) are standing next to each other. The system should infer a meeting and provide appropriate documents for their discussion.
- Scenario 3: A salesman ("Salesman1") is attending a meeting in Frankfurt and he would like to view data related to sale fulfilment for the Frankfurt Organisation.

Queries are created for each of the above scenarios and stored under the names sap1.q, sap2.q and sap3.q respectively. The queries are subsequently tested using reporting data stored in N3 documents of various sizes (replicating existing triples for performance analysis). This testing will show whether the retrieved data is actually extracted from defined SPARQL queries and if they conform to the users' requirements and more importantly whether the performance of such a system is adequate.

The query used for Scenario 3 (sap3.q) is shown below in Figure 6:

The query has some similarity to SQL with select/from/where terms. The interesting aspects of the query are that the files (domain ontology and InfoGraph) are on the Web – and can be placed anywhere. The resulting output of the query is able to be rendered on a number of devices (simple ambient and mobile output in the case of this research). An example of the output can be seen in Figure 7. The choice of device used is based on proximity detection (altering the query in some cases).

4.3 Performance Analysis

Three scenarios (three queries) are executed (see Table 1 and Figure 8) - each query is executed ten times for each of the N3 files listed below (mean timings being reported). The results are encouraging with adequate performance when running even with 20,000 triples (detailing 7000 BiGraphs). Obviously, the underlying network speed is a large dependency here and the figures presented are taken from a campus network, local N3 store and internet sourced domain ontology.

Although the performance results are encouraging, the process by which the artifacts came about is of equal or more interest. This process is presented as an UBIS ONTO framework – presenting both a list of concerns and steps to engineer the ontology. The interplay between the domain ontology, N3 Business instance data and the queries – namely where and when knowledge and rules are created, extended and stabilize – is apparent as each artifact was developed and subsequently integrated.

Table 1. N3 Input file sizes

DataSet Name	Document	Lines	Description	Query time
Small size	7	95	N3 list of 7 document	2.278 seconds
Medium size	70	244	10 times of N3 list (document name changed)	2.409 seconds
Large size	700	1452	100 times of N3 list (document name changed)	2.786 seconds
Extra large size	7000	24004	1000 times of N3 list (document name changed)	5.246 seconds

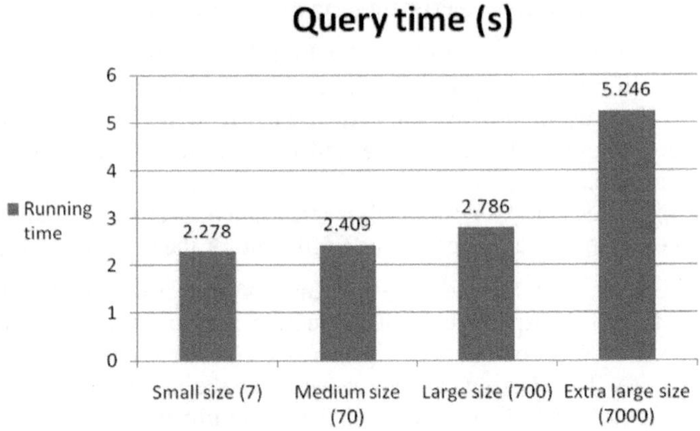

Fig. 8. SPARQL Query execution time

5 UBIS ONTO Framework

Reflecting on the process that unfolded while developing the presented artifacts, a number of areas required analysis and subsequent decision making (see Figure 9). The starting point is the source documents/data sources that underpin current business reporting functionalities. It is this data, coupled with user requirements/scenarios, that

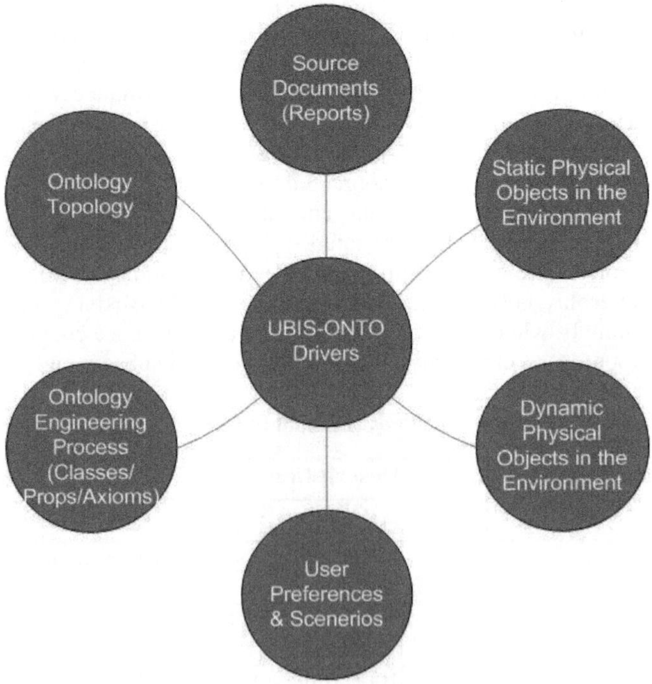

Fig. 9. UBIS-ONTO Evolution drivers

is able to direct initial domain ontology production. Once initial domain ontology has been created, a number of activities come into play in order to extend the ontology with necessary detail – taking into account the objects residing in the environment and the target ontology topology (placement of domain and triple based ontology over the network). In addition, user preferences and scenarios (how the user interacts with the system) direct ontology re-organization over time. It should be noted that personal data privacy and security are not within the scope of this paper.

5.1 Recommendations for Engineering

Based on the resulting research artifacts and the process by which they were developed, a number of steps are presented summarizing the UBIS-ONTO process (Table 2). The process includes many of the steps identified by Uschold et al. (1998), but extends traditional methodologies with the addition of two key steps: (a) detailed interpretation and integration within the ontology of proximity objects and measures and (b) a harmonizing process that re-organizes ontology and queries based on their use. The work also addresses weaknesses identified by Chen, Finin and Joshi (2003)

Table 2. Ontology Engineering Steps (UBIS-ONTO)

	UBIS-ONTO STEPS
1	Source documents are interpreted – extracting classes and properties from structural labels (headers, headings etc.)
2	Review and organize interpretation of the domain - with output into an OWL ontology. Identification, organization, re-naming, re-categorization of classes and properties.
3	Add additional detail to classes and properties. Detail in this case is driven by projected future query requirements.
4	Analyse the physical environment and identify objects (static and dynamic) of interest.
5	Transform instance data in N3 triples (automated where possible). Transforming current reporting data into a single or network of triple files/stores.
6	Extend triple document/store with proximity definitions – with interest in particular concepts when “near” to identified objects. This will include the definition of “near” with respect the objects in question.
7	Develop SPARQL queries (and support presentation adaptors) to support identified user scenarios.
8	Harmonize ontologies and queries in use – moving indentified groupings and/or patterns into the domain ontology.

through the use of commodity semantic web technology and by: (1) adopting OWL and N3 as an easy to use knowledge representations platform supporting data sharing and 2) a focus on the ontology (as opposed to software) in order to better support the dynamic nature of contextual information and the environments (i.e. less if any impact on software systems). The ability to distribute business data across the network (in separate N3 stores) is also better able to support transactional flow – placing aggregate data in separate stores and more dynamic content nearer to source if hosting options are available. Ontology centered approaches also provide a level of independence from hardware and software – a more general advantage highlighted by Pendyala and Shim (2009).

6 Conclusion

The paper presents a novel approach to mobile business data reporting that interweaves proximity sensors, business data warehousing and semantic web tools. The resulting system and methodology is relatively light weight allowing business data to be stored over the network and displayed when and where most appropriate to the user (radically different from current approaches that rely on centralized data cleansing, loading and storage). The paper focuses on how ontology tools can be used to realize a UBIS business intelligence vision – virtually integrating business data on the Web for presentation on mobile or ambient devices. The practical work includes experimentation that emphasizes the viability of the approach in terms of performance. The research itself is exploratory in nature and much is left to investigate. One key area for the future is testing the approach in a real-world business environments (moving beyond the SAP test data being utilized here), and investigating the evolution of ontological artifacts (including queries) over time.

References

1. Baumbach, J., Brinkrolf, K., Czaja, L.F., Rahmann, S., Tauch, A.: CoryneRegNet: An ontology-based data warehouse of corynebacterial transcription factors and regulatory networks. BMC Genomics 7(24) (2006)
2. Bose, I., Mahapatra, R.: Business Data Mining – A Machine Learning Perspective. Information & Management 39, 211–225 (2001)
3. Campbell, A.T., Eisenman, S.B., Lane, N.D., Miluzzo, E., Peterson, R.A., Lu, H., Zheng, X., Musolesi, M., Fodor, K., Ahn, G.: The Rise of People-Centric Sensing. IEEE Internet Computing 12(4), 12–21 (2008), doi:10.1109/MIC.2008.90
4. Chen, H., Finin, T., Jishi, A.: Using OWL in a Pervasive Computing Broker. In: Proceedings of Workshop on Ontologies in Open Agent Systems, AAMAS 2003 (2003)
5. Chen, H., Perich, F., Finin, T., Joshi, A.: SOUPA: Standard Ontology for Ubiquitous and Pervasive Applications. In: Int. Conf. on Mobile and Ubiquitous Systems: Networking and Services (August 2004)
6. Daniel, H., Albert, P., Mike, P.: RFID, A Guide To Radio Frequency Identification. Wiley, USA (2007)
7. Gruber, T.R.: Toward Principles for the Design of Ontologies Used for Knowledge Sharing. International Journal of Human and Computer Studies 43(5/6), 907–928 (1995)

8. Gruninger, M., Fox, M.: Methodology for the design and evaluation of ontologies. In: Proceedings of the Workshop on Basic Ontological Issues in Knowledge Sharing held in Conjunction with IJCAI 1995, Montreal, Canada (1995)
9. Hevner, A., March, S., Park, J., Ram, S.: Design Science in Information Systems Research. MIS Quarterly 28(1) (2004)
10. Mizoguchi, R.: Tutorial on Ontologial Engineering Part 2: Ontology Development, Tools and Languages. New Generation Computing 22, 61–96 (2004)
11. Nunamaker, J., Chen, M., Purdin, T.: System Development in Information Systems Research. Journal of Management Information Systems 7(3), 89–106 (1991)
12. Pendyala, V.S., Shim, S.S.Y.: The Web as the Ubiquitous Computer. Computer 42(9) (2009)
13. Raman, B., Chebrolu, K.: Censor networks: a critique of "sensor networks" from a systems perspective. SIGCOMM Comput. Commun. Rev. 38(3), 75–78 (2008)
14. Ridhawi, Y., Harroud, H., Karmouch, A., Agoulmine, N.: Policy Driven Context-Aware Services in Mobile Enviroments. Innovation in Information Technology, 558–562 (2008)
15. Salguero, A., Araque, F., Delgado, C.: Ontology based framework for data integration. WSEAS Trans. Info. Sci. and App. 5(6), 953–962 (2008)
16. Simson, G., Beth, R. (eds.): RFID Applications, Security, and Privacy. Addison Wesley, United States (2006)
17. Schmidt, A.: Ubiquitous Computing: Are we there yet? Computer 43(2) (2010)
18. Stanford, V.: Pervasive computing goes the last hundred feet with RFID systems. Pervasive Computing 2(2), 9–14 (2003)
19. Uschold, M., King, M., Moralee, S., Zorgios, Y.: The Knowledge Engineering Review 13, 31–89 (1998)
20. Weiser, M.: Hot topics-ubiquitous computing. Computer 26(10), 71–72 (1993)
21. Weiser, M.: The Computer for the 21th Century. Scientific American 265(3), 94–101 (1991)

Disintermediation in the Tourism Industry: Theory vs. Practice

Laddawan Kaewkitipong

Faculty of Commerce and Accountancy
Thammasat University
lad_k@hotmail.com

Abstract. It has been several decades since disintermediation was first known (although under other terms), and it seems that disintermediation has become increasingly intense, particularly in the tourism industry where many large hotels and airlines have successfully utilized the Internet and website as a direct channel to sell to their customers. This paper examines disintermediation issues and situation and argues that in practice disintermediation, despite becoming increasingly intense, it will just require travel agents to acclimatize rather than to be removed from the tourism value chain. The review of both academic literature and practical survey research shows that effect of disintermediation on Thai tourism SMEs might not be as extreme as it has been on European tourism SMEs in the near future. Three in-depth case studies of Thai tourism SMEs are summarized and presented to show how travel agents act to respond to the disintermediation. The cases highlight the need for more study on customer behaviors which are likely to vary depending upon region and many other factors. Ultimately, this paper calls for future research on customer behaviors and strategic alignment for tourism SMEs.

Keywords: Disintermediation, Reintermediation, Internet adoption, Tourism.

1 Introduction

The research reported here is part of a larger research programme studying the use of e-business technologies by Thai SMEs in the travel service sector. Since the tourism industry contributes significantly to the Thai economy, a thorough understanding of the industry's supply chain and the effect of e-business adoption on tourism enterprises is especially important in this Internet era. The Internet has opened up new opportunities for all players in the industry to present themselves, offer their products online, and improve many of their business activities. As several large tourism suppliers have begun utilizing the Internet as a direct selling channel, the competition between suppliers and travel agencies is thus inevitably increased. Hence, it is important to contemplate how travel agents should respond to this threatening situation. The travel agents have to be better able in offering distinctive value to their customers, based on a well-defined and robust business model. Of primary interest in this paper is disintermediation in both global and local (Thailand) contexts. This is of significance in two ways. Firstly, since large numbers of small and medium-sized travel agents are active in this industry, the disintermediation effect could be vast, and hence making this issues worth

M.L. Nelson et al. (Eds.): Sustainable e-Business Management, LNBIP 58, pp. 160–171, 2010.

further examination. Secondly, prior research on Thai tourism industry, albeit being one of the most important industries for the country's economy, is limited.

Extensive review of literature on disintermediation and three in-depth case studies provide a basis for this paper. The paper is structured into 4 parts. The first part starts with a consideration of the stakeholders in the tourism supply chain. There are considerable tensions here as companies of very different sizes are required to both compete and collaborate. Part two reviews literature on disintermediation issues both in general e-business literature and in tourism industry literature. Part three discusses the disintermediation situation facing the three selected Thai tourism SMEs and how they attempted to survive the crisis. Due to limited space and word length as well as the fact that interpretive case based research has become has become a well-established part of the IS filed (Walsham, 2006), detailed discussion concerning the selection of case based methodology in which adopted for this research is omitted. Finally, part four discusses and summarizes the research findings, implications, and future research.

2 Tourism Stakeholders and Supply Chain

Of particular interest to this paper is the combined sector of travel and accommodation, which is heavily ICT dependent (Buhalis and Licata, 2002). This sector, also known as the travel service sector, has a similar structure to conventional retail/wholesale businesses. It comprises a number of stakeholders, including suppliers, intermediaries such as tour operators, travel agencies, and customers or travelers. Final products of this industry are usually made up of more than one product or service e.g. a hotel room, a flight ticket, and a tourism activity package, and therefore effectiveness and efficiency of each stakeholder seem to affect the others (Yilmaz and Bititci, 2006). The whole tourism value chain can be illustrated as shown in Figure 1.

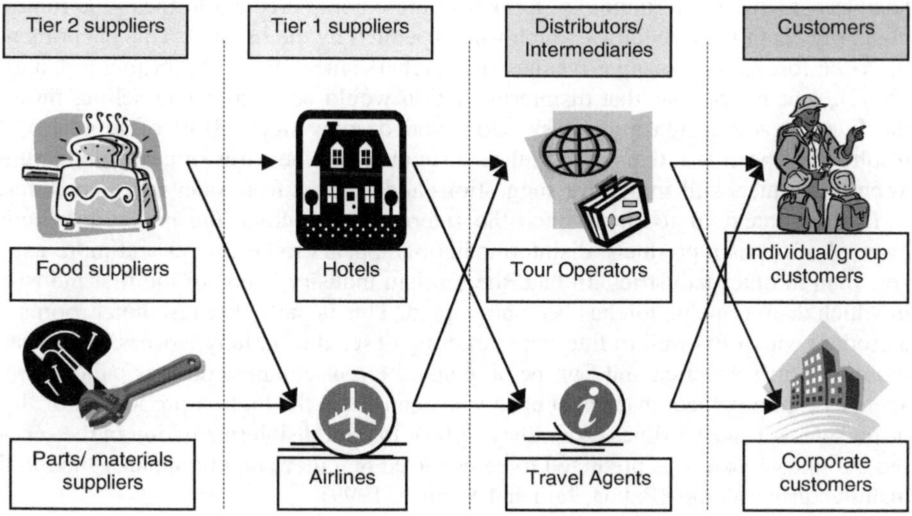

Fig. 1. Tourism Value Chain

According to Lafferty and Fossen (2001), integration among players in the tourism industry, particularly in the upstream part of the value chain is critical, but this appeared problematic mainly because of substantial differences in nature of airlines and hotels businesses. The airline sector is characterized by a strong sense of international competition, while hotels and restaurants are more location-based business and have no need to compete with hotels in other areas. Major concern of hotels is yield maximization, but they, unlike airlines, can survive low occupancy in some periods. These conflicts thus made the integration difficult and unsuccessful.

Another problematic area is between suppliers and travel agents/tour operators. Whilst the former attempts to cut distribution costs, the latter wants to obtain as highest margin as possible from the distribution services they provided. Nevertheless, since tourism product is intangibility, perishability, inseparability and interdependency (Yilmaz and Bititci, 2006); suppliers like hotels and airlines will still need to diversify their risk through a number of distribution channels rather than relying only on their own website. Despite the conflicts, Yilmaz and Bititci suggested that various tourism organizations need to work together as a value chain to add value and deliver product/service to the customers.

Overall, it is not surprising that stakeholders in the industry have some conflicts of interest. Hotels and airlines rely somewhat on travel agents as distributors; however at the same time they also seek to cut the intermediary costs as much as possible. The important point is that these conflicts in the long term could erode the relationship between the suppliers and the intermediaries and could eventually in the worst case disintermediate the intermediaries. Next section reviews the issues of disintermediation both in theory and in practice.

3 Disintermediation in Literature

Disintermediation is terminology termed in the e-commerce era to mean the removal of supply chain intermediaries which was expedited by the Internet. This phenomenon has been foreseen by many e-business researchers since 1990s. According to Chaffey (2002), speculation was that disintermediation would occur as direct selling through the Internet was increasingly easy. However, despite much effort of suppliers, the results have been less than spectacular, particularly in the cases of car manufacturers as end customers still sought for suggestions and services from sales representatives.

In the context of tourism, since the Internet has become the major distribution channel of tourism products, disintermediation appears to be clearer and more extensive than in other industries. In fact, the tourism industry is one of the first industries in which disintermediation has been attempted. This is partly because hotel rooms are a product which fits well to Internet marketing (Tse, 2003).Many airlines, particularly those in North America and Europe, attempted to cut commission fees paid to travel agents, despite the fact that travel agents has generated the highest proportion of flight ticket sales for most airlines (Alamdari, 2002). In fact, disintermediation in the service sectors like tourism was predicted to be occurred in a more rapidly manner than in the manufacturing sectors (Palvia, Jain and Vemuri, 1999).

Nevertheless, the views concerning disintermediation in the tourism industry have been mixed. Although the tourism suppliers have attempted to disintermediate the intermediaries by developing their own online channels to sell directly to the ended customers, travel agents, enabled by the Internet, can also reintermediate themselves back into the tourism supply chain mainly through the model of infomediary or aggregator. Clearly speaking, these travel agents specialize in the business of information, not of products. They search, aggregate, organize and sort information of various special travel deals offered by suppliers for online travelers (Beirne, 2005). Hence, disintermediation seemed to be overrated as many intermediaries have found their ways to fit into the supply chain and able to add values to their services (Rosenbloom, 2007).

From the supplier perspective, cutting intermediary costs is a desirable goal, but hotels usually have less expertise in distributing their products/services than travel agents or tour operators. Nevertheless, in the Internet era, small hotels can avoid the set-up costs of online booking development by adopting larger travel agents' website, whose online booking features are readily available (Brown and Kaewkitipong, 2009; Earl and Mandeville, 2009). Having their hotels listed on travel agents' sites is considered a good opportunity for them to be found by travelers worldwide. Besides, this allows hotels to cut web maintenance costs and the cost of transaction handling. On the airlines' side, effective and efficient distribution of their products is crucial because, as mentioned above, with their high operational costs they cannot cope with the low number of bookings as hotels can (Lafferty and fossen, 2001). Nevertheless, airlines have sufficient resources to develop their own channels and offer added values such as loyalty reward program for their customers and therefore can be less dependent on travel agents in terms of product/service distribution.

From the intermediary (travel agents and tour operators) perspective, while the Internet allowed suppliers to contact directly to travel consumers more easily than ever, many online travel agents also realized that they could add tremendous values to the travel consumers by providing all the information the consumers may need in one place. According to Buhalis and Law (2008), e-business technologies allow the travel agents to add further value to their services by empowering the customers to not only search and book single components, but also to assemble and book whole travel arrangements in real-time by means of web-based technologies. Agrawal, Agrawal and Singh (2006) suggested infomediary as an appropriate business model for non-physical products like flight and hotel reservation which requires marketing value added into the product distribution. Nevertheless, despite many alternatives to add values to their services, online travel agents are still facing challenges posed by suppliers' move to online. Many online travel agent sites have been used merely as price-comparison sites, and then the customers jumped to suppliers' sites for direct purchase (Euromonitor, 2008).

In practice, EyeforTravel research (2007) found that European suppliers are advancing their online strategies and are changing the landscape of the online travel marketplace. The research forecasted that by the end of 2010, online travel agents will be accounted for approximately 29% of Internet bookings declining from 31% share in 2006. On the bright side however, the European market saw an increase in online bookings in package tours growing from just € 1.4 billion in 2002 to be € 5.9 billion in 2006. Also in the hotel sector online travel agents were able to increase the market share and this trend tended to continue. This was because in Europe, unlike in the US, 80% of hotels were small or medium sized and did not possess a strong brand, and hence online travel agents' views would play a significant role in influencing the customers' perception towards particular hotels. This means that despite a harsh situation of disintermediation, there are gaps for online travel agents in this fragmented market. This is also held true in the context of Thai tourism industry where small hotels accounted for approximately 87.6% (NSO, 2004).

In sum, we can see that the Internet acts as both a blessing and a challenge for many stakeholders in this industry. Although the Internet allows the travel agents to provide a more informed service to their customers, at the same time it empowers the travelers and suppliers to directly contact each other and hence can disintermediate the intermediaries like travel agents. The huge number of online travelers also encourages hotels as well as other suppliers, such as airlines, to reconsider the adoptions of the e-business technologies not as an extra cost but as a strategic investment (Buhalis and Licata, 2002). Consequently, as the searching and buying transactions are made easier, and travelers become more computer literate, it may well be that the travel agencies' power on the distribution channels will be diminished gradually unless they can offer value added advice, such as travel advice which satisfies the customer needs (Lewis, Semeijn, and Talalayevsky, 1998; Bennett and Lai, 2005). Such a situation is also discerned in the survey of European online travel market, conducted by Eyefortravel in 2007 that revenue generated by online travel agents is eroded by the more online-aggressive suppliers.

From the traveler perspective, buying direct from hotels or buying from intermediaries are choices influenced by several factors. Different groups of online buyers have significantly different views towards and against disintermediation of hotel reservation. For example, those who are frequent buyers showed a more positive view towards online booking of hotel rooms and a less positive view about the service provided by travel agents than both occasional and moderate buyers (Law, 2009). Travel style, age, and nationality were found to be factors influencing buyers' preference to contact face to face with travel agent to obtain tourism information (Gronflaten, 2009). These different views and groups of online buyers spare rooms for intermediaries to remain in the supply chain. In Thailand the majority of transactions were made via traditional travel retailers with online sales representing less than 2% of total sales in 2006. It was also reported that inbound travelers generated the most online sales in this category, as European and American travelers, the majority of tourists who visited Thailand, tended to be more familiar with online booking methods (Euromonitor, 2008). This highlights the different booking behaviors between Thai travelers and European and American travelers and adds to the points made by Law (2009) that consumers' behaviors might differ due to physical regions. A better understanding of these behaviors, apart from specialization and focus, will be important for the survival of travel agents.

4 Disintermediation in the Context of Thai Tourism SMES

In the context of Thailand, Brown and Kaewkitipong (2009) reported that small and medium-sized hotels have begun adopting their own website as a direct selling channel and this created tension for travel agents, particularly small and medium sized. In this paper the three in-depth case studies (TA I, TA II and TA III) are presented as examples of attempts and different approaches to survive the disintermediation. This has been done in three possible ways: i) through the better integration and closed relationship with hotels; ii) through the introduction of management fees philosophy; and iii) through the value-added services such as insightful advices on complex itineraries (Alamdari, 2002). Additionally, tourism SMEs could benefit from the low operation costs due to their smaller size and therefore can continue their businesses even on the low margins. Case study method is deemed appropriate since it is the individuality, complexity and context-based issues that are of particular interest to this research (Starbuck, 1995; Yin, 2004).

TA I was an online medium-sized travel agent focusing on selling hotel rooms for travelers who would like to visit Thailand. The company had developed a web-based application to facilitate activities throughout the supply chain, including supplier management, production/operation, sales and marketing support, and customer relation. Intensive use was on dealing with bookings and queries. The incoming bookings and queries were stored in an online database which can be tracked and viewed by a reservation team. Products' information, such as room types, room rates, list of hotels, and attractions of each place, was also stored on the database, enabling various websites (of the company) to retrieve these data for displaying purpose. Importantly, the application is also used to manage the inventory on the database.

For customer relationship marketing, the company's websites keep track repeated actions such as the top-search hotels, the top-selling hotels, and returning customers. These data were statistically analyzed so that the marketing team can then create newsletters or even offer promotions which were of particular interest to the customers. Despite these efforts, the company found the situation had become more difficult in terms of both competition among travel agents and relationship management with suppliers. This was due to the move of hotels to direct sales to travelers, making price even more sensitive. It became more difficult for TA I to sustain the equal amount of revenue to that of the previous year.

> "The other day one of my friends just called me to complain about the room rate on my website that it was higher than what he found on the hotel's website. The worst thing was that it was the hotel we had a contract with and thus they were not supposed to do this." (The Managing Director)

> "The problem was not direct sales of hotels on their website. It was when they offered even cheaper price than they gave us." (A Marketing Manager)

In response to the increasingly high competition, the management decided to develop a Travel Agent extranet system to link with hotels and an XML interface to link with a wholesale travel agent. The systems were perceived as a means to obtain more room allotments and access to a wider choice of hotels (through the wholesaler); they were part of a business strategy to improve the supply chain. The Travel Agent extranet system enabled the hotel to log on and manage its allotments and room rates whenever needed without having to call or fax to several agents when the rates and inventories were changed. This was more flexible and convenient for hotels given that their rooms are perishable products and prices are varied due to demands.

After the implementation of the Travel Agent extranet system, around 60% of hotels which had contracts with TA I moved to the extranet system as they were pleased with the flexibility offered by the system. In this way, room rates offered on TA I's site became more competitive and up-to-date. Besides, less staff was needed to input room rates and hotels' information. Results were clearly positive. Well over 50% of bookings were from allotments allocated through the Travel Agent extranet system; this helped TA I maintain a good relationship with its suppliers in a sense that the company could help the suppliers sell and distribute their products more efficiently and effectively.

TA II was a small-sized travel agent focusing primarily on selling flight tickets to corporate customers. The company was established in mid-2003, the period in which tourism industry was facing a downturn. The competition in the flight ticketing business was commonly high, and the margin which could be marked up per ticket was quite low. This was because the market was fragmented, shared by a large number of travel agencies. Consequently, the company had to obtain a large volume of tickets in order to create sufficient revenue and satisfactory profits. Strategically, the company chose to compete with its competitors by offering quality of service and building a close relationship with customers rather than by offering lower prices. For corporate customers, although low cost was important, convenience, reliable, helpful advice, and well-rounded services was more important since corporate customers usually have no or little knowledge about the destination they need to travel to. Besides, they usually had limited time to arrange their trips. Therefore, for customers' convenience, the company developed a website which provided an online request form for flight booking and basic information about flights and airlines. Another important value added that the company offered to its customers was a monthly report summarizing money that a corporate spent in a certain month and detailing costs of each trip. This service, albeit provided with an extra fee, was popular among many corporate customers.

> "We provided a monthly report for our customers on an agreed format. This service was actually the value added we offered to our customer. ... Many customers liked it a lot, and they did not mention anything about the service fees, so I assumed I offered the right service which my customers really needed" (The owner-manager)

Nevertheless, despite the management report service, the company found itself needed to expand their products/services to be able to provide more values for the customers. Based on the fact that well-rounded services were important and that hotel bookings were likely to yield higher margin than flight bookings, the company thus expanded its product to include hotel bookings by mid-2006. This was primarily done through a B2B extranet system of a larger wholesale travel agent since the system required no extra implementation and installation, thus enabling both low operational cost and a wider range of products/services. Adding hotel booking service allowed TA II to please its customers; the revenue generated through hotel bookings reached almost the same amount of the revenue generated through flight bookings. Later in 2007, an online hotel booking system was developed and plugged in to the company's website in order to offer alternatives for customers who preferred self searching before asking for any help. According to the owner-manager, although an online booking system generated an extra cost and many customers still called after browsing the system, it proved to significantly save time for a customer service team since the customers had done some research and narrow down their choices. This highlighted a variety of customers' preferences and behaviors which travel agents like TA II cannot afford to ignore but need to do their best to well respond to those preferences.

TA III was a micro-sized travel agent focusing on selling flight tickets to individual as well as corporate customers. The company was founded in 1997, only a few months before the 1997 Asian financial crisis. With the micro scale (two employees and an owner-manager who did not manage the company full time) and gradual investment, the company survived the harsh crisis and obtained an increasingly bigger network of customers. Facing the same situation as TA II, TA III had to keep its operational costs as low as possible and needed large volume to cover the costs and to be profitable. An owner-manager attempted to use email as a main channel to respond to customers' requests or queries instead of calling customers back; this was to cut telephone costs. Besides, the owner-manager attempted to cut delivery costs by encouraging his customers to receive e-tickets via email with an offer of slightly lower prices. Apart from the low operational cost approach, the company also attempted to create good relationship with its customers by offering advices on complex itineraries and information about visa application for specific countries with no extra charge. This appeared very helpful in retaining customers; well over 40% of the customers were repeated customers or friends of existing customers, and therefore the company did not need to do much advertising.

However, in early 2005 the company became under threat posed by an increasing popularity in low-cost domestic airlines which cut intermediaries out of their booking process.

> "Since the low cost airlines had thrived, we saw a significant decrease in domestic flight sales. We had to cut operational cost even further, and we also tried to offer other services such as hotel reservation and tour package arrangement...However, I think our strength was still the expertise in planning and managing complex itineraries. " (The owner-manager)

Since domestic flight bookings accounted for approximately 30% of the company's total revenue, the move of travelers to book low-cost domestic airlines were problematic for TA III. The owner-manager thus decided to develop the company's website and also adopt the affiliated online booking system provided by one of the well-known wholesalers. With this concept, the company could offer online hotel booking on its website without any implementation but a link to the provided online hotel booking system. Results were however not as expected. Most customers still preferred to call rather than to complete a booking online, but at least the company could increase revenue through hotel booking services.

> "There were also some customers who had tried the system online but eventually called the company because they did not want to pay by credit card on the Internet or did not want to pay too many days in advance to reserve the room." (The owner-manager)

Such cases were perceived as unsatisfactory to the owner-manager; however, since there were no fixed costs incurred in linking to the booking system, the company was not affected much by the low acceptance of the system by the customers. This confirmed that there were still customers who preferred personalized services and hesitate to book online without making any personal contact with a seller either it be a travel agent or a hotel.

5 Conclusion and Future Research

This paper responds particularly to the need to study the tourism industry as an end-to-end value chain (Yilmaz and Bititci, 2006). The end-to-end value chain view provided an appropriate lens to investigate into the issues. Through the consideration of the tourism stakeholders and the tourism value chain, this paper underlines that disintermediation is not an issue between suppliers and intermediaries only. Rather, it is essentially about customers too since they are the most powerful component of the tourism supply chain, especially in this Internet-enabled era (Bennett and Lai, 2005; Buhalis and Law, 2008). The three case studies reflect interrelation among the three main components of the tourism supply chain, while other prior studies focused more on the relationship between travel agents and suppliers and ignored the importance of customers.

Although the number of case studies was limited, the literature review confirmed that disintermediation has been overrated (Rosenbloom, 2007). This was because 1) the tourism market is fragmented (Costa and Baggio, 2009); 2) it is unlikely that the Internet will be able to replace travel agents entirely as technology-assisted services cannot match the level of personal services (Law, 2009); and 3) tourism products/services by nature can be sold worldwide, and hence it is likely that significant differences of customers' preferences and behaviors caused by particular geographical regions will continue (Gronflaten, 2009).

Due to the fragmented nature of the tourism industry, no one distribution channel is likely to dominate in the near future, and this means that hotels and airlines still need to rely on a number of travel agents to reach the marketplace (Middleton and Clarke, 2001). Therefore the challenge for the tourism suppliers is to manage the tensions associated with dual distribution channels (their own and that of travel agents) that are potentially competitive with each other (Brown and Kaewkitipong, 2009). Law (2009) also agreed with this point by stating that ongoing cooperation with partners is critical for hotels to be benefited from a stable business return. For travel agents both traditional and online, they need to be highly effective and efficient in distributing tourism products and services (Rosenbloom, 2007).

The issues of technology-assisted service versus personal services also need further consideration. Through the three case studies, this paper has highlighted that customers are varied in profiles and preferences. Therefore the three travel agents were able to generate profit through different approaches and strategies. For example, in TA I where the majority of the customers were foreigners, online bookings were completed with minimal personalized service, whilst in TA II and TA III where the majority of the customers were Thai, it can be seen that many customers had little idea about connecting flights and thus preferred personalized suggestions about routes and airlines to general information on the Internet. This adds particularly to the points raised by Gronflaten (2009) that distinction needs to be made between information sources and information channels. Simply speaking, the differences in the customers of TA I, TA II, and TA III were actually at the level of choices of information channels (Online vs. Offline) rather than information sources (TAs vs. Suppliers). This means that in practice it was preferences for information channels not information sources that concerned those customers. Therefore, despite attempts of suppliers (hotels and airlines) to cut intermediaries by selling directly to customers through their own website, completed disintermediation is unlikely to occur. Hence, a thorough understanding of tourist information search behavior is vital especially for intermediaries that need to improve their services for tourism consumers (Gronflaten, 2009). Also, strong relationship with suppliers is equally important for travel agents as a middleman. This can be achieved through attempts to create trust, commitment, quality communication and information exchange with suppliers (Medina-Munoz and Garcia-Falcon, 2000, 2002; Yilmaz and Bititci, 2006; Costa and Baggio, 2009).

As tourism intermediaries need to be more effective and efficient, this paper calls for more research on business and IT strategic alignment particularly for small and medium sized tourism enterprises. IT will be pivotal, because it reconstructs a new interactive interface among tourism providers, tourism intermediaries and tourists, and it has pervasive effects on the creation, production and consumption of the tourism products/services (Hjalager, 2010). More importantly IS strategy in alignment with business strategy will help not only large but also small and medium-sized firms to achieve the strategic value enabled by the technologies (Schlenker and Crocker, 2003). There was also evidence that the higher performance or value of IT will be achieved through strategic fit between business and IT/IS needs (Ross, Beath, and Goodhue, 1996; Henderson and Venkatraman, 1999; Byrd, Thrasher, Lang, and Davidson, 2006). Therefore, managing a strong IT-business relationship is critical for the delivery of a successful outcome and ultimately an increase in company's revenue (Clarke and Doherty, 2004). Nevertheless, research in this area which focuses specifically on the tourism SMEs perspective was still limited. More research is thus considered worthwhile.

Ultimately, it should be noted that the findings and implications are indicative based on the three firm cases from a larger research programme and generalisability is limited. Overall, however, this research contributes particularly to the debates of disintermediation in tourism industry. Significance of the developing country context is not obvious from these three case studies except in terms of customers' preferences. Therefore, another interesting area for future research could be on consumers' behaviors in different region (Law, 2009) as it is important that the intermediaries understand and can identify their customers' behaviors in order to best fulfill their needs (Tse, 2003). Also, it is interesting to conduct further studies on some other developing countries which have similar Internet penetration rate to that of Thailand in order to understand underlying factors resulting in different behaviors of customers.

References

1. Agrawal, D.K., Agrawal, D.P., Singh, D.: Internet Based Distribution Systems: A Framework for Adoption. Decision 33(1), 21–46 (2006)
2. Alamdari, F.: Regional development in airlines and travel agents relationship. Journal of Air Transport Management 8, 339–348 (2002)
3. Beirne, M.: Meet the AGGREGATORS. Brandweek 46(22), 24–32 (2005)
4. Bennett, M.M., Lai, C.K.: The impact of the internet on travel agencies in Taiwan. Tourism and Hospitality Research 6(1), 8–23 (2005)
5. Brown, D., Kaewkitipong, L.: Relative size and complexity: e-Business use in small and medium sized tourism enterprises in Thailand. Journal of Enterprise Information Management 22(1/2), 212–231 (2009)

6. Buhalis, D., Law, R.: Progress in information technology and tourism management: 20 years on and 10 years after the Internet Internet – The state of eTourism research. Tourism Management 29, 609–623 (2008)
7. Buhalis, D., Licata, M.C.: The future eTourism intermediaries. Tourism Management 23(3), 207–220 (2002)
8. Byrd, T.A., Thrasher, E.H., Lang, T., Davidson, N.W.: A process-oriented perspective of IS success: Examining the impact of IS on operational cost. Omega, 448–460 (2006)
9. Chaffey, D.: E-Business and E-Commerce Management: Strategy, Implementation and Practice. Pearson Education Limited, Essex (2002)
10. Clarke, S., Doherty, N.F.: The importance of a strong business-IT relationship for the realization of benefits in e-business projects: the experiences of Egg. Qualitative Market Research 7(1), 58–66 (2004)
11. Costa, L.d.F., Baggio, R.: The web of connections between tourism companies: Structure and dynamics. Physica A 388, 4286–4296 (2009)
12. Earl, P.E., Mandeville, T.: The Competitive Process in the Age of the Internet. Prometheus 27(3), 195–209 (2009)
13. Euromonitor, Travel and Tourism in Thailand Report (2008), `http://www.portal.euromonitor.com` (accessed December 20, 2008)
14. Eyefortravel, European Online Travel Report in 2007, EyeforTravel Research, London (2007)
15. Gronflaten, O.: Predicting Travelers' Choice of Information Sources and Information Channels. Journal of Travel Research 48(2), 230–244 (2009)
16. Henderson, J.C., Venkatraman, H.: Strategic alignment: Leveraging information technology for transforming organizations. IBM Systems Journal 38(2/3), 472–484 (1999)
17. Hjalager, A.M.: A review of innovation research in tourism. Tourism Management 31, 1–12 (2010)
18. Lafferty, G., Fossen, A.V.: Integrating the tourism industry: problems and strategies. Tourism Management 22, 11–19 (2001)
19. Law, R.: Disintermediation of hotel reservations: The perception of different groups of online buyers in Hong Kong. International Journal of Contemporary Hospitality Management 21(6), 766–772 (2009)
20. Lewis, I., Semeijn, J., Talalayevsky, A.: The impact of information technology on travel agents. Transportation Journal 37(4), 20–25 (1998)
21. Medina-Munoz, D., Garcia-Falcon, J.M.: Successful relationships between hotels and agencies. Annals of Tourism Research 27(3), 737–762 (2000)
22. Medina-Munoz, D., Garcia-Falcon, J.M., Medina-Munoz, R.D.: Building the valuable connection: Hotels and travel agents. Cornell Hotel and Restaurant Administration Quarterly 43(3), 46–52 (2002)
23. Middleton, V.T.C., Clarke, J.: Marketing in Travel and Tourism, 3rd edn. Butterworth-Heinemann, Oxford (2001)
24. NSO, Report ICT 2004 (2004), `http://www.nso.go.th/eng/stat/ict/reportict47.pdf` (accessed April 22, 2005)
25. Palvia, S., Jain, C., Vemuri, V.K.: Distribution channels in electronic markets: A functional analysis of the disintermediation hypothesis. Electronic Markets 9(1/2), 118–120 (1999)
26. Schlenker, L., Crocker, N.: Building an e-business scenario for small business: the IBM SME Gateway project. Qualitative Market Research 6(1), 7–17 (2003)
27. Starbuck, W.: Learning from unusual events. Academy of management newsletter (1995)

28. Rosenbloom, B.: The Wholesaler's Role in the Marketing Channel: Disintermediation vs. Reintermediation. International Review of Retail, Distribution & Consumer Research 17(4), 327–339 (2007)
29. Ross, J., Beath, C., Goodhue, D.: Developing Long-term competencies through IT assets. Sloan Management Reviews, 31–42 (Fall 1996)
30. Tse, A.C.: Disintermediation of travel agents in the hotel industry. International Journal of Hospitality Management 22(4), 453–460 (2003)
31. Yilmaz, Y., Bititci, U.: Performance measurement in the value chain: manufacturing vs. tourism. International Journal of Productivity and Performance Management 55(5), 371–399 (2006)
32. Yin, R.K.: The case study anthology. Sage Publications, Thousand Oaks (2004)

Author Index

Author Index

GPSR Compliance

The European Union's (EU) General Product Safety Regulation (GPSR) is a set of rules that requires consumer products to be safe and our obligations to ensure this.

If you have any concerns about our products, you can contact us on ProductSafety@springernature.com

In case Publisher is established outside the EU, the EU authorized representative is:

Springer Nature Customer Service Center GmbH
Europaplatz 3
69115 Heidelberg, Germany

Batch number: 10704695

Printed by Printforce, the Netherlands